KNOWLEDGE

MAGAZINE

1994

2019

25

SPECIAL THANKS TO EVERYONE WHO PRE-ORDERED THE BOOK

Joe Addyman, Alfie Adelman, Matthew Alder, Justinas Aleksandravicius, Mikhail Aleksandrov, Carrie Allen, Stuart Allen, Moritz Amend, Allison Aniska, Yuliia Ashcheulova, Lee Attreed, Paul Audino, Marko Bajic, Clayton Baker, Damien Baker, Billy Barford, Frederick Barnes, Amy Barrett, Stuart Beattie, Cyril Becker, Stefan Bednarik, Nicolas Bernardi, Road Block, Mike Biondi, Adam Biggs, Clive Bishop, Steffen Boedeker, Kimberly Boncha, Chris Bowles, Ryan Bowermaster, Nick 'Brummy' Bragg, Milky Brewster, Grant Brothwell, Nathan Brown, Robert Brown, Ed Brown-Jackson, Alex Brady, Matt Brawn, Brian Burke, Bushpig, Stuart Burgin, Jules Burguieres, David Byrd, Riccardo Camera, Mauro Campana, Jon Carman,Tom Carpenter, Ross Causon, Tom R Chapman, Roger Charles, Nikolay Chernousov, Mike Choo, Paul Clarke, Philip Clarkin, Justin Clements, Lee Clinch, Russell Coe, Ruth Collins, Shawn Conte, Charlie 'Double' Cook, Mike Craske, Richard Crossman, Michal Cvik, Craig Czyz, Jan Dannenberg, Irish Dave, Tommy Davis, Victor de Groot, Ben Dellow, Bram Devreese, Zoe Dordoy, Jack Doyle, dubcomm, Matthew Duffield, Daniel Dwyer, Shawn Ellefson, James Evans, Simon Evans, Alex Eveson, Paul Falzarano, Phil Farmer, Synthetic Fauna (Costa Rica), Robert Fischer, Chris Fizik, Elisabeth Flores León, Tim Forrester, Natalie Fort, Matt Foster, Paul Francombe, Christopher Fry, DJ FuZion, Larry G, DJ Stevie G (Essence, Chrome, Jungle Fresh, Maximize crew), Erik Gaderlund, Leigh Garrett, Yohann Gilbert, Philip Gill, Marque Gilmore, Thushara Goonewardene, River Gosling, Stephen Gourlay, Sadie Graham, David Grant, Marcus Gränz, Cajetan Grill, Mike Grossman, Boutros Gully, Luuk Gyparis, Lee Hammond, Paul Harding, Leo Harper, Rich Harrison, Graham Hawkins, Justin Hawkins, Andy Hayes, Chris Hayes, Christa Hazlehurst, Tom Head, Joel Heatley, Jeffrey Hekele, Mark Hetherington, Danny Hinfray, Derek Holder, Craig Holmes, Philip Holland, Bryan Hollinger, Daniel Hoogerwerf, Alan Hopson, Tom Houlton, Louis Husson, Phil Hutchinson, JP Hutton, Eduardo Iniestra, Danut Iosif, Gergo Ivacs, Andrejs Jacko, Jade-Elize, Thomas Jackson, David James, Malcolm James, Anssi Järvinen, Mark Jenkins, Phil Jensen, Jinx, Richard Johnston, Wesley 't Jong, Joel Kane, Chris Karriker, Sharon Katanka, Jon Keane, Paul Khan, Tuomas Kiiskinen, Melissa Kimsey, Louis Kipper, Martinus Klein, Anastasia Klyushin, Paul Knibbs, Денис Компаниец, Franz König, Sanj Koria, Harri Korhonen, Jens Krakowsky, DJ Kryptonn, Arun Kullar, Dylan Lally, Tom Lambregts, Neil Lavers, Joachim Lea, Danial Leakey, Daniel Lee, David Leishman, Clément Lemay-Chaput, Rudolf Lex, Shane Lightowler, Trevor Linnell, Kevin Logan, Joseph Loria, Eddie Luck, DJ Mac One, Neil Macaskill, Ben Macmillan, Adam Mados, Martin Magnani, Christopher Malcolm, Ben Mander, Omar Marrero, Fabien Matheron, Daniel Matthews, Alexandre Maury, Michael McAleer, Joe McCarthy, Joseph McGahon, Andy McMenamin, Rajanvir Mehra, Master Jai Mehta, Adrian Michna, Jean Minasov, James Minnis, Maxim Mityutko, David Moore, Jane Moore, George Morris, Katie Morse, Hans-Joachim Münch, Lloyd Murphy, Damien Mark Murray, Jasmine Murray, Ryan Murray, Richard Musi, Sid Nar, Daddy Nature, Adam Nicholson, Dave Nicholson, Mags Nixon, Scott Nixon, Todd Norvell, David Ochoa, David O'Clery, Simon O'Leary, Liam O'Mullane, Lars Rønne Olsen, Tobin Olson, Scott Olszowy, Arkhip Osadchuk, Daniel O'Riordan, Paul-Sebastian Osterwohlt, Jennifer Page, Dev Pandya, Rupert Parkes, Mark Peacock, Daniel Pearson, Ewan Penticost, Richard Perrin, Ryan Perry, Hamilton Phipps, Hansueli Pichler, Juha Ponteva, Berend Posthumus, Chris Pothecary, Alex Powell, Kevin Prest, Samuel Probert, T Pröfrock, Tim Pugh, Ryan Purdon, David Quamina, Jeschi Quillao, Stu Raeburn , Cullen Thomas Rainey, Jeff Randall, Oliver Reed,Sophie Reid, Christian Reiff, David Reindl, Sue Richards, Dominic Ridgway, Ian Riley, Doug Rippy, Michael Roberts, Santino Roberts, Sophie Robertson, Phil Robinson, Jack Rolfe, Wiki Rolfe, Francois Romero, Cosmo Rompani, Giovanni Rompani, Hugo Rompani, Paul Rompani, Rosco, Ryan Rossi, Bret Ruch, Tom Rush, Jamie Russell, Robert Russell, Jukka Sammalvuo,Sukhdev Sandhu, Mark Sandstorm, Xen Serghi, Eric Schonbachler, Adam Scott, Hugo Schmit, M A H Schofield,Al Seen, Shannon Setzinger, Jack Sheets, Joshua Shoemaker, Chad Simer, Dave Sims, Darren Skeet, Ben Skultety, Elliot Smith, James Smith, Jason Smith, Theresa Smith, Tom Smith, Tom Snelling, Steven Snooks, Paul Soyka, Daniel Spencer, James Spink, Piotr Stasiak, Anthony Stephenson, Scott Strachan, Jack Strickland, Rhys Sutheran, Gergely Szabo, James Tansley, Leigh Taylor, Asia Thomas, Mr Thunders, Heath Tidy, Deniz Timsel, Lars Tingelstad, Oliver Titmus, Yuri Titov, Reinout Toonstra, Tukatz, Joseph Tyrrell, Jill Tune, Rhys Tyler-Jones, Kai Uchiyama, Carl Urban, Pieter Van Gucht, C Z W Vanstone, Roan Venter, Jason Vigil, James Vinter, Stephen Vivian, Raffael Voelker, Patrick Vollmari, Tighe Wachacha, Ian Walpole, Dominic Walshe, Etienne Wan (nEW meta), Alexander Ward, Blair Warren, Robert Webb, Florian Weigl, Matthew Wheeler, Thomas Widdowson, Benjamin Wiggett, Cass Wild, Henry Wilson, Chris Woods, Lincoln Wright, Kenley Yi, Daniel Yokoyama, Robert Young, William Young, Richard Yuzon, Jakub Zaremba.

WEB
kmag.co.uk
mixcloud.com/knowledgemag
facebook.com/kmaguk

EMAIL
info@kmag.co.uk

EDITOR
Colin Steven

MARKETING
James Rompani at Concrete PR

EVENTS
Miguel Estevez

DESIGN
Nick Butterfield
www.butterdesign.co.uk

WRITING
Matt Anniss, Marcus Barnes, Andres Barry, Dan Beale,
Brian Belle-Fortune, Ewen Cook, Tom Denton,
Ben Hunter, Martin James, Dave Jenkins,
Joe Madden, Layla Marino, Sarah Marshall,
Chris Muniz, Ben Murphy, John Murray Hill,
James Rompani, Colin Steven,
Paul Sullivan, Oli Warwick

PHOTOGRAPHY
Cleveland Aaron, James Burns,
Georgina Cook, Rich DaCosta, Sophie Harbinson,
Jackson Douglas Kerrigan, Tristan O'Neill, Sonia Shahid

NT'S PANEL SOUND ENGINEER
James Rail

© Velocity Press 2019

ISBN 978-1-913231-01-9

9 781913 231019 >

So here it is, 25 years after our first issue, ten years after our last magazine and five years since we called it a day - we're back!

Over the past five years, many people have told me I should bring it back, but I've always resisted the temptation as I don't want to revisit the past. So why am I bringing it back this time? Well, I feel we have unfinished business. Reaching 20 years was such an important milestone, but it was a bittersweet moment and I didn't celebrate it at all because I knew the end was coming.

Earlier this year I realised that 2019 was our 25th anniversary, so I wanted to mark the occasion somehow. What better way than with another issue? 2009 - 2014 didn't really represent what we were about, so I want to put that right with another print issue and to showcase the music that I love so much.

At first, I considered doing a magazine, but I want to make it really special and different. One of the things former readers always say to me when they find out that I edited Knowledge is that they still have all of their copies and can't bring themselves to throw them away. So if people can't part with their magazines then surely they would appreciate a premium book?

However, I was still unsure of what the reaction would be. Would anyone care? Would anyone buy it? I obviously thought it was a good idea or else I wouldn't be doing it, but a degree of self-doubt was at the back of my mind. Needless to say, I've been blown away by the reaction. A big thanks to the 300 plus people who bought the book on pre-order. Publishing is a cashflow intensive business, and this book wouldn't have been possible without your support.

Then there was the decision of what to put in it. The obvious and easiest thing would be a compilation of all our best bits, but that didn't seem right. Drum & bass has always been futuristic, so a totally nostalgic look back to the good old days didn't seem right. In the end, I decided to have a mixture of mostly new content alongside a few classic features that have stood the test of time and a few nostalgic bits. My favourite features in our magazine days always were the long form ones on a single topic with quotes from various DJs. So rather than have dedicated interviews with DJs, producers and MCs most of the features are like this.

The four panel discussions on women in drum & bass, radio, club promotion and record shops were lots of fun too. Head to our Mixcloud channel at mixcloud.com/knowledgemag to hear the full audio from them. Ultimately, this is the future for Knowledge, look out for me hosting more of these type of events in the future and live interviews with artists. Who knows, if people want it enough, there may even be more books! My own personal future lies with books. Outside of Knowledge I now run a book publishing company called Velocity Press that specialises in electronic music and club culture non-fiction. Check out velocity press.uk for more info.

Finally, I dedicate this book to Rachel Patey. Rachel co-founded the magazine with me back in 1994 and was an integral of our success, looking after the advertising, sponsorship and marketing. Unfortunately, she couldn't be a part of the journey this time but I wish her every success.

Colin Steven

CONTENTS

DYNAMITE MC
DJ RAP
GOLDIE
DJ DAZEE
IMPACT MC

DANNY WAV
NICKY BLACKMARKET
MC GQ
DJ MICKY FINN
STAMINA MC
SKIBADEE & RAKAN
JAKES MC

OWQUI MC
KYRIST

LONDON ELEKTRICITY

THTC
The Hemp Trading Co.

ECO FASHION REDEFINED SINCE 1999

PROUD SUPPORTERS OF DRUM'N'BASS
FOR TWENTY YEARS

10 YEARS OF
HARRY
SHOTTA
HARRY SHOTTA

RIYA

NAVIGATOR MC

PHOTOS BY RADSKI PHOTOGRAPHY,
CHELONE WOLF PHOTOGRAPHY,
AND FROM THE ARTISTS THEMSELVES

MC DEEFA
DJ HYPE
MC COPPA
KANE
RANDALL

N WARFARE CREW

FUNSTA
RESO
RUDIMENTAL
THE JUNGLE DRUMMER
MESSY MC
FATHOM AUDIO

THE FUTURE IS FEMALE

Words: Layla Marino
Photography: Sonia Shahid

THERE'S NO DENYING THAT FEMALES HAVE ALWAYS PLAYED AN IMPORTANT ROLE IN DRUM & BASS, FROM LEGENDARY FOUNDERS LIKE RAP, TAMSIN, KEMISTRY & STORM, WILDCHILD, FALLOUT, DAZEE AND DJ FLIGHT TO LABEL-RUNNING TRAILBLAZERS, HARDCORE UPSTART DJS TO WHERE WE ARE NOW WITH WOMEN WHOSE ALBUMS HAVE HIT NUMBER ONE IN THE CHARTS AND FEMALE COLLECTIVES PUSHING BOTH WOMEN AND DRUM & BASS FORWARD LIKE NEVER BEFORE.

The #metoo movement hit the drum & bass world in its own unique way. While there weren't a lot of public accusations and battle cries, many women who were already working in d&b, as well as press, labels and even male artists rallied to do more to bring the massive female talent pool in the genre more to the surface.

While visibility is increasing with more press coverage in publications like UKF and labels like Hospital and BCee's Spearhead Records jumping to sign more women, it seems to keep the momentum going the scene needs to really address what the gender gap actually is in d&b, as it's not always as obvious as in other genres or forms of media.

As part of our own panel discussion series for this book, we decided to put together a panel of female artists, both OG and newcomers, industry leaders and press to see if we could identify what the main issues are and what can be done to move the future forward with d&b females.

This section is ostensibly a transcript of that panel discussion, the participants were:

DJ Flight: *A DJ and producer with over 25 years in drum & bass who has had a residency with Metalheadz and radio shows on BBC 1Xtra and Rinse FM. She's also done her own pirate radio shows and podcasts online. She currently works with EQ50 Collective and is a producer for the non-profit Prison Radio Association.*

DJ Sweetpea: *A touring DJ for over ten years, has been producing and releasing tracks since 2014 on labels like Hospital, Addictive Behaviour, Dispatch, Med School and Terabyte Records.*

MC Chickaboo: *Well-known MC and vocalist who's been in working in drum & bass since the beginning and has made the crossover to many other genres like house, hip hop, electro and, most notably, soul and r&b, working with the legendary Soul II Soul for over 12 years.*

Hannah Helbert: *Well-known PR entrepreneur and owner of Elevated Sound PR. She's worked with most of the big labels, including RAM and Viper.*

Alicia "Alley Cat" Bauer: *Also involved with EQ50 collective, DJ for 20 years and agent for ESP booking agency.*

The event was moderated by myself, Layla Marino: Freelance writer and contributor to publications like UKF, DJ Mag, Bassrush/Insomniac and Your EDM, focusing on drum & bass.

Not at the event but also contributing their thoughts to the discussion points were DJ Rap, Reid Speed, Collette Warren, Dazee, Joanna Syze, Karen Iris of Iris & Quadrant and AudioPorn newcomer, Nvrsoft.

FIRST DISCUSSION POINT: THERE ARE ACTUALLY A LOT OF WOMEN IN DRUM & BASS NOT JUST ARTISTS BUT IN ALL PARTS; RUNNING LABELS, PR, PRESS, ETC. WHY DO YOU THINK WOMEN HAVEN'T BEEN AS VISIBLE OF LATE, AND WHAT CAN BE DONE TO INCREASE VISIBILITY?

Hannah: *So PR is quite dominated by women, but I would say the majority of meetings I go into with artists and promoters and labels, I am the only woman. There are really so many women working behind the scenes, and the press does tend to skew it as it's all men calling the shots. Incorporating women into the story more often would definitely help.*

Alley Cat: *From the agency side of things, the majority of people I deal with are men, that's just the reality of things at the moment. Especially promoters, so we'd love to see more promoters and agents in d&b. Years ago, when I first came here, there were more women, so I've seen it taper off. I'm not sure what happened, and there seem to be more male agents than female in my experience.*

Flight: *Wider exposure is also important. When people start thinking about and talking about women in d&b and we [Flight herself and EQ50] have all contributed to so many articles this year. There seems to be a lot more thought put into events like this, but it always seems to be the same people that are asked. So broader coverage would be great because there* are actually so many of us.

Collette: I think this lies within the people behind the press, events and labels. We need more promoters booking us as well and more labels getting behind the female producers and releasing the music, as well as vocalists having more of a main role rather than being the 'featured artist' all the time. Like when I did my EP on Innerground, it was my name at the forefront. We need more labels pushing us and believing that we can sell music just as much as men can.

Joanna Syze: I think some of what's been happening in the press this year in regards to support and highlighting of women artists has been really great. It's really unfortunate that it's taken 20 years for it to be taken more seriously, but there are no limits with how far it can go now. I know a lot of the articles have been about women artists this last year and that's great. I feel this type of stuff motivates more women to get involved in the industry. It would also be nice to have features on the many women working behind the scenes who are not only artists but label managers, or working for labels, marketing, booking agents and managers, events promoters, writers, photographers, etc. There are so many women who could inspire many other women to take a position behind the scenes in this industry. I think it would show a lot of women there is a place for them and also potentially open the eyes of males who maybe didn't realise.

Layla: So how do we think we can get that visibility from press and labels without it feeling like it's pandering or getting too negative?

Sweetpea: The female empowerment thing has been going on a year, maybe two now? It's definitely a good thing, but then you don't want a label to think it has to have a woman on their line-up or on their bill and, you know, bad vibes to you if you don't. So there's a weird sort of pressure on either end. But it's good that it's out there at all and I can see a massive improvement to line-ups and on releases.

Chickaboo: I think sometimes you just have to go for it and not worry whether it's tokenism or pandering. If there's an event where there's an all-male line-up, we're not allowed to point that out, but if an all-female line-up is put together we're being told we're man-bashing or being exclusionary and really what's that but misogyny and sexism? It's not about excluding anyone. We just want to be seen and heard and included.

Reid Speed: I think the best way to increase visibility, is that media outlets need to treat women as if we are part of the conversation, instead of constantly "putting a spotlight on" this woman or that female-collective. Instead, when the stories are written about the best things, top ten, et cetera, the new artists, the top labels, women need to be included wherever it's warranted by the work we are putting in.

Nvrsoft: I think we need to work on normalising women in d&b. A lot of press I see that includes women is female-centric, which is wonderful and great in a lot of ways, but I think we need to include more women in standard pieces, events, labels that highlight everyone.

Layla: What are some things you as individuals can recommend doing to increase visibility outside of the press?

Dazee: Get production skills, a unique style and sound and put music out. Sign up for a music production course - I teach on a degree course, and the ratio is still only about 1:10 students female. Do radio shows, work with a crew, put on your own nights. It's not enough to look cool and be able just to mix a couple of tunes together. I believe if you give back to the scene with music and show support for the sounds and artists you love, then your career will flourish and have longevity.

Chickaboo: I think supporting promoters is a huge one. I've done that at the beginning of my career, and I'll still do that. Promoters are always wanting to see the numbers. So if there's a night a certain promoter puts on that I want to work at, I'll make sure to show up as often as I can and support them just like I'm asking for their support. No part of this industry functions on its own. Networking means obviously talking to people and introducing yourself obviously but also being seen. The other advantage is once you do get to play there, you know the crowd and the vibe, and you know how to do a good job in your performance.

Sweetpea: I agree networking is still a massive thing and that goes for promoters, DJs, MCs, producers, everyone. You can't put on a successful night if no one has any idea who you are. I think that's how I got a lot of my gigs, just being up there at the front supporting.

Rap: It's all about the connections and who you know and the music you make. Making great music without having the business acumen to go with it won't get you very far. Get out there and make connections. You have to be in it to win it.

Sweetpea: Also DJ competitions, remix competitions, pop mixes up on Facebook and SoundCloud. You have a massive audience online; get in their faces too! You can even hit up online radio... release a monthly podcast. Find a crew or a group of people you connect with, try to make tracks together and even put a low-key night on just to get some play time.

Flight: I just echo what everyone has said here... how I got in with Headz was just to follow them around to every club. It's easy to get stuck behind a computer, and you've just got to get out there, even nowadays.

Collette: Pushing and helping each other as well. That stems from back in the day when Storm had the Feline brand, now we have EQ50. Mantra and the ladies are really pushing boundaries for women, and I'm also part of an all-female collective called KCDC which features myself, Kyrist, Charli Brix and Enada.

Alley Cat: From an agency point of view, I can say in terms of what sells at the moment, it's brands. Label branding is obviously huge, but artists can do the same and that's a way we can really shake things up by getting ourselves a logo or if you're putting on a night, make some merch. A few of us had a night called Feline that we played at ESP and, in hindsight, they were some really cool gigs and that was just a brand. EQ50 is also a brand. It's so easy to make your own merch. Get some t-shirts or stickers and pass them out or make a brand on Bandcamp.

Sweetpea: As much as I think there are more negatives to social media than positives - I definitely wouldn't be on there if I wasn't promoting myself - you can really use it to your advantage. It is a platform for people to see you. You just need to make sure you separate it from your real life. It's not real life, but it is a platform.

Alley Cat: Back in the day, you had to pass out mixtapes and call people or bug them on messaging services. But I do remember when I used to do that people said I was annoying or calculating. That aggressiveness doesn't get called out as much for men it seems, and so when that happened I did regress a bit.

Sweetpea: This is something that's not going to happen overnight. You're not going to send one track out, get picked up by RAM and then be playing Boomtown all in a weekend. I'm ten years deep now, and I feel like just the last two or three years I've gotten to this level.

Alley Cat: And also there's nothing wrong with going for a slow burn either. I mean I'm not the most popular DJ maybe, but I've been doing this 22 years now and I'm still here earning my living from drum & bass, so that counts for something. You can build it up slowly, branch out into other parts of the industry, play with different things and you can get that longevity.

Flight: Consistency and integrity as well, and you'll be in it for the long haul. I mean obviously most of us are not in d&b to be wealthy or famous; you can do that much better in a lot of places. If it's in your heart and your gut and you love it, that's all that matters anyway.

Chickaboo: And if you do keep going, other genres might even approach you. That's what happened to me and then suddenly you're doing even more than you planned. I was a d&b MC, and then I was approached by house music producers and then Soul II Soul came calling and I was with them for 12 years. So if you

> **"The music industry can really get to you with all the partying and drugs. It can get out of control and for your own sake, no matter what gender you are, if you want to be in it for the long haul, you have to be healthy and set limits for yourself. There's a lot of talk about mental health in music lately, and it's important to protect yourself"**
> - Flight

Alley Cat

Flight

Chickaboo

Hannah Helbert

DJ Dazee

Sweatpea

Collette Warren

DJ Rap

just keep going and stay open, you never know who's going to be attracted to your energy and what you do.

SECOND DISCUSSION POINT: HOW HAS THE MODERN SCENE AND THINGS LIKE SOCIAL MEDIA AFFECTED HOW WOMEN ARE AND CAN BE SEEN IN D&B? IS IT POSITIVE OR NEGATIVE?

Flight: I really think it's 50/50. The positives are that you have direct access to people now, whereas in the past you'd have to know someone or go hunt them down in the office, work the clubs, hand out mixtapes. If you were making tracks you had to put them on DAT tapes, getting things mastered and cut on vinyl was incredibly expensive, and then even to have access to the equipment. Now you can literally upload tunes and have people listening to them within minutes. On the flipside, however, the quality control has gone way down. Now you can just grab sample packs, download crack software that's not the best quality... so there's both positive and negative going on.

Sweetpea: I still think you need a bit of an edge up in some way. But I do think it's kind of cool in this generation, everyone has a laptop, and there are so many portable ways to make music and mix. So it's already there now, you don't even have to seek it out and wonder "how" you're going to do it.

Alley Cat: But then how do you get anyone to listen to it? A track being on SoundCloud doesn't mean it's going to be heard. I think people, especially young women, still need a stepping stone or an ally to help and listen to your stuff and give feedback. That's one of the reasons we started EQ50, and I want to encourage anyone who's in the EQ50 Facebook group to post your stuff for feedback. Even for myself, I sometimes get nervous about putting stuff out there.

Sweetpea: Today the market is so oversaturated, and it seems like all the same people are getting coverage in the press, especially digital press.

Hannah: Yeah, I think they're trying to work on that. UKF has featured a lot of US artists, and Layla just did that article on Kallan HK and Nvrsoft has been in, and Joanna had a feature...

Flight: I think there's a slight laziness with publications. I'm known to be quite cynical with a lot of press because I think they don't do enough digging and just tend to work with what's presented to them rather than actively seeking out good artists who maybe don't get as much coverage. The net needs to be cast a lot wider.

Chickaboo: Hannah and Layla, what do you think female DJs and producers can do to kind of cut through all the waves of white noise and get PR or press attention?

Hannah: Something I say to labels all the time who are trying to do their PR in-house is that they should designate a person to listen to the music and let artists know who that person is. Not every contact at a label is valuable if you're submitting tunes. Also, don't send in things that are unfinished or not your best stuff. If you're sending to a label make sure it's finished and it's as good as it can be. Don't just spam people.

Flight: Even as a DJ or someone who has label connections, I can tell if something has just been a copy and paste job or I'm part of a long BCC chain. If you really want to get your track on my label, really think about who I am as an artist and what I'm going to vibe with the most and if it's appropriate.

Hannah: Also, always get a second opinion about your tracks from a mate or maybe someone you know who does have releases on labels, just make sure the quality is there right the way through. I try to make myself available, my ears are always open and I'll try to help and say contact certain labels or don't bother with them. It's important to get some guidance before you just start sending everything out. And that's not just for producers and DJs but any women who want to work in the industry. You don't learn the workings of this stuff overnight, and it is really important to learn how to communicate with others in the industry or just even get your foot in the door.

Sweetpea: That's why it's nice to have people send me mixes or send me tunes for feedback. They just have to have the right approach to it. But if people want that bit of guidance, I really enjoy giving that back to people because I know I didn't get here all on my own.

Layla: Something I've found in my experience has been that the male artists or labels who send me releases, they really just don't care what they're sending to me in terms of quality or it being a copied email, they'll just keep bugging me until I talk to them one way or another. Women are a little bit more conscientious and don't want to make a bad impression. I've never had a female artist or label head come to me and bug me or think they are as entitled to my time as much as almost all the male artists and label heads do. To Flight's point, I'd love to cast a wider net but digital formats with publishing nowadays it just moves so fast, and I have to get things listened to, pitched and published within a matter of days or even hours. So all these points are helpful to get things seen but also just don't be scared to get in there and mix it up and be "annoying" if you want to.

THIRD DISCUSSION POINT: THE GENDER GAP IN DRUM & BASS - IS IT AS BAD AS OTHER GENRES?

Layla: Obviously, it's been a great thing for the #metoo movement to spread to d&b, and there are some definite issues that need addressing. However, some people have thought that this scene may be more open or the gender gap is not as bad as in other genres of music due to women not being so obviously objectified. For example, as in pop music or some of the more popular EDM genres, so I just wondered how all of you felt about that.

Flight: Well there is objectification to an extent; if you're a woman in drum & bass you will be judged on how you look and how you dress, and I think we've all experienced that in our time. Then also the idea that a female DJ is only on a bill or a female's track is only on a label because they've slept with so-and-so, and that still happens to this day.

Joanna: I was told back in 2004 that I should quit and just go play trance or house because it was more "female friendly", and you do tend to see that, even in EDM and all the other genres. Women are constantly being featured as equals to their male counterparts. Artist managers aren't scared to take on and develop a woman's career and see her net worth potential. In d&b you don't see this happening, and if it does, it's very rare.

Chickaboo: And then what about female artists who are just coming up and then sleep with a DJ, that can put a halt on their career progression. What about that? I don't know if that happens in other genres in exactly the same way, does it? In pop music, it seems like that actually helps a female artist's career. So with that, I've made a personal rule that I won't sleep with DJs or people I'm working closely with but does everyone need to do that? Like Hannah being of the younger generation, do you guys feel the similar pressure in terms of how to handle yourself?

Hannah: I'm not sure it's going to halt your career nowadays, but people definitely talk and judge and even rumours are made up, and that's not right. I think when that happens the best thing to do is confront it because they're the ones who are in the wrong. Don't be scared to call them out. If you're in these environments where everything is hedonistic, attraction happens and you may end up sleeping with someone but whether you shouldn't or should is up to you and that person. Why it's a matter for the scene to comment on, or a matter that affects anyone's career is beyond me.

Chickaboo: If something does happen and you're talked about you don't have to let it ruin you. We can always start again because they [men] have always been allowed to start again. You just have to have the confidence to keep going. Don't beat yourself up about a mistake. If it's not true, you can shut it down, but even if it is, you can say "yeah, so what?"

Alley Cat: Definitely. A lot of men in the industry get absolutely shitfaced almost every party, and it's fine, and they don't lose face or gigs unless it gets really bad. If I do that once it's like a big deal and that's another double standard or objectification that happens quite regularly.

> **"** I think the best way to increase visibility, is that media outlets need to treat women as if we are part of the conversation, instead of constantly "putting a spotlight on" this woman or that female-collective.**"**
> - Reid Speed

Sweetpea: I think, you know, it's all an experience, but I've definitely had a couple of times I've been a bit more... wavy, let's say than I wanted to be. You just want to remember if that happens and recognise it as an experience and learn from it. That's true for everyone. It's still a party, you can still have fun. At the end of the day, it's all about being safe as well and for DJs, you obviously don't want to get super-smashed before your set because you have a job to do.

Flight: The music industry can really get to you with all the partying and drugs. It can get out of control and for your own sake, no matter what gender you are, if you want to be in it for the long haul, you have to be healthy and set limits for yourself. There's a lot of talk about mental health in music lately, and it's important to protect yourself.

FOURTH DISCUSSION POINT: IT SEEMS AS IF WOMEN ARE DOING A LOT IN TERMS OF REACHING ACROSS THE POND AND PUSHING D&B TO BE MORE INTERNATIONAL. WHAT DO YOU THINK WOMEN ARE DOING AND CAN STILL DO TO HELP GLOBALISE D&B?

Chickaboo: I got out in America because Knowledge Mag organised a US tour in 1999, and from there I got an agent and carried on touring and touring. So I think it takes someone taking a chance on an artist to bring them to another area. That was huge at the time. Nowadays if you don't have coverage in a place where other markets get exposed to you, whether it's in press or radio or a track with a label, there are very few people that will take a chance on a tour.

Nvrsoft: My breakthrough came directly from help from my mostly male peers, who worked to help me get to places where I could create and seize opportunities. Everyone needs to work together – it's very hard to break through alone. When you see and recognise talent, and you're in a place to help give them support or a "break", it's important to do that.

Flight: I've toured the US and Canada numerous times, and it was because I had the radio show on 1Xtra and the Metalheadz residency, but my name definitely grew from that. So I think it's important not to ignore it but you also do need an 'in' usually. There are a lot of comparisons to make between the US and the regional gigs here in the UK. The scene there is much smaller, but the people who show up are really into it, so there's a cool intensity there. I've had a really positive experience in the US.

Collette: You just have to push yourself to do this. I have been touring in America for the past few years every summer, but this is down to me pushing myself and reaching out to promoters. They are more than happy to have you, you just need to get yourself there, and believe in yourself and do some research on different promoters across the globe. Obviously, the other option is to get an agent that will do all this for you, but I like doing this myself as then you get the personal approach and relationship with each promoter.

Alley Cat: I have two perspectives. As an artist, I have an American passport so touring for me was pretty easy comparatively. From an agent point of view, getting a visa as a touring artist is very expensive, so you do have to have a label backing. You need a lot of press and a sponsor... it's a lot. In terms of women being represented over there, how many female artists have that? Then you have to go out there and get enough gigs to cover the cost.

FIFTH DISCUSSION POINT: HOW DO YOU SEE WOMEN PUSHING D&B INTO THE FUTURE AS WE RAMP UP OUR VISIBILITY?

Rap: To a point, it's really up to us. If you make hit song after hit song, nothing will stand in your way. Having said that, we all know it's harder for us. Like everyone else I've experienced sexism and the problems that go with it, but it just makes me push harder, like adding fuel to my fire. To be honest, I have more of the guys on my side than anything, and many of them are my family. People like Kenny Ken, Fabio and Frost have my back. But this scene doesn't owe me a living. I do not believe in feeling entitled; this is a gift that requires a lifetime of hard work. That said, I love DJs like Lady V Dubz from Girls Take Action, she really cares about women and creating a collective. We need to support each other more and follow that example.

Nvrsoft: One huge change I'd like to see is a change in rhetoric from artists/MCs and patrons about women. I hear so many degrading lyrics about women, and see so many female artists get negative comments regarding their gender. I don't see enough men actively stand up against hate speech. I think if we all stopped allowing and actively supporting rhetoric that degrades women, that would cause a huge change; both in how women are seen and treated and in how women feel about coming to try and participate in our community.

Flight: I also wonder where are the men to answer these questions? They're often the ones in the positions of power, so we really do need them to start moving with us. It's a two-way street, really. We need to invite more men to these conversations to find out why they're not promoting women as well. Some are doing an okay job, but they could be doing a lot better.

Iris: On an individual level, just being an ally can really go a long way. Listening to women when they speak about their experiences, standing up for them when they are speaking about these experiences. For those who have a larger impact on the scene. We can find ways to get women involved, whatever that looks like for you. Book women for your events, give them constructive feedback on their tunes, ask their opinions, etc. Some of this does require more leg work for sure, but the more diverse we're able to make the genre the better and stronger it will be.

Joanna: I don't think this is just a woman versus men question. This is about people working and making music to support and grow their local music scene. We don't want there to become a movement where we accidentally isolate ourselves by the very act of wanting to be included. It should be about music and music has no gender. So absolutely the best way to push this music worldwide is by everyone, male or female, doing their part and not being scared to push those boundaries.

Reid Speed: I think us "legacy" artists have done the thing, we came out and were unafraid to take up space in this male-dominated industry and created paths to relative success. It's up to the new generation to keep pushing the envelope of these spaces and to really master the technical side. We can all trust that we are good enough and to keep putting ourselves out there; to keep stepping up as producers, DJs, presenters, PR people, journalists, A&R, label management. To keep occupying these roles both in front of and behind the scenes, to shift the dynamic to a place where it's no longer "male dominated" any more.

Dazee: I think the future is looking bright in terms of the numbers of female artists repping d&b - well, in Bristol anyway. I'm working with a whole team of young women who are really hungry for it, but they are putting the groundwork in: interning on my radio shows, studying on music or event courses, helping out with Ruffneck Ting nights and they all bring something to the table already in terms of style and skills. In fact, I'm picking up ideas from them! These will be the ones that succeed as they have a real passion and are prepared to work hard and hopefully won't suffer from the effects of a career that comes too quickly and they weren't ready for.

> **"I don't think this is just a woman versus men question. This is about people working and making music to support and grow their local music scene. We don't want there to become a movement where we accidentally isolate ourselves by the very act of wanting to be included."**
>
> - Joanna Syze

Iris

Joanna Syze

Nvrsoft

Reid Speed

FOR THE RECORD

Words by: Marcus Barnes
Photography by: Cleveland Aaron

I'M STANDING AT THE BACK OF A SCRUM WHO ARE ALL VYING FOR THE ATTENTION OF THE GUYS BEHIND THE COUNTER AS PLUMES OF SMOKE FILL THE AIR AND THE FAMILIAR BREAKBEATS OF A TUNE I HEARD ON KOOL FM OVER THE WEEKEND BLAST OUT OF THE SPEAKERS. IT'S 1996, SHY FX'S 'WOLF' HAS BEEN CAUSING UPROAR AT JUNGLE RAVES ACROSS THE UK AND EVERYONE IN THE SHOP WANTS A PROMO COPY.

Running things on this dreary Saturday are Nicky Blackmarket and Ray Keith, I'm tagging along with a school friend who plays jungle. We're at Black Market Records, the legendary Soho record shop, one of several on our hit list for the day - like many others, doing the rounds to add new music to the bag ahead of radio or club gigs.

Without being too sentimental, these were halcyon days, when youth was on our side and travelling around London to hunt down white labels and promos was a weekly practice. In the mid-90s almost every high street across the UK had a record shop on it, famous brands like Our Price and HMV could be found alongside a plethora of independent vendors. For jungle heads, stores like Lucky Spin/Section 5 in Chelsea, Jungle Fever Records in Hackney, Boogie Times in Romford, Black Market and Unity in Soho, Mash on Oxford Street and many more were packed every weekend.

When jungle music was in its infancy, CD turntables had only just been invented. The DJ's weapon of choice back then was a pair of turntables (usually Technics SL-1210s), and their artillery was records. Vinyl pressings, white labels, promos, dubplates, these were the ammunition for every

> **"** I remember when Deep Blue came in, 'The Helicopter Tune'. We ordered in God knows how many. Boxes and boxes. So many boxes we didn't even know where to put them all. Within four days the whole lot had sold out. **"**
>
> - Nicky Blackmarket

DJ worth their salt in the jungle scene.

Playing on CD decks was unheard of, and USBs hadn't even been invented yet, let alone software like Traktor or Serato. In this vinyl-driven era, record shops were intrinsic to the growth and proliferation of the culture.

In light of this, Knowledge organised a panel discussion at one of London's most iconic record shops, Rough Trade East, to get the lowdown on record stores new and old. Panellists included Nicky Blackmarket and Ray Keith, two of the most familiar faces from the seminal Black Market Records, Jack Christie from Container Records and Jon Smith from Intense Records.

EARLY EXPERIENCES

"Back in the day I would save up my dough every week, £150, and go 'record hopping'," Ray Keith says as we explore the panellists' early record shop experiences. "At that time I was living in Clacton-On-Sea, I was working on King's Road and I spent all my f****** money on records, like every single penny. I'd get up on a Saturday morning and drive up to London, stopping off at JiFS in Chadwell Heath, which is where we'd get all our bootlegs from. Steve Davis would be there every week! Then we'd go on to Black Market, City Sounds, Music Power, Vinyl Zone, Trax, Groove, and if there was any chance I had some money left, we'd hit Bluebird. That was the ritual every single weekend, I would spend hours in those shops." Ray recalls picking up a record that changed his life, during this period - it was 'Beyond The Dance' by Derrick May, "I got that on a white label," he says.

"I went in to a shop on Edgware Road and said to the guy behind the counter, 'Have you got the tune that goes,

→ → Marcus Barnes, Nicky Blackmarket, Jon Smith, Jack Christie, Ray Keith

'Duh-duh-duh-duh-duh'?", Ray explains. The shop assistant told him he didn't recognise the tune but to wait. "Four hours later, the shop's about to close, and he plays the tune. I was like, 'Mate, that's the tune!'. He says, 'I've only got one copy'. And that's what it was like, you'd give your left arm for the record you wanted. He looked at me, probably with a sad expression on my face, and said, 'Ok, go on then'."

Nicky Blackmarket takes us back to 1982, Groove Records in Soho. The shop, which was on Greek Street, was run by Jean Palmer - a legend in her time - who imported all the latest US releases. Groove was one of the very few record shops to stock early hip hop and house cuts, way ahead of the curve and it's thanks to Jean (and her sons Tim and Chris) that they had such a progressive collection. "I was about 15. I rode my BMX down there, no helmet, nothing. I'd saved up my pocket money just so I could go and buy some records," he says. "Jean was a woman who knew everything about everything. At that time it was the electro boom. It was all about saving your hard-earned cash and spending it all on records. That's still with me now, that mentality. It's never left me."

Jon from Intense Records tips his hat to Nicky and Ray, being a devotee of Black Market in his teens. "I owe a lot to these two because, when I was 15, we'd come up to London and do 'the circuit', as we'd call it: Black Market, Unity, all the Soho shops," he recalls. "You'd stand and wait for ages, waving your hand trying to get their attention, 'Ray! Ray!'. I remember going see Nicky play one Friday night, going to the shop the next day and asking, 'What was that Congo Natty one you played last night?'. He puts his hand down under the counter, pulls a record out and says, 'This one'. I was like, 'Yeahhh bruv!'."

Jack remembers going to buy an album on vinyl, taking it home and being scolded by his mum. "I went to Banquet in Putney and bought a Nirvana album. When I brought it home, my mum told me to take it back because 'vinyl's dead'. It wasn't until a couple of years later when I started getting into drum & bass that my mates told me about Black Market. I went down with my birthday money from my 17th or 18th and spent the lot."

"I think I was pretty terrified. Back then I looked a lot younger than I was and there were all these big geezers round the counter," he adds. "I left with some good records though, one of them was 'Mothership' on Dread actually."

BLACK MARKET RECORDS

Black Market Records opened in 1988 and closed in 2015. Nicky worked there for 25 years, with Ray joining him for 19 of those years. Alongside Ash A-tack and Clarky, they were the core team who manned the counter, serving up fresh jungle and d&b to eager DJs and collectors every day of the week. At the height of the jungle explosion, almost every one of the main streets in Soho had a record shop on it, with a wide range of musical styles on offer, from electronic music to jazz and classical. Black Market would be one everyone's rounds as they trawled Central London trying to track down the elusive white labels they'd heard on pirate radio or in the clubs.

"People would come in, and they'd trust us," Ray says. "We were like their handlers, so people would come in and they'd say, 'Nicky, I've got £100 in my wallet, sort me out, you know what I like'. You built that personal, one-to-one, relationship with the customers."

One of the core aspects of record shops was the interpersonal relationships between the staff and their customers. The more you went, the more you got to know each other and the more likely you were to become privy to the more exclusive delights behind the counter. Sometimes only a handful of white label promos would be dropped off by a label or artist, so only a very select few would be lucky enough to get hold of them. It was a time when artists were actually able to make a living from music sales. An era when illegal downloading was impossible, unheard of.

> **"** It was a community, it was a culture. I was there 19 years, and it was the best thing I ever did. It wasn't work for us, we loved being there.**"**
> – Ray Keith

"I remember when Deep Blue came in, 'The Helicopter Tune'," Nicky says. "We ordered in God knows how many. Boxes and boxes. So many boxes we didn't even know where to put them all. Within four days the whole lot had sold out."

It was a raucous, often chaotic, hub where junglists would travel from far and wide to get their fix. Careers were launched and reinforced by Black Market, new artists would befriend the staff, pass on their music and have it played out that weekend at some of the top raves of the time.

"There were times when the shop was a cloud of smoke," Ray laughs. "Groove[rider] would be in the back, there'd be about 50 heads in the shop, and it was like, 'What the f***?!'. It was an amazing time because there was no social media. We found people and supported them. I remember DJ Fresh coming in with his trousers hanging down past his pants, handing us a CD. It was a hub."

"We were the Internet!" Nicky adds. "It was a lifestyle and it was fun."

"It was a community, it was a culture. I was there 19 years, and it was the best thing I ever did," Rays adds. "It wasn't work for us, we loved being there. We were young men growing up together. We smoked a lot of weed and played a lot of records. There'd be a big cloud of smoke, someone would pass you a tenner, and you'd be so stoned you'd give them twenty back!"

Financial issues led to the shop's closure in 2015. Nicky and Ray had already left by that point, but the legacy remains strong. Both Jack and Jon are former customers who now have their own record shops, countless artists and labels got their break through the shop, and it was one of the cornerstones of the scene itself.

"The fact that the shop lasted so long still amazes me," Nicky tells the audience. "We never thought about where we were going. The shop would be rammed, we'd play a big tune on the decks and then dish out 20, 25 copies of it like a pack of cards! Those memories will never fade."

"It was just great to meet so many people," Ray adds. "I have people come up to me now asking if I remember them, but there were so many punters that came through, and I might have a bit mash-up, I don't always remember. It was a special time, it was a happy place for 19 years for me."

SURVIVAL OF THE RECORD SHOP

Whether you have a grumpy old man at the counter or a vibrant bunch of youngsters, there are core aspects of a record shop that are universal and separate the great ones from the not-so-great ones, keeping them alive and kicking. The panel discussed this, based on their own experiences on both sides of the counter. What qualities did Black Market possess that kept it one step ahead? What is it that keeps Container Records going in such a challenging climate, and how has Intense Records lasted 20 years?

"It's the love of the people behind the counter," Ray states. "We lived and breathed it. For 19 years I was with Nicky more than any other person - we worked together all week, then we'd fly to Germany together on Friday night, off to Canada Saturday, somewhere else Sunday and back to the shop on Monday!"

"That's why I like All Ages in Camden," Jack agrees. "You can tell a lot of love has gone into it. Their curation is impeccable, and that's what you get with most good record shops. It's the curation. When you're searching online, you're driven by your own focus and targets, even if you're browsing. In a shop, you're walking into a place that has been curated with the expertise of the staff."

> **"** You can't remember your first download, but you never forget your first record.**"**
> - Jon
> (Intense Records)

"People want to interact, to see other people and talk to them," Ray adds. "Part of being a human is that interaction. How many times have we been in a record shop and stumbled across something that took you by surprise, or a tune you'd been searching for for ages? Or a tune that you'd forgotten about? Shops have to diversify, but as long as they're selling records, it's all good."

"I actually model our shop on Black Market," Jon tells us. "The main ingredients are; decks behind the counter, a load of records on the shelves and a big soundsystem."

In an age where, despite vinyl sales increasing every year, it's very tough to keep a record shop open, those in charge have to diversify and explore other venues to keep the business afloat. An ability to accept change and move with the times can be crucial in a shop's survival.

"We've survived 20 years through being stubborn," Jon explains. "My accountant told me to shut up shop years ago, so I sacked her and got a new one! We do events, we do a monthly record fair, so we get other sellers in, hire a pub next door do a barbeque and get bands in there. Second-hand music is a big, big thing for us now. We get

people bringing in their collections all the time, so we buy them and put them straight on Discogs. Locals will see a crate come in and swarm the place like vultures."

With all of the changes that have occurred in the way music is sold and distributed to the public, streaming services in particular, you can still find at least one record shop in most big towns and cities. There is still a demand, a need, for physical stores. But what do the owners get out of it? What they get is beyond money. What lies at the heart of the most successful and influential record shops is the pure love that exists at their very foundations. It's the people, the experiences, the real-life connection and interaction... the music and the physicality of the records and the space.

"I just love it. I love record shops," Jack enthuses. "It's an amazing thing to be able to hook someone up with music you know they're going to love. You get to be around music all day, getting to know about new releases. It's hard work, and it's not the best pay..."

..."You get paid?!" Jon interjects.

"But I'm here voluntarily, I keep getting up every morning because I love it," Jack concludes.

"Music doesn't have a language, it's love, it invites people," Ray adds. "It's f****** hard because you need to make enough money to keep the doors open. Sometimes you might have to sell the record you had your eye on just to make ends meet. It's not easy. If you don't embrace change, then it's not going to work for you."

"Meeting people is a big part of it, you're a community," Jon says. "The young artists who've come in the shop and we've ended up booking to play for us at our events, being part of their progression is great. My wife Jen, she used to come and buy records, now we're married."

"Yeah, the people, the friendships you make, the artists who you see develop," Jack responds. "The other day I had this kid pop in who's been coming for two years. He always comes in and is quite pushy about playing his beats on his phone. They were a bit shoddy, but he went away for 10 months and came back just the other day, played me some new stuff and I was so impressed I asked him if I could have some of the tunes to take with me to my radio show the next night.

Of course, there's a strong feeling of sentimentality when it comes to record shops. In some respects, they are representations of a bygone era, intrinsically linked to the human spirit. The smell of an old record shop can provoke strong memories, as do the records themselves. Music lovers have such a powerful connection to their music, digital or physical, it has the power to transport us to the past in a flash, or help us transcend the present moment to lose ourselves for a few minutes. It soothes our ills, lifts us up when we're down and amplifies a good mood. It's a companion that never lets us down.

"You can't remember your first download, but you never forget your first record," Jon states emphatically.

May all the record shops of the world keep the spirit alive, creating more memories, sharing more unforgettable moments and bringing people of all walks of life together in unison...

PROMOTING PASSION

Words by: James Rompani

Photography by: Sophie Harbinson

WHAT TRIALS AND TRIBULATIONS DO DRUM & BASS CLUB PROMOTERS FACE? ON THE SURFACE, MANY RAVERS HAVE THIS PRECONCEIVED MISCONCEPTION THAT PROMOTERS ARE ROLLING AROUND WITH CARRIER BAGS FULL OF NOTES AND DRINKING CHAMPAGNE.

Where this may have been a reality at some events in the early 90s, many factors are at play. Weeks, often months, of hard work and graft go into organising an event, everything falling into the fate of one day/night, where things like the weather, nature and transport links can all play a huge factor to the success and outcome of an event.

At the same time, the promoter is often at the bottom of the pecking order; always at the mercy of agents, club owners and punters, trying to find a balance to keep all corners happy whilst at the same time often being responsible for creating opportunity for rising talent to take to the stage (only for the said talent to then be later priced out of their budget once they rise to fame and are in the hands of agents).

It's safe to say there have been many external factors that have changed methods and tactics when it comes to selling tickets and spreading the word about your event. Before Facebook and MySpace the landscape was certainly favoured towards physical promotion; now in the digital age, there are numerous options and avenues down which you can go to get your message to potential ticket buyers.

But as agents get a tighter grip over acts and DJ fees continue to rise the average ticket price on the door hasn't increased in relation to this, pricing many small promoters out of the game when trying to book certain acts.

We gathered a crack panel of some of London's most experienced drum & bass and jungle promoters to find out what really goes on behind the scenes: Sarah Sandy (Swerve), Clayton Hines (Renegade Hardware), Paul Ibiza (Jungle Splash), Billy Daniel Bunter (Unity In The Sun) and Jack Robinson (Pack London).

→ → James Rompani, Sarah Sandy, Jack Robinson, Clayton Hines, Paul Ibiza, Billy Daniel Bunter

Please introduce yourselves panel...

Sarah Sandy: *Next year will be 30 years since I set up Groove Connection, one of the first DJ agencies. I did my first party in 1990 and have promoted many different events over the years. Started Speed in 1994, which was a reaction to the end of Rage and the jungle scene was getting really big. It ran for three years until Bukem left to set up Logical Progression. Following that Fabio and I set up Swerve. It was weekly, then went down to monthly and now it's much more infrequent, but we're still doing it.*

Jack Robinson: *I've been promoting for 15 years now. I started off promoting monthly dubstep nights in Leeds as a student which led onto doing them in different cities, which led onto starting Outlook festival in 2008. Since moving to London, I now run Pack London, which is a company that does promotions for everybody. We recently took over doing the bookings for Fabric Live on Fridays, and it's been a real pleasure to work with that venue.*

Clayton Hines: *I started putting on parties in 1995,*

> **"People think it's glamorous - you're out there off your face with everyone counting the cash but ain't that, this is hard work."**
> - Billy Daniel Bunter

my first party was at The Key in Kings Cross. In 1996 I started Trouble On Vinyl, and in 1997 we got a residency at The End club for our other label Renegade Hardware. We were there for 11 years and ended up being the longest residency at the venue. It really put our label on the map. After that, I bought Breakin Science and had that for a couple of years before I sold it on. I'm lucky in that I've experienced all sides of the promotion scene.

Paul Ibiza: *I've been in this game since 1988. I started out running Ibiza Records label but promoting come along with it, and I've been promoting Jungle Splash since 1994.*

Billy Bunter: *Next year I'll have DJed professionally for 30 years and unprofessionally as a promoter for 25 years. I always said I never wanted to be a promoter and that it's a mug's game, but I did and I've never let it go since. I love partying, I love drama - and promoting brings loads of that - and I have an addictive gambling nature. It takes a special person to be a promoter and take all the risk. You also have to be passionate to push the music and artists that you love.*

What qualities does a good promoter need?

Sarah: *Resilience. You've got to keep coming back because you get so many knock backs and you have to be passionate about what you do. I'm the ultimate raver still. You have to believe in it, you have to love the music. You have to keep going, and you really don't know until on the night whether it's going to work or not. Sometimes you'll sell loads of tickets in advance and it's guaranteed, but a lot of the time you really don't know if it's going to work. If you have the passion, then you don't give up, you just keep on going.*

Paul: *Got to keep reinventing yourself. As the years go by crowds change and you have to reinvent yourself, or you get stuck in old school mode. The new kids on the block come on the scene and take the scene further. You may need to change the way you do things.*

Billy: *You've got to love looking after and entertaining people. You've got to put yourself on the frontline, it's not about the adulation of everyone loving your party. All of us have had trouble at our front doors. It's about putting yourself out there on the frontline looking after your crowd and what you've built up. It's not a fairy tale thing where you walk into a venue where you get 2000 people spending £30 each, and you walk away into the sunset with all the money. Do you believe in it that much that you will stare every problem in the eye and take it* on to make sure that people have an amazing time?

Jack: Always being able to look at what's changing. Look at how music is changing and treat things with an open ear or eye. Just because that worked last year or just because that artist was good for you doesn't mean you have to pay double this year with no album out or any promotion. You have to keep your ear to the ground, follow what the kids are listening to and understand how the scene changes. What things can you look at to judge the value of an artist? You need to do the research to see how much artists are worth. You need to build narratives around your event as well.

Clayton: You've got to have passion for it. Most promoters I know don't make as much money as what people think. It's a slog. When you're going home, and everyone has made money apart from you, it isn't a good feeling. I started promoting because I like to party not to line my own pockets. Eventually I fell out of love with it, and that's why I stopped.

Billy: Promoting is the most unforgiving side of the music industry. All of the panel have made far easier money in other areas of music than promoting. Many times we've had the raw end of the stick.

Jack: We're the arse end of the industry, when the shit goes down, it all falls on us basically.

Billy: People think it's glamorous - you're out there off your face with everyone counting the cash but ain't that, this is hard work.

> **"I've got a disdain for agents. I see why they're there, but most of them are failed DJs and producers and it's the last thing they can do to stay part of the scene."**
> - Clayton Hines

Is it more saturated these days? Have platforms like Facebook allowed new people to come and have a crack at promoting?

Jack: When Facebook first came around, there was a big explosion of student promoters. You could invite all your friends and you didn't have to go out flyering. Facebook wasn't monetising it and wasn't a billion-dollar company at the time. I promoted the first Outlook festival on Facebook for free. I just got everyone I knew to invite all of their friends. 30,000 people invited to a festival in Croatia for no money. You could actually game the system, but now you don't get anything for free. Whereas a lot of new promoters came in about ten years ago nowadays there are no young promoters taking risks with anything because they can't get the artists. If someone farts on YouTube, then they're two grand. You can't spot an artist any more. If someone has got a bit of hype then they're online, they've got an agent, and they're already quite expensive. They've got a million plays but are they actually that well known? What million people have played that? There's definitely been a big drop in people taking risks, new music being pushed, and the scene evolving. It's the older promoters who have stuck with it and some of the more corporate promoters who treat it as a long term thing who keep the scene moving forward, but they do it in a less risky way. They just book the same bread and butter artists they know.

Sarah: Yes, and they're just monopolising the whole

thing really. There are certain artists I think I was pivotal in breaking through into the circuit. As time has gone on and more people have come into the game, suddenly I could no longer get those artists to play for me. I find that weird. I talk to artists and they want to come and play for me, but they're not allowed to. So there's a lot of games that come into it.

Billy: It's interesting what you say because some of the parties that I'm the front person of I make sure that all the DJs are my closest friends that I've known for years. Agents are never involved, there's no paperwork. They're always my favourite parties to do. I also have other projects where I'm a silent partner or overseeing the marketing. The other week we were quoted five grand for an artist who in my head I think is £300.

Sarah: We were there right at the beginning, so we were setting up a whole new game. A lot of people told me to lock everyone down, but realistically you couldn't do that, this scene is global now, it's so big. We were right at the cutting edge of something that was so creative. I felt it was going to blow up. One person and one agency could never control that. So everyone who came to the game from that moment on we had to welcome them in. But then you get to a situation, and I think a lot of it is very male, but as soon as they've got something it becomes their territory, and they don't want you to be able to have it. A new agent would come up and they'd do what you're doing but at a bit more militant, put the prices up even more and stop you being able to book their DJs. This became a ridiculous game with everyone outdoing each other until now where you've scaled up and up and up and you've got the proper big boys in the game now, the really big record company agents and the big backers. A lot of us who started the whole thing off don't stand a chance any more.

Clayton: As promoters we created monsters, and now they're biting us on the arse.

Paul: I've seen it all before with DJs and what you have to do now as a promoter is make your brand powerful. Don't worry about the DJs, work on your brand and the DJs will want to play for you.

How has the internet changed promoting for you?

Billy: I love the internet age of promoting. 15 years ago I would produce 100,000 flyers for an event, now we're doing 10,000. Before I used to be outside a club flyering and it's like pissing in the wind. I love content and stories from the promoters and DJs, and I love the fact that now I don't have to wait to ask the record shop how many tickets I've sold. I'm always on the pulse of my sales. We purposely sell the majority of our tickets on our website so that we retain the data. We don't abuse the database, we use it sparingly. Marketing changes so quickly and it's back to mailing lists for us.

Jack: We've been running a flyer pack for 12 years, and every year we think about stopping it because it's a lot more difficult to do than it was eight or ten years ago. Promoters would pay £50 to get their flyers in the pack and it would go to ten raves. With Facebook rising as quickly as it did promoters now think 'why should I spend £50 on flyers this weekend when I can advertise on Facebook for the same amount and sell a bunch

of tickets?' Now we're seeing physical coming back though, both flyers and posters. The cost-effectiveness of Facebook means that every promoter in London is bidding on the same people, so if you pay a flyerer to go to an event, it's probably going to do better for you.

How important is it to find the right venue?

Jack: In London, it's been tricky the last few years, a lot of smaller venues have disappeared, which means you don't have the breeding ground for the smaller artists. You don't have the ability to try and test something, and that's across most cities. Warehouse Project and Printworks come with these huge line-ups, which means smaller artists don't have that space. A fifth of UK venues shut in 2018 and most of them were small venues. You have to find somewhere that's going to work transport wise, and you need owners who are on board with the idea of pushing new music and not just slamming the place full of drunk people. It's always easier to get bigger bar spends for genres other than drum & bass, they've never been a big bar spend crew although this has changed as the age is rising a bit. Places like Steelyard, Village Underground, Fabric and Ministry still hold strong, but there's definitely a lack of smaller venues able to compete in the last few years, and I think

the scene really misses that.

Clayton: I agree that the lack of venues is a problem. Ten years ago you had about seven or eight venues in London that had 500/600 people capacity so you could start off small and test your night. If it worked, then you could move it to a bigger place.

Sarah: A lot have closed, but there are still small venues. I am a small club promoter, I prefer the more intimate vibe. I don't think I've ever promoted anything bigger than 1,000 capacity venues. Between January and August, I've been to about 20 different clubs in Hoxton and Shoreditch but you can't get in them. They're much more into having their passing trade on a Friday and Saturday. And if they do give you a chance within two events, they tell you they're not making enough on the bar. They don't want you to have any money back off the bar, and they don't like you charging their door either. They're more worried about getting the drinkers in so it becomes so difficult for a small promoter to do anything.

> **"There are certain artists I think I was pivotal in breaking through into the circuit. As time has gone on and more people have come into the game, suddenly I could no longer get those artists to play for me."**
>
> - Sarah Sandy

Jack: When you've got big numbers, you go for what you can rely on artist wise and don't take risks. What's always been enjoyable for me is when we work with an artist for a while watching them progress from supporting a 200/300 capacity club to headlining a

1000 capacity venue. You build them, but you need to have those smaller clubs to be able to take risks. The Arts Council has a lot of money available for live music at the moment, bursaries of £40,000 plus to various venues in London that do live music, but that money isn't available for dance music even though clubbing tourism in the UK is huge.

Paul: If you can find a good venue I'd say keep it because the venue is king in the rave game. If you have good staff and get on with the management, then stay where you are and work the venue. I've seen the changes. The small clubs keep the scene going.

Clayton: It's not as easy as that though. How many times have you spoken to a venue owner and they've told you your night will be exclusive for that genre but then they've let similar nights in?

Tell us the trials and tribulations of dealing with agents...

Paul: You've got good agents, and you've got bad agents...

Sarah: I like to think I'm one of the good ones. I was trying to help these guys establish a career instead of being used. The majority were black guys who were at the top of their game and needed to get some respect. I tried to implement a wage structure for them, and I don't think I was out of order trying to increase it, but I don't believe in the exclusivity thing. I think with good planning and everyone agreeing and just not clashing people could still do everything that way it gave everyone a chance to do promotions still. I never thought it was a good idea clashing things on the same night. Things have changed up now, though.

Clayton: I've got a disdain for agents. I see why they're there, but most of them are failed DJs and producers and it's the last thing they can do to stay part of the scene. Agents are supposed to work hand in hand with promoters but as time has gone on, it's almost like they're putting on your dance. You call up trying to book someone, and the agent talks to you like you're a piece of shit. They tell you what other DJs they want on the line-up, and it's like 'hold on, it's my dance'.

Billy: I'm fortunate because I'm an old skool promoter, so they're all my mates. Paul is right, though, it's as simple as there are good and bad agents.

Jack: There are certain agents who get the game, but they're also here to work with the people providing them with the cash. So they'll play promoter against promoter, but they'll

> **"We're the arse end of the industry, when the shit goes down, it all falls on us basically"**
>
> - Jack Robinson

do it in a semi-fair way. There are other agents who just squeeze it past the point, and it doesn't work for anybody. They also pit promoters against promoters to the point where someone outbids, but they've gone too deep. I've seen promoters and clubs go bankrupt and it's because those agents have squeezed the goose that laid the golden egg. Just because someone paid ten grand for said DJ doesn't mean that they're worth ten grand.

For me, it's really nice when you work with an agent and an artist over a long period of time and you have a narrative of building an artist. You all feel you're on the same side and everyone knows what the aim is. Agents are important and it just depends how they treat the promoter because at the end of the day we're still paying their bills, and sometimes it feels like that is forgotten.

Paul: *Prices for DJs are out of control.*

Billy: *Everyone wants to outdo whoever has gone before. You've got to look after your pennies to look after your pounds.*

Paul: *Promoters shot themselves in the foot as soon as they started doing back-to-backs, it became too much. You couldn't reverse it back. Some guys will pay big money, and once they do, then it's hard for everyone.*

What advice do you have for someone looking to get into promoting?

Clayton: *Start off small, do it with a couple of friends and for the passion. If you're doing it to make dough then forget it.*

Jack: *If you want to go into promotion then think 360. Promoters killing it these days are the labels. Look at Hospital, they're a label, agency, promoter... they do all of it.*

RADIO ACTIVE

Words by: Colin Steven
Photography by: Sophie Harbinson

→ → Uncle Dugs, Chef, Lady V Dubz, Eastman, Colin Steven

RADIO, PARTICULARLY PIRATE RADIO, IS EMBEDDED IN DRUM & BASS CULTURE. BACK IN THE EARLY TO MID-90S WHEN JUNGLE/DRUM & BASS WAS EMERGING AS A DISTINCT SOUND FROM HARDCORE, PIRATE RADIO WAS ONE OF THE FOUR PILLARS THAT KEPT THE SCENE ALIVE THROUGHOUT ALL THE CHANGES IN SOUND AND POPULARITY. IN THOSE PRE-INTERNET DAYS, THE ONLY WAY TO ACCESS THE MUSIC WAS VIA GOING TO EVENTS, BUYING RECORDS OR TAPE PACKS, READING FANZINES OR LISTENING TO PIRATE RADIO (ASSUMING YOU WERE LUCKY ENOUGH TO LIVE IN A CITY WITH PIRATE STATIONS).

However, times and technology change and the advent of the broadband era around the turn of the millennium brought about new legal ways of broadcasting. Internet radio stations became the new pirates with hundreds of stations appearing across the globe. Many predicted that internet radio would kill off pirates, and while there are obviously far fewer pirates than in the golden age of the 90s, many stations like Kool London continue to thrive.

These days through podcasting, live streaming on Facebook and on-demand websites such as Mixcloud you can have a radio show without even being on a station. Is this the future of radio?

Radio continues to be crucial to the advancement and spread of drum & bass culture, so we organised a discussion on its past, present and future. On the panel were Eastman (co-founder of Kool London), Uncle Dugs (Rinse FM), Lady V Dubz (Rough Tempo), DJ Chef (Pyro Radio) and myself, Colin Steven, as moderator.

Tell us about your early experiences with radio...

Uncle Dugs: *I started raving in 1991 and found pirate radio through raving. I knew of it before but wasn't really interested in it. It wasn't until Kool switched on in 1991 that I found a station that I felt was speaking my language. From about 1991 to 1997 it was the biggest thing in my life. All I wanted to do was get on that station. The Kool DJs and MCs were our pop stars and heroes. I'm on legal station Rinse FM nowadays, but I've journeyed through the pirates. Kool was the biggest platform that got me to where I am now. I actually rang Eastman and although he didn't want to see me leave he gave me his blessing. Kool is the most significant station as a listener and in my career to get me where I am today.*

Lady V Dubz: *I've been a DJ for twelve years. Before that, I was a raver and I still am now! Kool was obviously a massive part of my growing up. Anyone who was into drum & bass/jungle then Kool was the station. Everyone always wanted to be on Kool, but you weren't always that lucky. My first show was on Wax FM and to get there you had to go into this tower block on Woolwich Common. The studio was on the 13th floor and the 1210s were over the sink! I was lucky enough to get a couple of slots on Kool eventually. Recently I've done a few cover shows on Rinse for MC Stamina, but predominately I'm on internet station Rough Tempo these days.*

Chef: *I've been around the pirate radio scene for as long as Dugs. The first station I was on was Girls in south east London. It was primarily a house station but liked a bit of jungle and I got my first opportunity on there. Through the years, I played on loads of others but always trying to get to the pinnacle, which was Kool. Friends who were on the station like Marley Marl and Remarc would take me to the studios when they were doing shows. This was the place I wanted to be. Finally, after doing many shows and stations across the dial, I got the chance on Kool and I stayed there for 13 years. Nowadays I'm fortnightly on Pyro Radio. I still love radio, I think it's a very important medium that still needs to exist.*

Eastman: *I started off in pirates late 70s as a teenager. I had a friend who used to run a reggae soundsytem, and after he sold it, he started reggae and rare groove radio stations. Those days he lived in a tower block so he'd go on the roof, throw a wire over the side into his balcony and into his front room and the decks. He didn't even lock the rigs up, he'd just put them on the roof and get away with it for ages. I remember playing reggae on there for six hours straight.*

About 1990 I got to know my friend's brother, Smurf and in 1991 he approached me with an idea for a station. He was having trouble with other pirates who were kicking his aerial down so he wanted to

> **"Even trying to find the station was part of the buzz as often it would change location. I loved it. I still prefer it now to the internet radio show I do. You can't beat being naughty!"**
>
> — Lady V Dubz

link up with someone who could look after him. Smurf originally wanted to call it Rush, but Rush FM launched about two months before us. So we had to think of another name, and I said Kool - we're not rushing about, we're just cool.

Smurf was the engineer and he taught me everything. We progressed through the years and things changed. The internet came into force and funnily enough I was introduced to the internet through Pyro Radio or Pyrotechnic Radio as it was known back then. They were the first station really going for it on the internet. We even broadcast a few Kool shows on it. Through that, I realised we also had to be on the internet as well because things progress.

Luckily enough 28 years later we're still here, but it's about longevity. With Kool, all I ever look for is to be relevant with what's going on. Some people say we're not what we used to be, but I don't want to be what we used to be! We always move on and progress, you can't keep doing the same thing over and over.

Back in the day mainstream radio, or the media in general, didn't want to touch jungle, did they?

Chef: *Original pirate stations from the 60s like Caroline set the trend. They played music that the mainstream stations wouldn't play. Rave pirates followed the same pattern, it was an outlet for music* that wasn't being accepted by mainstream media. So if they didn't want to do it, you did it yourself.

Uncle Dugs: *I never realised for a long time how lucky I was because I thought pirate radio was everywhere. I didn't realise people drove down from other parts of the country to listen to radio. We just took it for granted. There were other pirates around the country but on the whole, ravers had to rely on Radio 1 and people like that, and they didn't give a shit about our music.*

Pirate radio stations back then were the gatekeepers and had a lot of power...

Eastman: *Nowadays we get told not to play certain tracks on the radio but back when we started the labels sent us records like mad. Radio helped shift units. Radio was a big outlet for rave events, records, artists, everything.*

Chef: *Pirates have influenced what mainstream stations do. Brian Belle-Fortune set up One In The Jungle on Radio 1 back in the mid-90s and copied the Kool format.*

Uncle Dugs: *Looking back now I can appreciate how important it was to have the One In The Jungle show on Radio 1, but at the time I didn't listen to it. For me, it wasn't real, it was a watered-down version for your parents' ears. At the time, I didn't like major record labels or stations. Everything that was not us I didn't like or care about because they didn't represent us.*

We were never about money, it was about believing in something you loved so much. I can appreciate the significance of it now, though.

Tell us more about the buzz of doing pirate...

Lady V Dubz: *Even trying to find the station was part of the buzz as often it would change location. I loved it. I still prefer it now to the internet radio show I do. You can't beat being naughty!*

Uncle Dugs: *I don't do pirate any more but that feeling when you hear a bang and wonder what it is! You turn the music down and look for an escape route. Usually it's nothing but now and again it is something. That's the buzz.*

Eastman: *You could lose all your vinyl back then, nowadays you just lose a USB stick or whatever.*

Uncle Dugs: *Do studio raids still happen?*

Eastman: *Now and again. What they tend to do now is hit all three at once: studio, midpoint and block. But it tends to be the people who take things for granted.*

Chef: *It was the excitement of going to these mad locations in the middle of nowhere at night. You couldn't bring a record bag, so your records would be in a bin bag or a Tesco's bag. We were lugging vinyl. You couldn't do a four-hour graveyard shift with 20 records.*

Eastman: *We once had a studio in Clapton at the back*

> **"**Radio is about personality, and we're lucky on Kool that we've got some really good personalities. When I do my show I talk about how I feel, it's about your personality.**"**
> - Eastman

of a reggae dance. Our studio was cordoned off, but when they had reggae dances we had to turn our set up louder. There was also a little crack pit connected to it, and at the side of the alley you had bare crack man dealing this and that. I had DJs phoning me up telling me they couldn't go down, but I told them to shut up and go down. They knew we were there and to leave us alone. Down that same alley, they used to dump all the rubbish. Probe and IC3 phoned me up one time and told me to come down as there were rats in the alley and they couldn't get out! I went down, and they were huddled up in the corner of the alley, and I had to kick up the bags of rubbish to make sure no rats were there!

Dugs, you have plenty of similar stories in your book, don't you...

Uncle Dugs: *Yeah, the book is called Rave Diaries & Tower Block Tales. It's about my life in music, and a big chunk of it is pirate radio. I started out on my local station Conflict in 1995 and within a few weeks me and my mates were running the station. Slowly but surely we learned how to use the equipment. We'd never done anything like that before - it's not like plugging in a stereo in your bedroom and it all just comes on. Like anything, if you're into it, you learn as you go. We made loads of mistakes, but we got better and better and I made loads of contacts.*

I ended up on Rinse when it was still a pirate in 1999, and I managed it when garage, grime and dubstep was being introduced. Watching kids coming along in tracksuits with holes in it and eating McDonald's because that's all they could afford to flying around in private jets, playing America and doing tours was a great thing to watch. It's something that gave inner city kids a future, and that goes for every generation of pirate radio.

Coming out of Rinse and finally getting onto Kool and concentrating on DJing again and then going back to Rinse when it was a legal station, I feel like I've lived a hundred lifetimes and I've had the best time. All I ever wanted to do was be on Kool and play at Jungle Fever. Radio has always been the heartbeat of everything that I've done. If I had to choose between rave and radio, it would be radio all day long. We're a bit of a weird breed radio people. People don't understand why you would go up a tower block and risk your freedom and records to play to nobody for 12 hours through the night. I've done shows where I've not had any texts or phone calls, and I've loved it exactly the same as when it's popped off because I just love it. I can't explain it.

What qualities does it take to run a station?

Eastman: *Thick skin for one. I also put on Jungle Fever and I might make six people happy and 40 people are cursing me! I don't care, they can call me names behind my back. It's strictly business. If I upset you, I don't mean it. You've got to be strong-willed, strong-minded and a leader. You have to have passion for the music and what you're doing. You can't let people take the piss or treat you like dirt. You've got to be able to stand up for yourself because otherwise, people will take over what you're doing.*

Chef: *It was tough love. Sometimes if a DJ couldn't pay his subs money you had to tell them they couldn't do their show next week, which is heartbreaking.*

Eastman: *You've got to know when and where and what to say. You can't just be a hard, horrible person all the time. You have to show love and guide some people and bring the best out in them. Loads of people might have a problem outside of radio, and we talk about it over a coffee. Because I'm a bit older, they look to me for that and I do that.*

What qualities does it take to be a good radio DJ?

Lady V Dubz: *I think there's a lot of character missing from shows now. Back in the day, I used to love locking into a radio show, and the DJ would have a nice chat, read out the texts and give you info. It's all about the MCs, and I'm probably guilty of that on my Rough Tempo show too, especially since the internet has come about and the video side of it.*

Eastman: *You've got to take control of your show. It's the same with my lot. If it's a MC orientated show, I tell the DJ to introduce the show for the first half-hour and then get the MCs on.*

Lady V Dubz: *The weird thing is when I do my show on Rinse I do that format – a little chat at the beginning, an interview and then get into the mix.*

Eastman: *Radio is about personality, and we're lucky on Kool that we've got some really good personalities. When I do my show I talk about how I feel, it's about your personality.*

Chef: *Funky Flirt is one of the best radio characters ever.*

Uncle Dugs: *Flirt started on Sunrise, so he does everyone for history. He's done every job. If there was*

"I'm not a fan of the video side of things because I believe that radio should be heard and not seen. You build the image in your mind."

- Uncle Dugs

a pirate radio hall of fame, he'd be at the top for me.

Chef: *Food Junky is mental too, his energy is incredible. You get to see it now, but when it was just the audio you thought the geezer was bonkers! He would make you laugh and you'd want to listen.*

Eastman: *It's about expressing yourself and being real.*

Talk about how the internet has changed things for better and for worse...

Uncle Dugs: *I was on Rinse when the internet first came about. There was a guy called DJ SL, not the SL from Kool, and he used to do something a bit like what Tune In do now. So he would stream half a dozen stations of really bad quality, and* the stream would break but there was a guy called Megatron who lived in San Francisco and he used to message us. That was the first time I experienced that, and that side of it was great. When I do my show now, fifty per cent are from outside the UK, but quality control has gone right out of the window. Anyone can broadcast now. You've got a million internet radio stations that are a bag of shit and people Facebook Live every minute to one viewer that's their mum downstairs. We're in a now generation for music, people want it now, and they can have it now but it doesn't mean they're good at it.

Lady V Dubz: The whole Facebook Live thing is dead now anyway because Facebook clocked onto its success and want to monetise it.

Chef: They want to close down the music you play as well, if you play a certain tune then they'll shut down your stream.

Lady V Dubz: It got out of hand, and maybe Facebook changing its algorithm is a good thing as people aren't bothering as much now.

Uncle Dugs: I'm not a fan of the video side of things because I believe that radio should be heard and not seen. You build the image in your mind.

Chef: It's changed, the DJs have to perform now, and it's become a visual thing now.

Uncle Dugs: There is a place for the visual side if you have MCs or it's a talk based thing but just watching a DJ is boring. Another thing I've really noticed is that it's become less about the station and more about the individual show. Now you're filming yourself doing your show for your own social media channels. Previously we used to listen to stations like a football team. I supported Kool like I support West Ham. I did listen to other stations, but Kool was my team. It came across to the listener. Even if the DJs and MCs all hated each other, we never knew that.

Eastman: There's a lot of good and bad on the internet in general. It's a big part of progression. You can't go backwards now. It's here, so you've got to accept it and make the best of it. Everything is technology. People that start digital stations now and I don't know why. Why waste your money and pay three grand a month to the government on a digital licence for one area when you can do exactly the same on the internet for a grand a month and be worldwide. Digital is shit, the signal is worse than FM.

How has podcasting and being able to access archived shows changed things?

Chef: There was nothing worse than missing a Super Sunday with Brockie and Det, and unless some had taped it, you missed it. Now with archives, they're all there for eternity or until the server gets switched off!

Eastman: All our shows are archived now but some people I speak to say they don't have time to listen live

and they'll just catch it on the archive. I'm like "No, listen live!"

Chef: With streaming services like Mixcloud my history of radio now lives somewhere and it can be accessed at any time.

Lady V Dubz: Radio has played a big part of people being able to see what Girls Take Action are doing. Radio has always been an important part of what I've done throughout the 12 years I've been DJing. Loads of more females out there are doing their thing now which is the whole idea behind GTA – we're not taking over, we just want to be a part of it and to show there are so many girls out there that get overlooked. The podcast definitely helps.

What about the future? Can radio stations stay relevant?

Lady V Dubz: I think that stations still need to exist, but there does need to be less competition. There are stations popping up left, right and centre but only the strong survive though.

Chef: I teach media to kids about 16, and one of my first questions is if they listen to the radio and usually none put their hands up. I then ask how many are forced to listen to the radio when they're in the car with their parents and about half the room put their hands up. This generation doesn't know the radio as a medium, they've lost the appreciation of what radio is because of on-demand.

Eastman: They haven't got time. They just hear what they want to hear. I love talk station LBC because I like to hear all different conversations and I listen to BBC World Service because I hear music I wouldn't hear anywhere else. With a lot of 14 to 25-year-olds, they just want to listen to exactly the tune they want to hear.

Uncle Dugs: Don't you think when a kid finds a style of music that they like that's when they find radio? Radio is still where it's at for someone who's into dance culture.

Eastman: There's so much choice now. We're not going to be first on the list of people getting into drum & bass now, as I doubt they've heard of us. That's just how it is.

What advice would you give someone wanting to get into radio?

Lady V Dubz: Don't be boring, come with some interesting content for your show. Try and do something different that other people aren't doing.

Uncle Dugs: Don't be scared to be yourself.

> **"**This generation doesn't know the radio as a medium, they've lost the appreciation of what radio is because of on-demand.**"**
> - Chef

HYBRID MINDS

Words by: Ben Murphy

RECENTLY DRUM & BASS HAS OPENED UP TO ENCOMPASS A MULTITUDE OF NEW INFLUENCES, WITH A HOST OF DJS, PRODUCERS AND LABELS PUSHING EXPERIMENTALISM AND FRESH LEFTFIELD IDEAS TO THE FOREFRONT. WE SPEAK TO THE LIKES OF DBRIDGE, ICICLE, SINISTARR, DEXTA, A.FRUIT, TIM REAPER AND SPECIAL REQUEST ABOUT HOW AND WHY THEY'RE MIXING ELEMENTS FROM FOOTWORK, TECHNO AND OTHER STYLES TO PUSH D&B FORWARD.

"**N**owadays it's a pretty much 'anything goes' environment when it comes to making bass music, which is refreshing," says Detroit producer Sinistarr, considering the new wave of hybrid drum & bass sounds that he and many others are contributing to in 2019. "In my view, knowing and respecting the history and heritage of genres and subgenres is ethically important, but they are foundations – not mandates for how a style should be made going forward."

More than ever before, drum & bass has opened up to encompass a multitude of new influences, with a host of DJs, producers and label owners pushing experimentalism and fresh leftfield ideas to the forefront.

In 2019, club crowds are more accepting of a mixture of jungle-adjacent styles, and switching between tempo, sounds and rhythms is no longer unusual. Sinistarr blends d&b with his home city's techno tradition and speedy electro; Sherelle and Fauzia spin a powder-keg mix of 160bpm beats of all kinds; Om Unit and Itoa take elements of footwork and half-time and reconstruct them amid frenetic breaks; Lakeway flits between grime and d&b in the space of one track; and Tim Reaper snaps rolling Amen breaks to thumping 4/4

kick drums for exercises in frantic jungle tekno.

Labels from dBridge's Exit to Fracture's Astrophonica regularly release beats that blur the boundaries between genres, while Med School, Rupture and Western Lore have all disrupted tradition with their experimental fare recently. They, and many more, are making drum & bass sound the most exciting and vital that it has in years.

Since its birth in the hardcore rave scene, jungle/drum & bass has been a compound, made of parts of hip-hop, reggae, funk and techno reassembled into something new, with a speed and sound unlike anything else. While in recent times some areas of d&b have become too narrowly defined, and settled into an orthodoxy of simplistic beats and ultra clean mix-downs, the current set of adventurous DJs and artists are upsetting this sameness and making music with the same pioneering, anything-goes spirit that created jungle/drum & bass in the first place.

"If you look at how it first came about, that was the beauty of jungle/drum & bass, that it was able to fuse any and everything together," says dBridge, an artist who has dedicated himself to pushing the genre forward with his productions, DJ sets and releases via the long-running Exit label. "You can have such differing sound sources and artists, combined into one track. That's important now from my point of view. I listen to so much varied stuff, and it does have an influence on me. I like to be able to fuse some of those elements. As a genre, d&b still has so much possibility in terms of what it can do."

Via Exit, dBridge has put out everything from Skeptical and Dub Phizix's halftime beats (the classic 'Marka', for instance), to Itoa's what-do-you-call-it productions and Sinistarr's recent ghetto-tech electro collaboration with DJ Stingray, 'Untitled', which found common ground between the genres thanks to their similarity of tempo.

This creative freedom is something dBridge has pursued for some time, as in the late 2000s, he teamed up with Instra:mental to create the micro style, Autonomic: a sound which drew from science fiction, analogue synthesis, electropop and film soundtracks for inspiration, and spawned a cult podcast series, a

> "Nowadays it's a pretty much 'anything goes' environment when it comes to making bass music, which is refreshing"
> - Sinistarr

Fixate

Om Unit

Special Request

Sinistarr

D-Bridge

Chris Dexta

A Fruit

Icicle

clutch of singles and a FABRICLIVE mix. For dBridge, being stuck in one sound stifles creativity.

"When I first got into this, I was making hardcore, then it was jungle," he says. "As I got older, I realised that I just wanted to make music, and try different things out, as any producer wants to do. I don't really do what's expected any more. It's something I've needed throughout my career, to be able to do this."

One of the reasons the scene now is vibrant, dBridge reckons, is that new artists are unsaddled with the baggage of the past, and its strict list of d&b dos and don'ts. To them, genre rules and restrictions are meaningless, as they've grown up listening to all kinds of sounds and are unafraid to take ideas from anywhere.

"There were always purists in the past, saying, 'you can only do this', all these rules that they tried to put in place about what defines it," he says. "But I think what I like about the new producers coming up is, they don't really have that. They're fusing things together in the spirit of what jungle was - but it's not jungle. So you've got kids like Itoa and Fixate applying these different rhythms and these sounds you kind of recognise."

Part of that new generation is Moscow producer A.Fruit. Her vividly hued track 'Please, Arrive' for Med School zings with warm techno synths, while tracks like 'Bright Spot' cut up micro breakbeat snippets into footwork rhythms, heavy sub bass lunges pushing it onward.

"I've always been more interested in the leftfield sounds of this genre," A.Fruit says. "Studying and working on audio engineering has also affected my way of feeling the music. Just at the time when I needed some fresh inspiration to understand what kind of sound I wanted to produce, I discovered footwork music. It inspired me to create the type of hybrid sound I'm really into."

Another A.Fruit track, 'Secret Trick', finds her disrupting time signatures, moving between 130 and 160bpm with a subtle, though brain-scrambling sense of temporal displacement. A.Fruit's crisp though unconventional sound comes in part, she says, from her background in video game sound design, giving her a fastidiousness and experimentalism when making d&b.

"My video game soundtrack work definitely affects my perspective," she says. "I'm very sensitive to what every little sound feels like - sometimes it's even annoying. But I guess this experience with games also makes my music sound a little bit more interesting, it helps me to see the details from different angles."

If A.Fruit's aim is to shift the focus to other rhythms and sounds, then Fixate is taking familiar formats and redrawing them in fresh ways. With releases on Diffrent Music, Exit and 1985, he's made waves recently with a remix of Double 99's speed garage anthem 'Rip Groove', keeping the original's warping synth bass and snapping it to a rapid Amen break for maximum devastation. His collab with Dub Phizix, meanwhile, the aptly named 'Hotfoot', has bubbling, speedy footwork percs over a clipped halftime beat, while a sludgy bass slurps around below: another track sitting in between tempos and genres.

Itoa, meanwhile, is a contemporary whose minimalistic, skeletal beats, as on 'You're The One For Me', dash abruptly across different speeds: a highly physical sound with shades of grime, footwork and disorienting shards of jungle breaks.

This cohort of artists is a source of inspiration to DJ and producer Chris Dexta, A&R for Med School and founder of the Diffrent Music label. Also citing "Profane, Om Unit, Silent Dust, Fybe:One, Dominic Ridgway and Pepsi Slammer" as artists shaking up the genre, it's their leftfield experimentalism and absorption of other styles that Dexta reckons is making drum & bass more exciting.

"I find it magical when someone who's heavily into jazz music starts drawing time signatures from their favourite bands," he says, "or someone who's into ambient sound design uses textures and layers rarely used in the d&b realm - it offers up something interesting for the listener. A lot of the d&b music I've heard over the last five or six years seems like it's stuck in a loop, or just getting louder. Others must be noticing that as well, and that's why they're playing around in the void, bringing some vibe and funk back."

Dexta's Diffrent label has put out a wide variety of distinctive releases, ranging from Fearful's cinematic, found sound-laden beatscapes to Lakeway's grime collisions and the lyrical wordplay of Sense MC. Artists creating these engaging musical chimeras is why the imprint was established in the first place.

"The label was set up to create a platform for something alternative in the scene," Dexta says, "at a time when there wasn't much experimental d&b music going on - well, at least not showing up on my radar. Now, nine years later, there has been a positive surge into the leftfield, which has led to an exciting breeding ground for new and established artists to enter."

If this surge in adventurous beat making and DJing has benefited the drum & bass scene, it's also encouraged a creative freedom for d&b artists to experiment beyond the immediate confines of their genre. Tim Reaper is a prolific producer whose many EPs and singles for Repertoire, Green Bay Wax, Skeleton and 7th Storey Projects have specialised in smash-out Amen break jungle and classic beat edits in the style of classic Dillinja or Photek.

More recently, he's searched further back for inspiration, influenced by labels like Basement Records and the early 'jungle tekno' sound, driven by 4/4 kick drums and a manic electronic energy, along with its ever-present breaks. His 'A2' track for vol.9 of the 'Globex Corp' series, a collaboration with Mr Sensi, is a thumping 4/4 piece with rolling breaks and gated, trance-like synth melodies, while 'B2' (with Dwarde and Gand) has rude hardcore acid blips and rushing hi-hats you might normally associate with original jungle tekno specialists Top Buzz. For Tim Reaper, making music like this is a different discipline, and allows him

> **"**I like to think that the new generation will take it in their own direction and not really give a fuck what... the old guard think**"**
> - DBridge

to work differently and employ more melody than in the edit-heavy, bassy tracks he normally creates.

"With that mind-set, the drums don't become the forefront of the tune and instead, the riff or the pads or whatever melodies are on top can take more dominance," he says. "When that's the case, I can flex more different sounds on top of it, because there's usually more room in the track."

Tim Reaper admits that in the past he's drawn influences from tracks that are very similar to his own stuff, and now has made a conscious decision to look further afield to freshen up his beats.

"I've been previously guilty (and still am to a degree) of being heavily inspired by other examples of the exact same music that I make," he says, "but I've found that it leads to quite derivative results, due to the limited sound palette you can get from being solely into one style. Most of my favourite examples of music from jungle's golden era and today's jungle have been tunes that sample sounds that haven't already been used before, and that really adds to the gene pool of the style, which can only be of benefit if there's more to choose from."

Other established d&b DJ/producers have stepped even further into alien territory, encouraged by the current warm climate for polymorphous sounds. Calibre has made house and broken beat for Craig Richards' Nothing Special label (2016's 'Grow' album), dBridge has made a similar blend of styles as Velvit, and Tim Reaper points to the fact that: "Dwarde's been making garage on the side for a few years and had his first garage release last year, with more coming, Kid Lib had a covert house release out last year, and Equinox has been making house and garage for years."

One genre that has had a particularly fluid exchange with drum & bass is techno. Breakbeats are again commonplace in techno DJ sets, while artists like Forest Drive West see no issue with making purist techno and drum & bass alike, releasing it all under one name. Fracture has recently dabbled with d&b speed 4/4 on the ferocious 'Dropping You', and DJ Tasha originally came from the d&b scene, so a bass attitude still pervades her underground kick drum fusillades and some of the releases on her Neighbourhood label.

Minimal techno sensation Shifted was originally one half of Commix, Instra:mental's Boddika went on to make his name as a techno DJ, and another techno artist, Randomer, started out on Med School, and today makes weird hybrid beats with a heavy sub bass focus drawn from his d&b years, while occasionally playing pure jungle sets.

Add to that the fact that late drum & bass pioneer Marcus Intalex had a sideline in bassy Detroit techno styles as Trevino, and there's a case to be made that the genres have a lot in common. For Dutch DJ/producer Icicle, the styles have become intertwined as mutual influences. Though best known for his suitably frosty d&b tracks, the sound design and synths of techno have been a constant muse on his tracks for Critical, Shogun and Outlook (hear the boiling 303 squelches of 2015's 'Acidic' for starters), while he's also made straight up 4/4 beats under the name Cadans.

"My drum & bass has always been quite techno influenced in terms of sounds, even from back in the day when Ed Rush & Optical did it, the old school tech-step stuff," Icicle says. "That's a really different way of working. It gives you a different perspective on dynamics, whether it's solid bass or pulsating rhythm. For me, it's always been an interesting way to flip it. It's so easy to get bored and stuck trying to do the same tunes, so what better than to try something else?"

For Icicle, the lo-fi, scuzzy direction that techno has gone has inspired the way he's made d&b lately, shunning sparkling production in favour of analogue grit and dirt.

"It's kind of an alternative to the Mefjus way of producing, which I always like doing, but it tires me out because it's so perfect and so well defined and super clean," he says. "Just to get a break from that, I went to techno. The last EP I did was a lot more saturated and not as modern sounding. I was trying to bring that organic kind of sound that there used to be. Also, the techniques that come with it, like using real tape for tape saturation, or using a modular synthesiser."

Detroit's Sinistarr has become renowned for his releases on Metalheadz, Inperspective and Creative Source, and has his own relationship with techno, just one of the many styles swirled into his diverse releases, which also touch on halftime, electro, footwork and hip-hop. For him, techno is an aspect of the cultural influence of Detroit, which permeates his work.

"The idea of Detroit outside of the city is stuck in a continuous homage or nostalgia kick to a bygone era," he says. "I think of my sound as a form of 'field reporting'... making sounds that are of a time and place in the city. Sounds you'd have to visit Detroit to really know about and truly understand. From influences inside the city, my music comes from a very black and multicultural sound - ghetto-tech to Motown, hip-hop, house and techno were my local influences, so I like 'cross-pollinating' those styles and sounds in my productions and adding my style to it, making something new and exciting."

For Sinistarr, the tempo, rather than the genre, is often the thing that binds all his musical interests together.

"Genre names are in place for reference at this point, mainly because there's 25-30 years of legacy behind it and counting," he says. "But there are always new ones being invented, or new experimentations in dance music happening, so I usually bypass the genre of what it is and just look at tempo."

Pointing to the jungle influences in the work of Chicago footwork artists like the late DJ Rashad and other members of the Teklife crew like Spinn and Taye, Sinistarr recognises these musical blends as an important cultural and transatlantic exchange.

"The footwork pioneers employing jungle in their works in the past few years is a great example of this, in turn bridging a major connection between Chicago and the UK - both tempos staying right in place at 160bpm."

Just as there is now a "revolving door" between producers working in different genres, there is also a greater opportunity for DJs and producers from outside the drum & bass scene to make their mark on it. A case in point is Paul Woolford, whose Special Request alias has been responsible for devastatingly heavy jungle, like the crushing 'Replicant' or the dark and rolling 'Black Ops'.

Once best known as a house and techno DJ whose metallic 2006 track 'Erotic Discourse' is considered a classic, as Special Request, he's been embraced for tracks that deal not just in drum & bass but also in hardcore, UK garage and electro. It's Woolford's expertise at crafting beats and as a DJ that have seen him spin at Metalheadz events, and seen his tracks played by traditional d&b DJs. Woolford grew up with rave culture, and he's spent many years working to achieve a sound he felt was good enough to share. Though he was initially unsure about how his d&b material would be received, he's paid his dues many times over.

"I had some concerns, but I also had the knowledge that I'm not a dilettante," Woolford says. "I'm sure there were people that thought I was, but other people's opinions are none of my business. Ultimately, when you do anything, you need to know you are doing it properly - inside and out. I've never been the sort of person to take shortcuts, and I didn't do that with this music. I'd been messing around with it since '96-'97 before I publicly released anything in 2013, so it had been incubating for a good 16 years beforehand, and further back, if you count all the years going out and absorbing the tape packs, right back to the genesis of it all basically. I'm blessed that I've been able to be a fan of something for so long, and then contribute to it in my own small way."

Woolford loves being able to make what he wants without being put in a pigeonhole, and reckons that the dismantling of genre constrictions brought about via Spotify or YouTube, and a differently structured media, have contributed to the new way in which young (and older) people consume music.

"For many years dance music was compartmentalised," he says. "We had so many years of the media being all-powerful and putting both producers and DJs in boxes, and at a certain point, there was a reaction against this. The power structures behind dance music have largely changed, and add to this the turnover of younger people participating every year, and taking up positions in organisations with different influences.

"Also, streaming has ensured that we can all listen to pretty much any genre at any time. There's no barrier or hierarchy to finding the music of anyone, pretty much. You don't have to be mates with the right person at the right record shop to find out what My Bloody Valentine's best release is. A whole generation have grown up having access to everything simultaneously, so this means that they see no reason why they shouldn't make one thing one day and another the next. Ultimately, the human mind needs to keep itself interested. Why wouldn't you indulge all your impulses?"

In addition to these cultural shifts, another reason that this hybrid music is bubbling, reckons A.Fruit, is that people are sick of the same old, same old, and looking for something new. "There are quite a lot of producers who got tired of hundreds of very similar sounding tracks, and more and more record labels are getting interested in experimental sounds these days."

Also, with jungle back in the headlines - as much due to the volume of great music being released as it is due to a degree of nostalgia - more DJs and producers are becoming intrigued, picking and choosing bits and pieces from it, or incorporating it into their own musical agglomerations.

"People are very open to a jungle influence and it's very cool again," Icicle says. "That's good, because when drum & bass and jungle make an impression on other genres, it's easier for people within it to switch styles - you don't need an introduction. People see what you're doing and they're like, 'cool'. It's a good time for that right now."

It's through musical hybridity that jungle/drum & bass first came into being, and the stylistic mixtures of now are how the genre will continue to not just survive but evolve. Though some consider these new combinations apocryphal to what real d&b is, dBridge makes a convincing comparison.

"My example is, what do you think your parents thought when you took their records and made jungle out of it?" he says. "I can imagine the looks on their faces. I don't want to be like that. Some people forget how things were born and how they came to be. There are some old gits who need to move on a bit. I like to think that the new generation will take it in their own direction and not really give a fuck what some of us, the old guard, think, and what we think it should be."

> **"A whole generation have grown up having access to everything simultaneously, so this means that they see no reason why they shouldn't make one thing one day and another the next"**
> - Special Request

> **"I find it magical when someone who's heavily into jazz music starts drawing time signatures from their favourite bands"**
> - Chris Dexta

EST 1991

KOOL LDN

LISTEN & INTERACT @ WWW.KOOLLONDON.COM

 @KOOLLDN @KOOLLDN @KOOLLONDON  KOOL LONDON

WHATSAPP & TEXT ON 0750 801 2 801

NEXT GENERATION LABELS

Words by: Dave Jenkins

HINDSIGHT IS A BEAUTIFUL THING. USE IT TO LOOK BACK OVER DRUM & BASS' NEAR-30-YEAR TIMELINE AND YOU'LL SEE INSTANT SWEET-SPOT YEARS WHERE WHOLE CLUTCHES OF LABELS SEEMINGLY POP-UP EN-MASSE AND PROCEED TO HAVE A HUGE INFLUENCE ON THE GENRE AND ITS MANY SOUNDS AND DIRECTIONS.

Take 1996: the year the world was blessed with the likes of Hospital, Playaz, Renegade Hardware, CIA and Chronic. Take the invasion of 2001-3 from a whole army of prominent imprints: Dispatch, Soul:r, Critical, Frequency, Commercial Suicide, Exit, Signature, Innerground, Breakbeat Kaos, Viper, D-Style, Quarantine and Radius to name a few.

Tomes could be written on the impact of these labels. Yet no one knew how much of an influence these labels would have at the time. How many now-headlining names they'd break, how many styles they'd incubate. They were just doing their thing; pushing, developing and ultimately contributing to a movement that was barely into its second decade. It's only thanks to hindsight we can look back at those eras and consider their significance.

Until, arguably, 2016-18. Another, much more recent sweet-spot during which a whole new wave of independent labels hit the genre so hard it was impossible to ignore. 1985, The North Quarter, Get Hype, Ish Chat, Guidance, Index, Souped Up, Sofa Sound, Hybrid Music, Entropy Music, Obsolete Medium, Footnotes... Each of these labels meant business from the off. They had their own agendas, stories, distinctive sounds and identities. Notably, they had their own artist founder at the helm: Alix Perez, Lenzman, The Prototypes, SpectraSoul, Ulterior Motive, Breakage, Serum, DLR, Hybrid Minds, Icicle, Rockwell... All of them doing their thing; pushing, developing, contributing. But now the movement is

almost three decades deep. And the significance is so strong hindsight isn't necessary.

"In one way it's a generational thing," considers Greg Hepworth, one half of Ulterior Motive, the act behind Guidance, a label that already in its short lifetime has championed new artists such as Kiril and Lovely and encourage the return of early 2000s dons Future Cut. "Look at the labels we were inspired by. They're first-generation artist-run labels. They brought us in, now we're in a new cycle. It's not a coincidence that most of the artists who are running these new labels came in kind of around the same era."

It's also no coincidence they've all reached a stage in their career where even being signed to the most impressive label isn't quite as fulfilling as it used to be. Amsterdam-based Lenzman has had a similar trajectory as Ulterior Motive. They both came through on Metalheadz around the same time, released debut albums in 2014 and both launched their labels within a year of each other. Like Guidance, Lenzman's The North Quarter made a strong impression almost instantly. Known for its extended releases and deep hip-hop references, The North Quarter has amassed camp of like-minded spirits such as Redeyes, Anile, Submorphics and FD who have all said in interviews how he's encouraged some of the best records they've ever made out of them.

"Signing with Metalheadz was a big deal because I looked up to them so much," explains Lenzman. "It still

is a big deal. But once you've done things like release an album and EPs on a label, from an ambition point of view, you find yourself going through the motions doing the same things you've already done. Setting up the label was a way of adding a whole other dimension to being a music professional and gave a lot more creative challenges to rise to and a lot more ways to express my own vision."

Lenzman's appreciation for the much wider creative scope created by having your own label is shared by everyone interviewed for this feature. The word 'vision' is thrown around like a reload at a soundclash, and for a good reason: releases and DJ sets can make a statement, but a label allows you to articulate yourself, your sound, interests and aesthetic to the very last detail.

"1985 is one of the best examples of that," offers Breakage. "The momentum Alix has developed for that in such a short space of time is amazing. The apparel, the nights, the releases, the artists he's championing. It's all so cohesive. You get this sense of who he is, and what his vision is, through everything the label does. It's a new label energy."

Breakage rides this wave of new label energy, too. His own label Index was launched around the same time as 1985. While Index is a platform for Breakage's own music, the same passion is just as strong. Since launching Index he's had his most prolific release period in years and cooked up some of his rawest, most natural

> **"Now is the true time of the independent. It's never been a fairer time for it, and we have all the tools: you can speak to your audience, monetise your own material that belongs to you and basically do what you want to do."**
> - DLR

Ulterior Motive

Serum

Breakage

The Prototypes

DLR

Lenzman

Jef MethLab

jungle records of his career. He's inspired and motivated. Not just by the creative capabilities of a label but also ownership, courtesy of advice from his old label boss, good friend and mentor Shy FX.

"When Shy was closing Digital Soundboy he told me I needed to have my own label," Breakage explains. "He told me I needed to own what I make. That blew my mind a bit. I hadn't thought about it before. It's just what happens – someone taking 'x' amount of percentage of the music because it's them releasing it and doing that side of the process. But it doesn't have to be that way. And the way the industry is now, if you're lucky enough to be making music for a living and having a following you can get your music to, it seems crazy to do it any other way."

It's here where we begin to understand a much more significant reason why this wave of indie labels has made such a splash. Yes, it's a natural stage of the cycle where artists have outgrown the process of a larger label that has also grown and developed its roster. But it's much more indicative of the industry climate that's amplified this. Serum agrees. His label Souped Up was so distinctive and influential in its entrance it won Best Newcomer Label in the Drum&BassArena Awards in 2018, just over a year after it launched. Prior to this, his broad sound was renowned for appearing on labels across the spectrum from his mainstay V to Dread to 31 to Low Down Deep, but now most of his solo material is on his own label.

"Selling on lots of labels in the digital age is a hard thing," states Serum who runs the label with Benny V. "If you're signing a tune and it's sitting there with a slow trickle through on websites forever, it doesn't make sense to do too many things for different people. It's better to build your own brand and have more control of that yourself."

"It's actually really exciting," adds James DLR. His label Sofa Sound is comparable to Souped Up in its colourful illustrated artwork, sense of fun and character and strong mix of new and established talent. "In the 1970s if I wanted to launch a psychedelic Sofa Sound label and be independent then I better know someone with millions who can inject shit loads into what I want to do. It would have been almost impossible. Same in the 80s and even in the 90s majors would snap up indies quickly. Now is the true time of the independent. It's never been a fairer time for it, and we have all the tools: you can speak to your audience, monetise your own material that belongs to you and basically do what you want to do."

It's true; resources such as distribution services, direct-to-artist platforms such as Bandcamp and social media have created a two-way DIY street that's never been as broad and effective for independent artists as it is now. There are also more revenue streams from multiple streaming platforms and syncing royalties. Merchandise and apparel have become a vital revenue source for almost all new labels and those with very loyal, engaged fanbases have set up Patreon accounts. All these streams, when owned and controlled by themselves, help artists – for the first time since vinyl sales collapsed 10 years ago – develop more of a consistent income and be able to invest in their own and the label's future.

For some, the label will remain a vehicle for their own body of work. Like Calibre, it's their own signature. For others, though, it's a chance to upkeep the tradition that brought them in and start to develop a camp of new artists and help bring them through. Greg Ulterior Motive thinks it's selfish not to sign and develop new talent saying it's "our duty to encourage new artists and explore this sound and see how far we can expose it to people."

Inspired by the crew-like culture of labels such as Full Cycle and Virus, DLR is of a similar mindset. Nick White from the Prototypes also admits that developing a label and crew like Breakbeat Kaos was always an aspiration for him and production partner Chris Garvey and its legacy is a big influence on their label Get Hype. He warns the independent route isn't for everyone, or should at least be timed right, but he also observes that the genre moves so quickly the rules the founding labels set 20-30 years ago no longer apply.

"I wouldn't advise any brand-new artist to set up their label without getting that stamp of authority from the labels they aspire to release on," he explains. "I think every artist needs experience of being A&R'd. They need to understand quality control, how to get your music out, who it's being directed to. We learnt loads from being signed to Shogun and Viper. That said, though. Things have changed a lot recently. Artists are coming through non-conventional routes and smashing it in a very short space of time. So what we're seeing now are the bigger labels scratching around chasing after these independent artists and trying to get them involved. It's more the labels on the look-out than the artists right now."

And the labels who have proven to be the sharpest look-outs for new talent in recent years provide the final piece in this new indie tale. While all of the labels listed so far in this piece have made a big impression and seem to be run with long-game tactics, it's only a fraction of the wider scene. There are just as many, if not more, burgeoning DIY imprints run by people who aren't well-known artists (or artists at all) but they are just as passionate about pushing, developing and contributing to the movement.

It's one thing for an established act with a reasonable-sized following to launch a label, but there are others who have started at much more of a grassroots level and developed into key imprints who are breaking the headliners of the future. Critical Music is the most successful example of this; while the label boss Kasra is well known as a producer and one of the top tier DJs in the genre now, he was just a passionate fan when the label launched in 2002.

Meanwhile, other more contemporary examples of labels that are not run by higher-profile artists, but are fuelling the genre with just as much new talent and ideas include Flexout Audio, Lifestyle Music, Overview, Delta9, Context Audio and MethLab.

"Look at what MethLab have achieved," says Serum. "I'm lucky. I launched Souped Up at a point when my name has a following, but and what [label co-founder] Jef has done without being a known artist in any way? That's a whole other level of hard work and a massive challenge."

Like Souped Up, MethLab also won a Best Newcomer Label accolade in remarkably short time after launching. One of the most provocative and boundary-blurring new labels to have emerged in the 2010s, it was founded by Jef Oswald and Tommy Broken Note as an extension of their DJ agency, it instantly grabbed imaginations and a loyal following through its high-tech aesthetic and eye for experimentation.

Most importantly, MethLab represents a much wider sea-change in drum & bass label culture. It's not just the artist-run labels popping-up en-masse and influencing the genre and its many sounds and directions, it's every new label looking to push, develop and contribute to drum & bass.

And they're doing it at a time when the landscape is fairer than it's been for years and the tools are more accessible than ever before. Crucially, the new generation of artists are switched onto this and aren't wasting time utilising those tools themselves. As such it's encouraging much more of an artist-led scene rather than a big label-dominated one. And the new wave of labels, artist-run or not, are the ones helping and encouraging the new talent first.

"The most exciting and innovative ideas often come from the new entities," agrees Jef MethLab. "The ones for whom people have no expectations and are busy delving into the huge pool of unknown artists, many of whom will go on to become tomorrow's sonic heroes."

Hindsight is great, sure. But for a genre that's often characterised by science, technology and the ideas of the future, foresight is a much more fitting and beautiful thing.

> **"Things have changed a lot recently. Artists are coming through non-conventional routes and smashing it in a very short space of time."**
> - The Prototypes

> **"Look at the labels we were inspired by. They're first-generation artist-run labels. They brought us in, now we're in a new cycle. It's not a coincidence that most of the artists who are running these new labels came in kind of around the same era."**
> - Ulterior Motive

FROM THE OUTSIDE LOOKING IN

Words by: Oli Warwick

IT'S NOT HARD TO SEE THE APPEAL IN BRISTOL. MARKEDLY SMALLER THAN MANY OF THE UK'S MAJOR CITIES, ITS CULTURAL IMPACT PUNCHES WELL ABOVE ITS WEIGHT. THERE'S BEEN PLENTY SAID ABOUT ITS MUSICAL LEGACY, FROM THE POST-PUNK DAYS TO THE TRIP HOP BOOM, THE RISE OF JUNGLE AND THE DUBSTEP EXPLOSION. MANY OF THESE EPOCHAL MOVEMENTS OCCURRED WHEN THE CITY REMAINED IN ITS OWN BUBBLE OUT WEST, FAR ENOUGH FROM ANY OTHER URBAN SPRAWLS TO DEVELOP ITS OWN UNIQUE VIBE.

From the mid-00s, as the cost of living in London, in particular, began to skyrocket, the convenient location of Bristol (two hours from the capital, good links to Birmingham and Manchester) and its storied past became an attractive proposition to artists looking to weather the pinch of a music industry struggling to adapt to the rise of the internet. Charlie Bierman, aka Break, was one such artist who, with his partner Kyo, was looking for somewhere he could settle and subsist on the shaky income of a full-time artist.

"When we first moved to Bristol in 2007, we were like, 'no one works!'" says Bierman. "Especially back then, when it was cheaper, your average person could work three days a week and still pay the rent. It was much less rat race than London. At first, it seemed very laid back and almost lazy in comparison."

With his career as a producer and DJ already in ascendance, Bierman had a pre-existing relationship with Bristol. Through his links with Fierce, he'd gotten to know Bristol d&b lynchpin DJ Die, so he knew the city could offer a natural home for his own artistic development. When jungle and drum & bass came charging out of the 90s, there were key crews in

> **"**It's just a big melting pot right now of artists and things coming together... it's a nice little vibe down here right now, I ain't gonna lie.**"**
> - Randall

Bristol conjuring up a distinctive slant on the sound that attracted acclaim worldwide.

There was the Ruffneck Ting lot, who gave rise to chart-baiting crossover outfit Kosheen, Smith & Mighty's More Rockers stable and the Full Cycle collective, who shook up the jungle scene and grew with the emergent sound of drum & bass before forming the Mercury Prize-winning Roni Size/Reprazent. The discernibly 'other' sound rumbling out of Bristol was a magnet for artists from elsewhere.

"Jason and I used to go up and see [Full Cycle's] Die and Suv and Krust and Roni," says Total Science's Paul Smith. "We were really inspired by those guys who were living in Bristol. We would hang out in the studios. We heard so much music that never got released that was so good. It literally would blow my mind when we would go up there."

Both members of Total Science forged their own path from their roots in Oxford, but as the buoyant scene of the 90s and 00s thinned out, they found themselves a little isolated and in need of a change. They moved to Bristol around 2014. Jason Greenhalgh eventually moved back to Oxford, but Smith laid fresh roots in his newly adopted city.

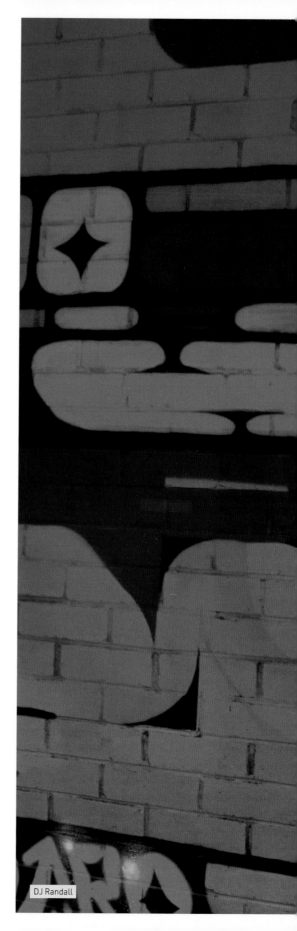

DJ Randall

Break

"My only experience of Bristol was in the night, at the clubs!" laughs day-one d&b titan Randall. "Obviously I knew the history about Bristol, but I didn't really have a connection. It was just playing for promoters and doing events in Bristol. I never saw any of the culture in the daytime, how Bristol actually was, until I moved there."

Similarly to Total Science, Randall's motivation to move in the 00s was as much about life circumstances as music. The affordability of the city and its relatively central location in the UK made practical sense, and the unique mood on the streets made for a welcoming change of scenery. It's also worth noting this coincided with the rise of online communication, which wrought massive changes in the way scenes functioned.

"The world of the internet was just kicking off with AIM," says Randall, "and you had the demise of [legendary dubplate cutting studio] Music House, so the connection to DJs like we used to have before was just becoming online. It was an easy transition in my head. [Bristol] was more easygoing, people were easier to connect to and have a laugh with. It was just a nice vibe, and I liked it."

Much is made of the welcoming nature of Bristol's creative community. Compared to the competitive, self-interested pressure that can be felt in other places, a common topic speaking to anyone engaged in any scene or artform in the city is the widespread enthusiasm for collaboration.

"That's the thing I got out of Bristol when I moved there," says Smith. "There's a lot of creatives there and they want to work with each other, whereas in other cities it's not so open."

When Smith moved to Bristol, he found himself in a studio session with contemporary Bristol d&b producers DLR and Mako, and was pleasantly reminded of the communal vibe he'd experienced with the Full Cycle crew in the 90s.

"I didn't have all these connections when we moved to Bristol," he adds. "Everyone was so welcoming and friendly - I just instantly got a good rapport with all those guys. It made sense to try and do a night together."

By "those guys," Smith is referring to a kind of supergroup alliance of producers and DJs including Randall, Break and Total Science as well as DLR, Mako, Hydro and Kyo, who came together to form the Collective night. Held intermittently at The Crofter's Rights on buzzing nightlife hotspot Stokes Croft, it's an intimate session that seeks to consolidate the community aspect of the scene with some of the city's major players.

"We started Collective a few years ago as something slightly more undercover, built by other DJs and people in the scene," says Bierman. "We wanted a regular night in that vein of [Metalheadz at] Blue Note or [Movement at] Bar Rhumba.

"People play their new tunes, the crowd is open-minded, we can book who we want and play what we want, and it doesn't have that short attention span you might get at some events. We've met people who have given us demos and hung out with new producers. That night's helped them feel like there's a good avenue for that stuff in the city. There's music courses in Bristol that are really good, and I think that also helps develop and germinate new talents."

Compared to the multi-room mega-rave sessions you can find elsewhere in the city at Motion or Lakota, Collective is the quintessential Bristol social. It may be spearheaded by a bunch of transplants to the city, but endeavours like this firmly place those involved at the beating heart of its d&b scene. Similar sessions happen across the myriad genres you can hear pulsing out of Bristol, where dedicated heads eagerly flock to hear the latest sounds. It's a reassuring real-world kickback against the detached nature of online engagement.

"These types of places are the only places where we can connect again," says Randall. "When we're doing nights like Collective, all of us are together, and we're just listening to music. Similar to what Bailey and Need For Mirrors do with Soul in Motion. Why not have a little place you can test out new music? We used to have it back in the day, it was called AWOL, then we had places like Metalheadz."

Given its diminutive size compared to other cities, much of Bristol's club landscape is made up of these pint-sized spaces, and Collective follows a string of iconic get downs tailored towards the heads rather than mass appeal.

"The first guy that booked me in Bristol was Ben from Intrigue," says Bierman. "His night has been going a long time. At that point, it was regularly at a place called Dojos, which was quite a small little club. It just had that cool atmosphere where people were definitely there for the music. You'd see a lot of heads at that night, and bump into a lot of DJs and musicians.

"Then Run had their night at Native, which was another institution which we didn't really know about from London, but that was a similar vibe in a small club

"We started Collective a few years ago as something slightly more undercover, built by other DJs and people in the scene. We wanted a regular night in that vein of Blue Note or Bar Rhumba."
- Break

with wicked sound. I was meeting people like Krust, and hanging out with Die, who I grew up buying their records and was a massive fan of. It was great to get into the Bristol scene quite quickly."

Beyond their Collective sessions, all the associated DJs have their own endeavours that feed into the current Bristol d&b culture. Bierman's Symmetry label throws larger scale events at Trinity Centre, one of the spiritual homes for d&b, dubstep and dub in Bristol. It's the same spot, in a 19th-century church, that hosted many a Ruffneck Ting dance back in the day. The mid-sized space is synonymous with Bristol's long-standing soundsystem culture – a by-product of the city's sizable Afro-Caribbean population instrumental in shaping the city's sound.

"The Black Swan's another venue that's always had a heavyweight sound ethos," adds Bierman. "That gives the guys who build and run soundsystems opportunities to take them out. You get a lot of soundsystem-oriented nights in Trinity Centre – it's a really good venue for sound in general. We did do other venues like Thekla,

but Trinity's been the perfect spot for us because it's big but not crazy. It's like a classic old school kind of dance."

There are plenty of spots in Bristol synonymous with d&b, and often the vibe of the space informs the kind of sound you can expect to hear. The Black Swan, on Stapleton Road in Easton, has a distinctly wild outlaw spirit that encourages rougher strains of jungle and free-party-friendly hardcore. Iconic boat venue Thekla has long housed many of the mid-sized Bristol dances that centre around one key headliner, while rave rabbit warren Lakota can provide a platform to an assortment of local crews.

It's a sad sign of the times many of these places are under threat of closure, through the usual suspects like rampant property development and

noise complaints. But as with anywhere, the culture prevails, and new clubs emerge to replace old ones.

"We played for Lenzman's North Quarter night at a relatively new place called Loco, a great little spot," says Smith. "It's a proper old brick cellar just by Temple Meads train station... it reminded me of some older clubs from back in the day."

Everyone agrees there's no shortage of d&b nights in Bristol. Even as the scene may have ebbed and flowed elsewhere, it's been relatively consistent since the early days in the city. Compared with the situation when he left Oxford, Smith says there's no comparison.

"I was speaking to Ben from Intrigue," he explains, "and there was one weekend where there were four gigs on, the whole month had 11 or so shows, and it's quite a lot. It seemed a little saturated, but obviously, there's enough numbers to go around. In all honesty, it seems pretty constant – most of the nights we've played at have been pretty good numbers-wise."

This fierce volume of activity reflects the wildly diverse nature of drum & bass in Bristol in 2019. Gone are the days of the cohesive 'Bristol sound' – albeit a term up for debate depending on who you speak to.

"It's a less identifiable sound than maybe at one point," says Bierman. "Back in the day there was a particular crew of V Recordings and Full Cycle that had quite a noticeable sound – that wobbly jungle bassline with the skippy breaks, and then Full Cycle went a bit more into that strain of Bristol jump-up you could spot quite easily. If you do something on that vibe, people identify that as a Bristol sound. It's an inspiration for everyone in drum & bass, but there's so many different influences and crew within the city now the sound itself is more spread out."

Certainly not the low-key outpost it was in the 90s, Bristol in the 21st century attracts an ever-increasing array of heads both established and up-and-coming. The likes of Digital, S.P.Y. and Foreign Concept have made it their home in recent years, while the music colleges, in particular, encourage the flock of emergent talent adding to the legacy and evolution of drum & bass in the city.

"I've met people on planes when we're both coming back from gigs," says Randall, "and they've shown me the parties they're doing, and I'm thinking, 'Right, I've never heard of it, you been in Bristol that long?' It's just a big melting pot right now of artists and things coming together... it's a nice little vibe down here right now, I ain't gonna lie."

> **"We were really inspired by those guys who were living in Bristol. We would hang out in the studios. We heard so much music that never got released that was so good. It literally would blow my mind when we would go up there."**
> – Paul Smith (Total Science)

Total Science

TECH SPECS

Words by: Tom Denton

DRUM & BASS HAS A COMPLICATED RELATIONSHIP WITH TECHNOLOGY. ONE THE ONE HAND, IT IS FUTURE MUSIC, PUSHING SOUND DESIGN, SAMPLING, SYNTHESIS AND MIXDOWNS TO EVER-HIGHER LEVELS. OTHER GENRES GAZE AND DROOL ADMIRINGLY AT THE COMPLEXITY AND SKILL OF OUR SCENE'S PRODUCTIONS.

On the other, we're also steeped in hard-defended traditions. Try arguing in favour of the sync button to most d&b fans, for example, and they'll give you the very shortest of shrift. Even the now-ubiquitous CDJ was widely regarded as an unnecessary gimmick, leaving d&b deejays spinning on Technics as standard, way into the noughties.

"The CDJ was seen as a bit more mainstream, and drum & bass and jungle has always been a scene from the street, a bit like American hip-hop," explains scene pioneer Micky Finn, "Also, the industry thinks like that. Pioneer, for example, they would take the house scene a lot more seriously and concentrate on trying to get endorsements and working with those artists because they saw them as a bigger advertising board."

Maybe that goes some way to explaining why the big, important cultural changes in d&b since the turn of the millennium haven't come as a result of advancements in DJ or producer kit. The real technological tectonic shift has come as a result of software, not hardware. It's the twin forces of social media and digital music distribution that have altered the landscape, in ways which nineties-and-later-babies might find it hard to comprehend.

For one thing, there was a time when the most advanced social media app (although no-one said "social media" or "app" back then) was AOL Instant Messenger. This was in the time of dial-up, when Tom from MySpace was still just known as Tom and downloading a dub could be a long-term project.

But even 56 kilobits per second was advanced tech compared to the way things worked before that. In the days when the idea of selling out Wembley Arena would have seemed like a sectionable delusion, Andy C was putting in the mileage: "Back in the day, when we used to cut our dubplates on a Thursday, me, Hype and Brockie used to meet up and literally drive around London and the Home Counties to meet up with producers and get DATs of tunes."

Simon Bassline Smith, DJ, producer and label boss since the days of hardcore tells us how things worked for his operation in the pre-social media world: "The systems in place from a label point of view from what I had in 1991 when I started Absolute2... it's incredible. If I made a tune, I had to physically take the DAT down to London to get it cut. Whether it was going to be cut as a dubplate or cut to be released, I had to physically go to London and sit there for the process to take place. Then I had to physically get the artwork and put it in an envelope and post it to the people that were manufacturing the sleeves and the labels. It was all very snail-pace. My girl used to write up the PR sheets. We used to hand-write them, we'd hand-write about fifty: Carl Cox, here's the new Absolute tune, Grooverider, here's the new Nookie tune... looking back it was all quite caveman."

Caveman it might have been, but the low-tech days are still remembered fondly. Clayton Hines, founder of Renegade Hardware and Trouble on Vinyl and former owner of Breakin Science, tells us: "Nowadays ninety per cent of promotion is done online, which is strange, but you've got to move with the times. You do miss that physical hand-to-hand interaction."

"It's changed everything", Andy C adds, "Massively. For the better or for worse, I don't know. It think it's enabled the drum & bass community to come together in a way we could never have dreamed of back in the day. A journey of discovery back in the day for me would be standing in a record store, hearing a record, and you form a picture in your head of what the people must be like who made the record."

> "The fact that social media is there and people can explode quickly onto the scene, that's a great thing. If someone's good at something, if they make fantastic tunes or they're a brilliant DJ, why not? We should encourage it and embrace it."
>
> – Andy C

Andy C

Clayton Hines

Bassline Smith describes his first forays into social media. "The very first social media platform as a label which really turned everything on its head was MySpace, because you could put your tunes on there - five or six tunes - and you could put your photo on there, and your bio on there. Up until that sort of period, if someone wanted to see your bio or photo, they had to buy a magazine."

Let's just take a moment to appreciate that. If you wanted to see a photo of your favourite producer, you had to wait until they were featured in a Knowledge Magazine (other mags were available, but, of course, Kmag was the connoisseur's choice), go out to a newsagent and physically buy it. It was entirely possible to be a passionate fan of someone's music for years before you ever saw their face.

"You still had a database, but your database would be addresses," Micky Finn explains, "Sad as it is, it was a big bill, but that Royal Mail bill to send everyone a flyer in the post was taken into account in the budget. You had street billboards, they were huge, they were a must... it was all those big street posters outside clubs, paying the flyering companies... it was a personal thing - hand-to-hand."

It's easy to get nostalgic about the traditional ways of doing things, and it took a while for d&b as an industry to fully embrace social media. Simon Bassline

Smith was an early adopter.

"The first time I signed up to Twitter, you'd look for anyone who was drum & bass-minded on there, and it was less than ten people", he tells us, "Myself, I remember Zinc being on there early, I think El Hornet was on there very early. There was just a handful of people, and we didn't know what Twitter was or how we would use it."

Now, of course, we've all grasped the promotional power of social media. No-one has to wait for a bring-in these days, we can all release content and find our own audience online. Occasionally, though, we hear a note of caution from older heads about the dangers of propelling artists up the ranks too quickly before they've "paid their dues".

Here's Andy C's view: "I feel a sense of pride in where our scene is now, because of that passion and that journey and the foundations that were set. If the foundations weren't set like that back in the day, you could argue that the scene wouldn't be where it is today... the times they move on. The fact that social media is there and people can explode quickly onto the scene, that's a great thing. If someone's good at something, if they make fantastic tunes or they're a brilliant DJ, why not? We should encourage it and embrace it."

With more and more artists taking the opportunities offered by the digital world and releasing music

> **"Labels are definitely going to be extinct like dinosaurs soon because no-one's going to need them. If you can go online and do your own promo, and you've got BandCamp, what do you need a label for?"**
> - Clayton Hines

independently, perhaps we're about to see another major shift. "Labels are definitely going to be extinct like dinosaurs soon because no-one's going to need them," Clayton believes, "If you can go online and do your own promo, and you've got BandCamp, what do you need a label for?"

Scary stuff for label bosses. Bassline Smith has a more optimistic view, however. "I know for a fact that Spotify's model is to cut out the label and just deal with artist direct," he concedes. "But, the thing about it is, there will always be quality labels run by influential people with a deep understanding of the music because up-and-coming artists will need to be, will want to be, affiliated with someone who can guide them through the woods and the trees of the music industry."

Maybe that's the point. Even if social media and digital music distribution have changed the game, perhaps there's something valuable about that connection to those old analogue days.

Bassline Smith explains: "Back then, people going out and consuming music, in a way there was a lot more passion. People would go out at the weekend, they would hear a tune, and it would be a life-changing moment for them, they would hunt that tune... us as deejays we used to go round ten, fifteen shops, hunting tunes that no-one else had. Now we're just sitting at our

laptops and someone will ping us a tune in there... I'm not dissing it, it's how things evolve. Nowadays people are more interested in a video moment they can capture or a photo moment that they can capture more than they are in consuming what's going on."

And, as Andy C tells us, even the frustrating limitations of production tech could become an advantage: "A lot of the old classic tunes would have come about by unintentional accidents happening in the studio because of the limits of the technology, or because of people not quite understanding the technology. And limitations played a great role."

Relishing the struggle against limits and obstacles is a common theme in stories of those early days. "Tunes now, there's a very staple arrangement structure to tunes, so dropping the tunes together is a lot easier," Andy continues. "When you were mixing on dubs back in the day and there were three bar overhangs or two bar overhangs, it was a challenge, but it was a challenge you wanted to do. I dunno man, it was kind of that extra edge to the DJing and something that I vibed off. If you DJ so much, you want to go at it, do some crazy stuff every time you play, you know."

And the technical and technological limitations of the day meant that becoming a drum & bass artist was a much bigger commitment from the get-go, both

Simon Bassline Smith

Micky Finn

in terms of time and finances. Simon tells us, "When you take it right back to those points in time, very few people wanted to be a DJ. Everyone wanted to enjoy themselves, everyone wanted to be on the dancefloor. It was only the most passionate people about music that actually pursued it that step further. There were only a few people who were going that extra mile to find that music, who was making it, can I get it, can I play it?"

We don't want to be too misty-eyed, though. Maybe the game was more work back then. Maybe it was just a different kind of work, though. Perhaps all that's happened is those hours spent travelling between record shops and studios to get the latest dubs has been replaced by the hours online building a social media presence. And, quite possibly, we've only just scratched the surface of what this interconnected scene could become. "To be able to reach people in far corners of the world, that was a massive thing for drum & bass," Bassline Smith reminds us, "You started being able to bring the world drum & bass community together."

In all the talk about social media as a marketing tool, perhaps we've overlooked the fact that it's also

"Spotify's model is to cut out the label and just deal with artist direct. But there will always be quality labels run by influential people with a deep understanding of the music because up-and-coming artists will need to be, will want to be, affiliated with someone who can guide them through the woods and the trees of the music industry."
- Simon Bassline Smith

a place where communities can flourish. Facebook groups like DnB Talk and Drum & Bass Against Racism have become woven into the tapestry of drum & bass culture, and it seems likely that there are many levels of evolution yet to come.

Drum & bass' relationship with technology tells us a lot about the characteristics we share and admire as a scene. We love the foundations and paying homage to the old skool, but we're also excited about the future, eagerly seeking the latest dubs and the next big thing. We want to play with the latest tech, but only if it leaves our traditions intact. It's a balancing act.

If we become too obsessed with the old days, the scene would devolve into a small, exclusive "you weren't there, so you don't know" club, unwelcoming to new recruits. Focus only on the latest hot new prospect, though, and we lose sight of the decades of innovation and sheer graft that got us here. One eye on the foundations and one eye on the future: it's the drum & bass way.

EVENT HORIZON

Words by: Ben Hunter

WHEN YOU THINK OF A DRUM & BASS EVENT, WHAT COMES INTO YOUR HEAD? FOR SOME, THE DEFINING IMAGERY IS BOOMTOWN'S TOWERING BANG HAI PALACE, OR MAYBE THE TWISTED LEGS OF THE ARCADIA SPIDER. OTHERS MIGHT SEE ANDY C HUNCHED OVER THE DECKS IN XOYO'S MAIN ROOM, OR LSB WAITING UNTIL THE PERFECT MOMENT TO LET LOOSE AT SHOREDITCH'S VILLAGE UNDERGROUND.

Not everyone's imagery will be this glamorous, either. For many, their most memorable instances are of a half-empty room two in Guildford or the bassbin-laded basement of a student house party in Sheffield. From Bournemouth to Glasgow, drum & bass is experienced week-in, week-out by die-hard fans, not-so-die-hard fans and people who, for some mundane, unknowable reason, just happen to be there.

It's the way it's always been and hopefully the way it always will be. But as the world changes and drum & bass changes with it, events haven't been left untouched. In the same way that music is consumed differently now compared to the 1990s and even the 2000s, the live environment is undergoing a set of different but similar changes.

Across nearly two dozen conversations with promoters, artists, agents and venue owners, a picture has emerged of a drum & bass scene that has begun to move away from the local and into the national and the global.

In an age of ever-increasing connectivity, this is unsurprising. But the impact of this change is real nonetheless, and it's been felt most keenly by those operating on the local level, the people who were most likely responsible for that half-empty room two in Guildford, for example.

Local promoters represent the ability for anyone with some spare cash and a passion for music to get involved. They represent music on an accessible level, and they're intimately involved in drawing that crucial line - a cultural line of experience, memory and sensation – from people's Spotify accounts to their real, lived-in localities.

This is easy to say, but what is it actually happening? One obvious aspect is the widely-reported decline of venues and spaces with the ability and incentive to

> **"It's significantly easier to put on a destination party that's unmissable and only do it once or twice a year than it is to do a party every week."**
>
> - Josh Robinson
> (Hospital)

host small drum & bass nights. A recent casualty was long-time Sheffield institution The Harley, a part-pub, part-venue embodiment of an inclusive, accessible space, one in which numerous Sheffield-based promoters cut their teeth.

Ollie Gillespie was the General Manager when it closed in April this year due to rising costs and declining revenues, a common formula he ascribes in part to "changing student patterns," with students "going out and drinking less."

He also believes that The Harley's business model was flawed because to survive in this hyper-competitive context, venues have to adopt a "360-degree approach, like Gorilla and Deaf Institute do in Manchester and Belgrave and Headrow do in Leeds. You've got food, a great bar, great gigs and great clubbing all spread over multiple floors."

The obvious downside of this need to appeal to a much broader array of customers and tastes is a dilution of specific sub-cultures, such as drum & bass, and more niche groups of people can find themselves without a home.

This was the experience of renowned drum & bass vocalist Charli Brix. She runs the Bristol-based Shotgun Sessions, a weekly night that is on a temporary hiatus after the owner of its previous home, the Faraway Cocktail Club, decided to rebrand as a sports bar for financial reasons (just like The Harley in Sheffield strangely).

Her experience in Bristol is that as venues close, the remaining venues are "becoming harder to book as promoters are being pushed into a smaller pool." This problem is made even worse by her experience that "there are loads of spaces in town that won't go near d&b because of the crowd that it attracts," a

stigmatisation that lingers despite the now truly global nature of the genre.

The problem certainly isn't limited to Bristol or Sheffield, either. Between 2007 and 2015, 35% of grassroots music venues have closed in the UK, and a 2019 Parliamentary report concluded that venues of this kind are a "vital part of the music industry ecosystem" because they "give musicians in the early stage of their careers a space to hone their live acts and broaden their audiences."

This also applies to promoters and, as Ollie Gillespie tells Knowledge, you need "local promoters pushing new and interesting nights because ultimately that's where the best ideas and the newest, freshest sounds come from."

The role played by local nights in Hackney in the formation of dubstep is a primary example from outside the genre, while it's doubtful that jungle would have evolved the way it did without Metalheadz and Blue Note in the 90s. An erosion of activity on this level can have much broader ramifications for the genre, consequences that might only become apparent much further down the line.

The declining number of venues also makes it harder for promoters to differentiate their events from their competition, which creates an incentive to book bigger line-ups to stand out. This is where a second factor comes into play, and it's an issue that was frequently cited as the biggest obstacle for small promoters: the increasing cost of booking DJs.

This is a historically contentious issue, and it's almost certainly the case that some promoters have a tendency to unfairly blame agencies and managers for all manner of woes. However, as Peter Van Dongen, label assistant at Shogun Audio and co-founder of promotional outfit Arcane Culture outlines, "artist fees have gone up, while promoter budgets from top to bottom have loosely stayed the same."

A significant part of this is the increasing popularity of the genre. In the words of Critical Music founder Kasra, "the fact that there's a scene all over the planet, with touring DJs going around at the world at varying levels of success, would suggest that the music is more popular."

Josh Robinson, events manager for Hospital Records,

Charli Brix

Kasra

Chris Marigold

Peter Van Dongen

Particle

Peter Piper Maxted

Mantra

agrees: "Is d&b bigger now in terms of ticket sales and listening numbers, compared to 10 to 20 years ago? Without a shadow of a doubt."

With more popularity comes higher demand to see artists live and, as Mark Bauer, founder and director of ESP Agency explains, with "high in-demand artists, the fees generally go up a lot faster."

But popular artists costing more money isn't exactly new, and it would be unreasonable to expect artists not to capitalise on their own, well-deserved success.

As Chris Marigold, one-third of Blu Mar Ten and director of the Hospital Records-affiliated agency Clinic Talent tells Knowledge, "these are the people that generate the stuff that drives the entire machine," an argument made more salient by the fact that "it's become virtually impossible, aside for the very few, to generate any revenue from the sales of music."

Promoters need that music just as much as anyone else, and every single promoter expressed to Knowledge their belief that artists need to be supported.

So why have DJ prices become more of an issue? Daniel Burridge, co-founder of long-running Leeds night Overflow, feels "like there's a lot of variety, but there's an exclusive 5% of DJs, and unless you book them, you're going to lose money, like immediately."

Displace, a Sheffield-based promoter, tell Knowledge that "even when we try and curate a night that's aimed at filling a place like Hopeworks, it's not just the cost of it that's the difficulty, it's the numbers of it that are the problem."

If filling a club is more difficult, promoters need to maximise their chances by going for the bigger artists, leading to the type of situation mentioned by Mark Bauer in which promoters are "asking for the

same 4-5 headline artists, and those happen to be the ones that everyone else wants as well, including the big promoters."

Bigger promoters, therefore, gain even more purchasing power than they would've had already, a fact they consolidate through the use of exclusivity agreements. Andy Wade is the founder of London-based SINE Sessions, and he explained to Knowledge that big promoters "can go into London and speak to agents and be like 'we'll do three or four events in a year and we'll do that over two years, we've also got this festival that we're doing, and we'll give them a high-up slot."

In return, that artist won't play any other gigs in that city over that time frame. This dynamic is particularly prevalent in London and for Particle, an exciting new artistic talent and founder of London-based promoter Coded, it's gotten to the stage where he "literally can't run Coded any more as every big headliner is now exclusive to certain brands," something he sees as killing the London scene "from the ground up."

The negative impacts of exclusivity agreements are felt most sharply in big, highly competitive cities like London and Bristol, and it's mostly limited to the top tier of artists. But when artists and agencies have a guaranteed revenue stream from a smaller sub-section of promoters in a smaller sub-section of cities, there's less incentive to play in a wider range of towns, to a wider range of promoters.

The other side to this, of course, is that bigger promoters take bigger risks and when thousands of pounds and the livelihoods of staff are on the line, it's hardly surprising they look for assurances. As Josh

Robinson argues, they're "an essential part of an industry where the financial investment of booking an artist is as high as it is."

As prices climb, so do the benefits of exclusivity agreements and the two seem self-reinforcing, because this arrangement not only prevents promoters from booking the artists they need to fill clubs, it pushes promoters into a smaller pool of available artists, thereby increasing their demand and thus their price as well.

It also speaks to how some large promoters have influence over multiple promotional outlets, sometimes in ways punters are unaware of. One well-known promoter told Knowledge that most people aren't aware that a particular London-based events company are "behind a lot of the big drum & bass nights" in the city.

A quick flick down their Facebook events page shows that they're involved with events held by many well-known drum & bass labels. Staff listings on Companies House also show that they're affiliated with Pack London, an events marketing company who work with Fabriclive, as well as being affiliated with NVS Promotions, the events company responsible for Outlook Festival and Dimensions Festival.

This gives them a level of promotional reach and artist purchasing power that's impossible to compete with on a local level. Such a significant degree of horizontal and vertical integration between companies that ostensibly compete is common in the music industry, and drum & bass actually escapes relatively lightly compared to other genres by virtue of its small size.

The 2019 Parliamentary report on the live music industry highlighted the fact that Live Nation, a US-based events company, controls 25% of all UK festivals over a 5,000 capacity, a significant portion of the market. Diversity and plurality are the historical core of dance music, and as Leeds-based promoter Overflow co-founder Alex Wilson tells Knowledge, the context

> "There's always been adversity and interesting scenes have always found their way around these things. In fact, often they've flourished."
> – Chris Marigold
> (Clinic Talent)

now is "definitely pushing it all into one homogenised route, it's pushing everyone to be the same because it's what sells." This can only be bad for the genre, for music fans even more so than promoters.

But there's a much more interesting and important point to be made here, because while some companies might have significant power over line-ups, they don't have the power to stop fans from attending smaller club shows – the cause of the problem for small promoters. Because whilst some variation of the practices outlined above has always happened, the situation has become more acute for promoters over the past few years despite an increase in the genre's popularity.

The important change is much more structural and much more fundamental. Simply put, the new event market favours big events. Josh Robinson, events manager at Hospital Records, used to be the booking agent for Fabriclive from 2006 to 2010 and explained to Knowledge that back then, "there were queues around the block every single week, with everyone going out. You could easily put on a party one week and then the next week, and there'd just be more guarantees that there'd be x amount of people."

Whereas he now believes that "it's significantly easier to put on a destination party that's unmissable and only do it once or twice a year than it is to do a party every week."

The symptoms of this at Hospital Records are instead of six London shows a year as they did in 2010, in 2019 they're "doing three, next year it will only be two, and those shows are on a much larger scale."

This aligns with the experience of Critical Music founder Kasra, who says he now employs a "less is more approach," because "every time you do something it has to be really, really strong to ensure that it does as well as it can."

Peter Van Dongen, label assistant at Shogun Audio and co-founder of promotional outfit Arcane Culture, agrees: "I think people would prefer to save up for this kind of experience with their friends, rather than do the

Josh Robinson

traditional club night frequently."

This is also the perspective of Chris Marigold of Blu Mar Ten and Clinic Talent: "It does seem that young people might spend £60, £80, £100 on a ticket for a really big event where they feel they're getting really massive value for money, rather than two £10 events in a week."

The reasons for this shift are multi-faceted, complex and mostly reside outside of drum & bass. One crucial factor is that people are simply going out less, with £200m wiped off the value of the UK club market over the past five years amidst a 15% drop in the number of adults attending a club event at least once a month.

William Franklin, founder of events and artist management company Whitepark Music, thinks part of the reason is because "it's so easy now for someone to stay inside and watch Netflix, back in the 90s you only had like 10 channels, so as a kid all you wanted to do was to go out and party."

Peter Piper Maxted, founder of the Brighton-based label Overview Music, puts it succinctly when he says that "you can sit there and roam for hours on Red Dead Redemption and be completely amused for the entire night." There's simply less incentive to get out of the house.

Most importantly, perhaps, is that the economic context faced by young people in the UK today is the most tenuous it's been in decades. Tuition fees are the highest they've ever been at £9,000 a year, and homeownership rates have fallen by 38% since the mid-1990s, pushing more young people into an increasingly expensive rental market.

Annual wages are still £760 lower than before the 2008 financial crisis, with millennials the worst hit, and those unable to find wage-paying jobs end up in an expanding gig economy made up of short-term, highly insecure employment with companies like Deliveroo or Uber.

With incomes trailing behind inflation and cost of living, it's therefore not surprising that young people are going out less and that, when they do, they'd rather get their money's worth. The culture of modern consumption also plays a part and William Franklin remembers that when "Printworks came out, I saw it and thought 'holy shit, this is the best thing I've ever seen', and then a year or two later I was like 'ah, it's not that cool anymore'. You get used to it."

With more entertainment comes a shorter attention span, and in the age of instant streaming, music is one of the industries most affected.

It's incredibly important to remember, however, that there are still numerous small promoters putting on nights up and down the UK and as Andy Wade tells Knowledge, "there is still a healthy scene… there are still people wanting to go to the dark and dingy, good quality sound nights."

For Overflow's Alex Wilson, "we just do it on the basis

> **"We just do it on the basis that we're not going to make a profit, which isn't great for a business perspective but that's just the way that it is."**
> – Alex Wilson (Overflow)

Alex Wilson

that we're not going to make a profit, which isn't great for a business perspective but that's just the way that it is."

Peter Piper Maxted of Overview Music has a similar perspective, in that he doesn't "look at it as a money-making exercise, I'm just trying to do something cool, and anything extra is a plus. It's about the vibe and then hopefully in a couple years it might turn into something special."

Rupture LDN is the perfect example of a small night that did just that, albeit in a more favourable context. Mantra recounts how she and co-founder Double-O started over a decade ago in a "random little basement a few doors down from Herbal called Under The Bridge," a perfect space for "the vibe that we wanted, really electric, low ceilings, banging the walls and stuff, really intense."

For Rupture in 2019, nights "are busier than they've ever been for us, it's a young crowd as well," and this year they're "going to be pushing 8-9 events which we never would've done a few years ago."

The events picture is thus anything but clear-cut. For every small promoter who struggles to break through the many barriers, others might succeed. Chris Marigold makes the point that "there's always been adversity and interesting scenes have always found their way around these things. In fact, often they've flourished."

This logic applies regardless of whether it's the Criminal Justice and Order Act of 1994, stagnant wages or expensive DJs.

There is undoubtedly an important conversation to had about some of the negative elements tied up with the evolution of drum & bass, and these conversations are important, both for understanding and for improvement.

For Chris Marigold, this means "there needs to be, on all sides, a realistic recognition of the positions that everybody is in," and for Ed Priest, co-founder of Dazed promotions and previous events assistant at Hospital Records, "it should be a balancing act between demand, supply, the music, the promoter. It should be a qualitative, textural, fluid relationship."

Drum & bass is in one of the strongest positions it has been for years and while true equality between all levels of the scene is impossible to achieve, especially now, that doesn't mean promoters, agents and artists shouldn't give it a shot.

The control desk at Music House in 2001

DUBPLATE SPECIAL

Words by: Chris Muniz
Photography by: Georgina Cook

JUMPIN JACK FROST TOOK TO TWITTER RECENTLY AND POSTED: "MOST OF YOU NEW CATS WILL NEVER EXPERIENCE THE COMMUNITY AND BEAUTIFUL VIBE WE USED TO HAVE AT MUSIC HOUSE, WHERE WE ALL MET TO SHARE MUSIC AND ACTUALLY TALK FACE TO FACE."

While many "new cats" most certainly weren't around to cut tunes at the legendary cutting studio that Frost is referencing, the sentiment is a familiar one to any who came up through the years when dubplates reigned supreme. While Music House was a well-known dubplate cutting shop in London, what stands out about Frost's lament is the yearning for the days when DJs and producers were part of a "face to face" community centred not only on sharing music but on being a part of something special.

For the uninitiated, a dubplate can be thought of as a one-off record. Instead of being pressed to vinyl, however, tunes are "cut" directly into an acetate-lacquered aluminium disk or plate. The resulting dubplate is a one-of-a-kind pressing and, by its very nature, temporary in the sense that it's meant to last for only 30-50 plays. Long before jungle, hardcore, and drum & bass were a thing, Jamaican reggae artists were utilising the format to not only test out tracks on massive sound systems but to play special remixes and edits of popular tunes in an effort to outdo other DJs and sound system crews in the competitive soundclash culture of the '60s and '70s.

"My first experience with dubplates was in my early teens," Digital tells us when asked about the roots of his own dub-and-reggae inspired hits. "I had brought a reggae soundsystem tape home, and it was full of West Indian swear words like Bloodclaat! Raasclaat! I can still remember the slap in the head I got from my mum for playing it in the house. But amongst all the shouting and going on, every time the music stopped, the mic man would shout stuff like, 'You cyaaaaan play dis tune, only we have it!' 'We'll kill you with dubplate!' From this, I came to understand how dubplates were unique versions of popular songs and

> **"Back then, 10" dubplates were a sign of status and success. Not everyone got to cut other people's music, so it was a sign that you had arrived."**
> - TeeBee

pre-released music, adapted and used to excite the crowd in a soundclash competition."

The very same ethos that drove soundsystems like Bass Odyssey and Killamanjaro to tap artist/engineers like King Tubby and Lee 'Scratch' Perry to craft "dubplate specials" would be a sentiment that would carry over into the burgeoning drum & bass scene as each DJ sought to stand out with their own exclusive cuts. Music House in North London became ground zero for the drum & bass version of this culture as established and up-and-coming artists alike could be found there on any given day cutting the latest tunes before dropping them at seminal clubs like Metalheadz' Sunday Sessions at Blue Note.

One of the dons of this early era was none other than Grooverider, whose access to dubs was legendary. A true tastemaker in every meaning of the phrase, if 'Rider decided to drop your tune in his set at Blue Note (and especially if it was his last tune of the night), then it was almost guaranteed to go on to become a hit.

This is where the true power of the dubplate can be found. To modern audiences, it may seem no more than just a stone-age storage device designed to transport the tune from DAT to the club, but beyond the obvious ability to play out exclusives in a pre-CDJ world, dubplates carried a symbolic significance that far exceeded its utility.

The exclusivity of the tracks one had access to became manifested in the number and quality of dubplates you had in the bag, physical representations of your status within the social hierarchy of the drum & bass world.

Even now, TeeBee remembers how impenetrable the UK scene seemed from the outside looking in. It wasn't just that seminal figures like Grooverider,

Fabio, and Goldie were five-to-ten years older than he was, but that he was trying to break in as a youngblood from Norway that proved the most difficult challenge to initially overcome.

"When I first came to the UK with my own music, I was turned away several times," TeeBee explains. "The original hardcore/jungle scene was notoriously tight and quite rough around the edges. At first, I had someone very prominent refuse to take the DATs I tried handing him at a legendary London venue. I was told this was a UK thing, straight up. I left that night devastated, feeling like I'd been excluded from something I desperately wanted to be a part of."

TeeBee returned to Norway disappointed but paradoxically, even more determined to get his music heard by those in the know. "I got a haircut and persuaded my parents to send me to Hastings for summer school to sort my English out," TeeBee continues. "I stayed primarily with the locals, hanging around the local record shop. A major breakthrough happened the last week I was there. All those letters and phone calls had finally paid off, as none other than Slipmatt sent me a package of records to the local store! No one in there knew why there was a package from Slipmatt to a DJ TeeBee that no one had heard of. The shop owner turned out to be a rather big local promoter, and as a result, I was asked to open up for Randall at Heat at Hastings Pier."

TeeBee flunked a planned school trip to Brighton as he was practising in the record store for three days straight ahead of his gig, but the resulting experience was one that would bring him up close and personal to the mythical world of dubplate culture. "That night I understood dubplates properly," TeeBee remembers. "Randall rocked up with nothing but acetates. I looked at those spinning 10"s thinking this was the coolest thing I'd ever seen. Fast forward eight years and I left for my first USA tour with a box full of acetates. I was broke, dubplates were expensive, but so incredibly proud as I walked into the first gig of the tour in San Fran, and people lost their shit that I carried an acetate box. Back then, 10" dubplates were a sign of status and success. Not everyone got to cut other people's music, so it was a sign that you had arrived."

While often criticised for representing the best and worst aspects of the scene, there was no denying that what often looked like elitism from the outside only made it that much sweeter when you were finally accepted into the fold. Having a tune held back from release and rinsed by only a handful of top tier DJs not only made the full release of a track that much more exciting for the consumer but also fuelled the fire for producers hoping to break through.

Digital's anthem 'Deadline' released in 2000 is a case study in how a simple trip down to the cutting house could transform your career and the trajectory of drum & bass culture along the way. "I made that tune in 1998," Digital says with a smile. "I honestly thought nothing of it as I drove to Music House to cut it so I could play it the forthcoming weekend. I loved the tune but I thought it would be looked at as being odd because of the bongos and unusual flow, so I wanted to cut it first to get it out of the way before anyone sensible turned up!"

To say the tune took off is an understatement. The first time Digital dropped the tune the crowd got so hype that a fight broke out and with blood literally all over the dancefloor the police closed down the night. "That was when I realised I'd made something decent. It was the best reaction I've had for any track on a first play!"

Even TeeBee remembers the scene in Music House when 'Deadline' came through: "It was mayhem. Someone I didn't know was cutting for one of the big guys and I lost my shit hearing it in there for the first time! I wasn't the only one. Ray Keith, Bryan Gee, J Majik, Marcus Intalex, Klute and a few I didn't know were having a full-blown skank-out jumping around when it dropped! It was truly a special magical moment."

Flash forward a few years and TeeBee's own turn would come as Grooverider dropped TeeBee's "Space Age" at Blue Note and rewound it twice with TeeBee in the crowd. "I didn't even know Groove at the time! I had posted him DATs every month and the fact he had spent his own money to cut one of my compositions onto an acetate made me lose my cool, and I was a little more than excited when I introduced myself to him after his set. He couldn't have been nicer, and him and Fabio were pivotal to me climbing through the ranks early on."

Across the pond in Los Angeles, an alternate dubplate scene was taking off as a local artist named Oscar Da Grouch came across a vintage Scully lathe originally used to cut religious records in the

> **"Our whole scene has always been based around dubplate culture. From the early days of cutting acetate dubs to sending Dropbox links over WhatsApp, and DJ promo shoots via Label-Engine, FatDrop and what-not. It's just how our scene moves forward."**
> *- Dexta*

Midwestern United States. He and his mentor, Len Horowitz, one of the world's leading authorities on disc recordings systems bought and refurbished the lathe and launched Turnstyle Records in 1997. It quickly became the Stateside equivalent of Music House as local, national, and even the occasional international artist would cut plates as they passed through.

"I think this fuelled a lot of the LA-based DJs to step up their game and start producing their own tunes so they too could be part of this exclusive club," Oscar says. "Everyone knew what a dubplate looked like so as soon as they pulled one out of their record box, their status increased."

With the introduction of AOL Instant Messenger, dubplate culture began to become even more inclusive. No longer did one have to post a DAT to their favourite tastemaker, one could simply send the files over Messenger and hope for a response that way. "AIM changed everything," TeeBee agrees. "I got sent all this music from around the world by all these amazing artists, and I realised I wasn't alone in being from overseas. Dieselboy, Marky, the Phunckateck crew, the list goes on. Now when I arrived at Music House, I was stacked and not dependent on permission to cut from the DATs there."

Unfortunately, this was also the beginning of the end for traditional dubplate culture as the acceleration of technology would soon have far-reaching consequences on the way that DJs would deliver music to the masses. With the advent of CDJs and later, Serato and USB-sticks, dubplates and vinyl quite simply disappeared.

While this shift in technology allowed for widespread democratisation in the world of DJing and producing, what remained was the sense that one's status was still tied to your access to unreleased or exclusive tunes. With each dubplate costing anywhere from £30-£50 back in the day, the cost of testing out a new tune not only went down considerably but also reduced the inherent quality control metrics built in to a system that required you to part with hard-earned cash in order to cut a plate (what DJ Hype has infamously called a "shit filter").

It's a sentiment that Dexta from Diffrent Records agrees with as he launches into a new collaborative venture designed to "make dubplates great again". The service is called 1-800-Dubplate, and it's just what the name implies, a new-school dubplate cutting service for a world that seems hell-bent on a seamless digital DAW-to-club experience.

"Our whole scene has always been based around dubplate culture," Dexta muses. "From the early days of cutting acetate dubs to sending Dropbox links over WhatsApp, and DJ promo shoots via Label-Engine, FatDrop and what-not. It's just how our scene moves forward. Still, ever since the digital realm blew up and file-sharing became such a big problem with pre-release album leaks, YouTube rips, 'Russian Pirates' and the whole lot, people have changed the way they 'promote' their music. It seems that it is no longer about sharing music and building a natural organic vibe. I feel like we've got to go back to the start again."

At the other end of the spectrum are new-school producers like the San Diego-based duo Sub Killaz. Having earned their stripes with releases on imprints like Playaz, Souped Up and Biological Beats, their tunes have been rinsed internationally by a host of heavy-hitters ranging from Hype to Mefjus and everyone in between. Their experience in dubplate culture is the more common one these days, where "dubs" are transmitted digitally and played by tastemakers online or at festivals and clubs. The latter is the most coveted slot, especially when someone has a video of the tune being dropped so it can instantly be archived via Instagram, Facebook, or YouTube.

A quick scroll through the Sub Killaz socials and it's not hard to find video after video of their tunes being dropped by heavyweight selectors at festivals like Boomtown, Rampage, and Creamfields. If there's any doubt as to the power of their productions, the size and response of these massive crowds says it all. "As producers, you feel empowered by the dubs you create and having something other people want," Sean, one-half of Sub Killaz tells us. "All it takes is one dope video of you or one of your heroes dropping a banger to the right crowd and suddenly you're a household name in the scene. It's a powerful thing and we're grateful even to be noticed let alone receive some of the music we've gotten over the years."

> **"As producers, you feel empowered by the dubs you create and having something other people want."**
>
> - Sean (Sub Killaz)

Now that digital dubs are the norm and acetates are an even rare breed than before, the verdict is still out on whether this is good or bad for the scene and culture. The old days of a core crew of gatekeepers seems to have gone by the wayside but at the same time so have aspects of the "face-to-face" and "beautiful vibe" culture that Frost was mourning on Twitter.

"The whole structure of how our scene has changed," TeeBee says thoughtfully. "We've lost a vital part of our identity as a more corporate approach has become the norm in order to make a sustainable business out of the culture we love. We're trying to combat the promo-sent-a-week-prior-to-release by going back to the old ways of trading tracks with our peers. If that is a good or bad thing, only time will tell."

Returning to the "old ways" is something Dexta is keen on as well: "It's like when you're going out to play a gig. Do you want to take 400 tunes, promos that you've just downloaded hours before so you can play the same tunes as everyone else in your circle? It's a bit shallow, isn't it? But picking a bag of 30-40 records, tunes that you know like the back of your hand, a handful of dubplates of your own music or from your favourite producers that not many people have access to, that's what gets people excited! Let's have it!"

CHASING ANDY

Words by: Ewen Cook

WHY HAVE COUNTLESS GROWN MEN AND WOMEN SPENT THEIR ADULT LIVES OBSESSING OVER ANDREW JOHN CLARKE? FORMER KNOWLEDGE CONTRIBUTING EDITOR AND MIXMAG'S DRUM & BASS EDITOR FOR THE PAST DECADE, EWEN COOK REFLECTS ON 20 YEARS OF PURSUING D&B'S BIGGEST STAR – AND WHAT IT TELLS US ABOUT THE POWER OF UNDERGROUND MUSIC.

All my adult life, I've been chasing Andy C.

And I am not alone.

Raving fans, booth-hanging tracklist nerds, obsessive tapepack hoarders, copycat bedroom DJ fantasists, near-speechless young promoters, disbelieving warm-up DJs, fawning festival bill-proppers, starstruck journalists – an A-Z of junglist archetypes have all trembled, gawped and thrilled in the wake of the great man.

And I should know. Like countless others, I've been all of the above – a fact that tells its own story of how underground UK music scenes work: multi-faceted communities that allow, immediately on entry, anyone to create their own unique pathway of in-real-life memories.

Everyone's got their Andy story. Most junglists have several.

Here's to them all.

RAVING PILGRIMS

From the moment the penny dropped at one of DJ Chris Natural's legendary Lunarcy parties in Brighton's beachfront bunker The Volks in 2000, I was struck by how distant and foreign all mainstream music scenes and stars suddenly seemed, by comparison, to the raw raving experience. I'd air-guitarred to the Red Hot Chili Peppers, marvelled at the machine-gun bars of the Beastie Boys and grinned wide-eyed at Keef's spikes along with the best of them. I'd even successfully blagged my way into a Primal Scream afterparty and failed spectacularly to get any conversation out of a deeply unimpressed Mani. At the time, it felt like the Holy Grail of meeting one's heroes. Made it. Job done.

This could not have been more beautifully, laughably wrong.

Suddenly, with no previous link to jungle whatsoever, and after barely a few months immersed in all things 170bpm, I found myself trekking to see Andy C for the third time in ten days - culminating in a sprawling warehouse expedition a stone's throw from London's recently built Millennium Dome.

And instantly, it begins. I was convinced that Andy had recognised us that third time - pointing and grinning knowingly back from behind the decks at his sweating pilgrims. Pure nonsense, of course. But it was enough: to my young mind, an authentic interaction with a musical hero within weeks of beginning the journey. In just one moment, it had blown everything else out of the water. And it was just the start.

MIXING OBSESSIVES

In understanding drum & bass fans' devotion to 'The Executioner', it is impossible to overstate the importance of vinyl DJ culture in the late-'90s and noughties, when thousands of bedroom fantasists would scrap for limited numbers of white-labels at the record shop counter or on the burgeoning online portals of Chemical Records and Redeye - in order to try and emulate the latest Andy C dubplate wizardry they had heard in the club that month.

The drum & bass scene's infamous insularity and initial rejection of 'digital' mixing had its roots here:

like legions of Britpop youngsters strumming chords to Oasis's 'Wonderwall', many bedroom DJs wanted little more than to try and copy Andy C's mixes, and style, with religious zeal.

The core of this idolatry was rooted in *comparison*: the thrill came from DJs knowing they had *exactly* the same decks, mixer and, when they waited patiently enough, the same tunes, as their DJ hero. As Andy's style evolved away from the Randall-inspired rolling mixes of the mid-'90s towards his own airlock-tight formula of rapid-fire double-drops and ceaseless teases, his legions of DJ tutees would fetishise the first mix in his sets – which would invariably involve a brand new dubplate along with the 'big tune of the moment', which they too owned on white. Like

Lionel Messi visiting a local school to show off near-impossible ball skills, Andy C would perform miracles using exactly the same tech and music as his disciples – while they screwfaced their approval.

Tapepacks were white-hot fuel in this feverish climate, with each Andy C tape listened to on repeat – first out of the pack, ceaselessly battered and fiercely protected: *"Oi – careful with the Andy one!"*

TURNTABLE JEDIS

A word on sheer levels. Mixing three drum & bass ripsnorters at once, at breakneck pace, in a cacophonous club, under pressure, is a risky business. In fact, no one should attempt this in their own home without first warning the local council. Imagine driving a chariot, for the first time, with six bucking stallions lashed to the front of it, while the whole world watches you.

So how did Andy actually manage it in a pre-digital era? Mixing purists will tell you the best DJs never touch the record. Not Andy, however, who despite appearing to beat-match tunes by telekinesis alone was always happy to give the platter a nudge when needed – especially as his hair-raising three-deck style evolved. Nonetheless, there are simply limited numbers of people in existence who can corral multiple jungle tunes at once with a flick of their fingertips.

The magic, as far as we could work out, lay in Andy's revered 'pitch-chasing' technique on a Technics deck: intricately sliding the pitch control back and forth at lightning speed to synchronise a record within a few hundredths of a second. Many DJs employed this approach, but Andy's sheer speed bordered on the miraculous, and from the late-'90s inspired a generation of tapepack-clutching booth-hangers to try the same (with limited results). Drum & bass's three other marquee mixers of the noughties – Mampi Swift, Friction and DJ Marky – all had the technique refined to dizzying degrees, but none could quite match Andy's combination of bashy risk-taking and Zen-like control.

"How on earth does he do it, mate?" Week in, week out, hardened drum & bassers would also delight at Andy's uncanny ability to raise the volume of a club system that had previously sounded muddy or weak only minutes previously. Rumours of specially-cut dubplates, designed to maximise decibels, or of promoters instructing sound engineers to restrict levels until Andy took to the stage, abounded – but the truth was couched in a multitude of factors. Andy's legendary ability to squeeze the most from the mixer, and the crystalline clarity of his mixes, all served to make myth reality. Add to that the electric expectancy of a crowd whose buzz went nuclear as soon as the word went round that *Andy C was inside the building...*

And there he is: arriving late, at 5:30am on New Year's Eve 2001 at Legends of the Dark Black on the south coast, traipsing up the steps to the stage with a rueful grin to save the day. There he is, just one barely-visible hand appearing above the decks to tease a cheeky tune over the previous DJ's outro – then popping up to grin and wave at the few who noticed. Andy! Of course we noticed.

FLYER BELIEVERS

The very idea that despite being merely a fledgling promoter and bedroom DJ, the likes of Andy C could come to your night and play on a bill you have designed – a bill that includes yourself, your friends and crew – seems entirely ludicrous unless you inhabit the world of drum & bass, where fantasy is quite regularly reality. In less than three years, my Andy C journey had advanced from standing enraptured behind the decks at a friend's night in Portsmouth, watching as Andy delved deep into his extra vinyl bag filled exclusively with 'teases', studying his every move – to taking over from him onstage after a two-hour set in Plymouth, as my own DJ fantasy began to grow modest wings.

To go through the handover ritual witnessed a

thousand times from the distant mists of the back of the dancefloor feels preposterous, impossible, slow-motion – like being inside a montage moment from a film where everything speeds up and the good times just roll. Standing millimetres from the great man, headphones in hand, as he sets the last tune going and leans back to bellow directly into your ear in the time-honoured close-quarters clubland style, advising about mixer channels and needles and apologising for having the booth monitors up earsplittingly loud...

And then *there you are*, awkwardly placing your own first tune *on the very next deck*, fumbling for the headphone jack... And then, best of all, the moment witnessed *yes* a thousand times *but now it's you*: the final handshake, thanks, good luck...

I clanged my first mix something rotten.

FESTIVAL DREAMERS

A word on sheer *class*. It's midnight at the Brunel Rooms in Swindon, and Friction is late, and Andy is about to finish, and the promoter asks if I wouldn't mind filling in for half an hour. Wouldn't mind?! And yet... My warm-up set was hours ago, and the night has taken hold – *but there is Andy, talking me through the mixer once again and chuckling at my nerves...*

And there he is again – *there we are again* – this time onstage in front of thousands at Escape festival in Wales, and no he doesn't mind one jot as I tease ten seconds of a tune over *his* outro – *remember, Andy?* – and explain how he'd done the same himself years back and I'd promised myself that if I ever got the chance... *and now he is roaring with laughter and back-slapping and telling me to shut-up apologising*

and get on with it... and knowing, right there, that this whole thing, is truly made of dreams.

WORDS FOR LIFE

Full circle. My DJ journey done. But always already new beginnings. Because Andy C is kneeling down on the concrete floor serving the drinks. This is not a joke. In a cramped corner offstage at Amnesia, Ibiza, with 10,000 eager faces awaiting, there isn't a table within reach. "Wait a second," he laughs, placing two cups on the floor and rippling vodka into both. "Won't be a minute".

We have not met in six, seven years. My face must be one of literally millions that have passed by. And yet here he is, as humble and chirpy as ever, as we reminisce and chat about his and Chase & Status's newly forming Ibiza takeover. He chuckles as he gainfully tries to remember all the stories I gabble excitedly at him.

How many others have trembled, gawped and thrilled? All those hanging on his every word at London's XOYO, certainly – as his 10-minute speech at the end of 2019's return residency calls many of them out by name. *And here we go again.* We all smile. We all sing.

They say you should never meet your heroes – that you'll be disappointed. Let it be said right here that Andy C is adored, respected, revered by so many for very good reason.

Everyone's got their Andy story. Most junglists have several. Here's to them all.

And here's to you, Andy – the DJ who gives life to dreams.

ORIGINAL

JUNGLIST

CLOTHING

JUMP-UP WILL NEVER DIE

Words by: Dave Jenkins

IT'S THE DIRTIEST WORD IN THE D&B DICTIONARY, YET IT'S THE STYLE THAT GETS THE MOST RAUCOUS REACTIONS IN THE DANCE. IT'S GOT A HISTORY THAT GOES RIGHT BACK TO THE VERY START OF THE GENRE, YET IT ATTRACTS THE YOUNGEST CROWDS. IT'S HOME TO A FIERCELY LOYAL FANBASE, IT'S GOT ITS OWN ENTIRELY SELF-SUSTAINED ECO-SYSTEM, IT'S ARGUABLY THE BACKBONE OF DRUM & BASS. IT'S JUMP-UP. IT WILL NEVER DIE.

"What does 'jump-up' even mean?" asks Jon Midwinter from Bristol duo D*Minds. Jon and his partner Al Vickery's names are dented all over jump-up for almost 20 years as a major part of the subgenre's turbo mutations during the 2000s. "Those two words together don't make you think of anything in particular sonically. It's not like liquid or neuro or tech or minimal where you have a very clear idea of the type of sounds you will hear in a track. Jump-up could mean anything. It's just an energy that takes on all shapes and sizes. It's Saturday night bangers, mate. Tunes people can sing back even if there are no words to them."

That's the essence of jump-up in a nutshell right there. And the reason it won't die. While other subgenre pigeonholes connote a certain sound or style, the term jump-up defines a spirit. It can, and has, adapted, morphed and developed with every new generation. It's why jump-up means something different to every d&b fan.

For some it's the early jump-up jungle sound of 93-95, for others it's a sound related to Bristol (from any point between 95 to around 2007), for younger fans it's more likely to be the bouncy, riffy sound of Macky Gee or Hedex. It could be the Belgian sound, the Leicester sound, the tear-out sound. Like the devil, jump-up takes many forms. But one consistency runs deep.

"The whole basis is the intro and a bassline," considers Manchester's Ste Rowney. As co-captain of G13 Records, and a member of Standard Procedure with Propz and MCs Toddlah & TNT, he's been a staunch jump-up representor since the early 2000s. "It's a melody, it's a cheeky little swagger. Yeah, there are many variations in the sounds. It could be a big horn style, a higher ringtoney type of one, a warm subby one, whatever, but it's the melody that stays the same. If the main melody is in the bassline, there's a jump-up element to it."

Regardless of its myriad morph modes, jump-up will always be defined by its bassline hook. Right the way from DJ SS – 'Lighter', Shy FX – 'Wolf', Ganja Kru – 'Super Sharp Shooter' to DJ Hazard – 'Bricks Don't Role', DJ Guv – 'Warning' and Macky Gee – 'Tour', this has been the subgenre's most consistent key trait. It's the most consistent trait for any track to be called a 'banger' full stop. But there have been other defining characteristics that have shaped the genre hugely over the years. One in particular that had a huge influence on the style's earliest roots was its direct relationship with hip-hop.

"A lot of the original guys were all hip-hop heads before jungle was a thing or jump-up was even a term," explains Clayton Hines. He's perhaps best known for giving the world Renegade Hardware, a label that had a huge impact on the techy side of the genre. But his first label Trouble On Vinyl had just as much impact on jump-up. And did so fusing Clayton's two loves. "Hip-hop and drum & bass? It was a match made in heaven. Trouble On Vinyl was set up specifically for d&b with breakbeats and hip-hop samples. We aren't alone; a lot of labels were on that vibe. Pascal's Frontline were killing it, True Playaz, DJ Zinc. And, of course, DJ Kane and DJ Red who really pushed that sound and became the two key members of Trouble On Vinyl."

Other examples of this strong hip-hop influence include Bristol's Full Cycle crew. All b-boys growing up, Krust, Die, Roni and Suv were huge hip-hop heads, and Krust spent years learning turntablism before he even considered producing his own records. Their Dope Dragon label, in particular, was home to many hip-hop sampling cuts and Dynamite MC's key role at the forefront of Reprazent are all evidence of their hip-hop roots.

Another strong force on this side of the sound were Micky Finn and Aphrodite. Their tracks like 'Bad Ass' and remixes of Jungle Brothers were major crossover points for the genre's exposure to more mainstream. Meanwhile, on the underground frontline you had Kartoons. Run by Nicky Blackmarket, it was responsible for one of this jump-up era's most enduring anthems: '2 Degrees' by the late great DJ Trend and DJ Target.

"Trend was way ahead of his time," says Blackmarket who founded the label to represent the sound his shop Blackmarket Records was best known for. "'2 Degrees' was just this mad 60s Hammond organ and all these sounds mixed into the jump-up melting pot. But that's what jump-up has always been. Just like jungle, it's just been a massive melting pot where you can just throw all them elements in, but as long as it's got that bassline, it's true to the sound."

> **"There have been times people have slagged it off, or it hasn't been accepted, but if anything it's thrived because of that and created the most loyal fanbase you'll get in this music. I can say this, being in the scene for as long as I have, jump-up will honestly never die."**
> – Nicky Blackmarket

Clayton

Hazard

Nicky Blackmarket

Original Sin

D*Minds

And as we move into the 2000s, a whole load more ingredients were added to the pot. During the late 90s / early 2000s the dominant d&b sound was much darker and technical with camps such as Virus, Prototype, Ram, Headz and acts like Bad Company, Fierce and Matrix all pushing their machines beyond their perceived technical means. A fine line of soulful and liquid drum & bass was also emerging at the time from the likes of Creative Source, Hospital and, a little later, Soul:r. The term word 'clownstep' reared its provocative head around this time too, exacerbating jump-up's dirty-word status even more.

"Fucking purists," sighs Clayton Hines. "They always had something to say about it. Forums. Too many people talking too much shit and not doing anything like it is today."

"They were great times," smiles DJ Hazard. "Clipz, D*Minds, G Dub [Original Sin & Sub Zero], Twisted Individual. We all made some good tunes back then. All of us. I'd love to relive that time again." By now the time is the early-to-mid 2000s and jump-up had retreated, regrouped and come back with a sound that tore the face off the entire scene. Hazard and everyone he mentions were some of the key names that took jump-up to entirely new levels during the 2000s with obscene basslines, an energy and a raw, balshy 'fuck you' feel that ushered in a whole new generation of fans.

"From my own point of view I could see a gap that needed to be filled in terms of the music I wanted to hear," says Original Sin who explains how the jump-up at the time didn't quite have the energy he was looking for. "I never set out to make any particular style of drum & bass. It was just me mixing up the elements I loved about the music and putting them together. I'd also say that 2000s DJ culture had a big influence on me. Double drops, teasers with classics. Little moments that come out of nowhere. I thought 'if that's what gets the dancefloor hyped, I'll do it in my tunes.' Like little surprise elements to throw people – little cheeky noises you'll hear for four beats and nowhere else."

> **"Jump-up could mean anything. It's just an energy that takes on all shapes and sizes. It's Saturday night bangers, mate. Tunes people can sing back even if there are no words to them."**
>
> – D*Minds

anything about it themselves. Clownstep, which didn't even come about through a jump-up tune, was really damaging for what people understood jump-up to be. But then guys like Twisted Individual and Hazard came along and blew everything up. Without them, jump-up wouldn't be anything like it is today."

Just like the predominant DJ nature of hip-hop, the brutal and fast-paced d&b mixing style that came into its own in the 2000s (and remains dominant to this day) did indeed have a major influence in the new jump-up sound. Not just in tracks like the extra bass tease on Original Sin's 'Therapy' or the trippy reverse fills on 'Cheater Cheater', you can also hear that influence on tracks like Clipz's famous 'Rubbish' or the lunatic switches on Hazard's 'Machete'. Tongue-in-cheek switches amid the skin-melting basslines, strange samples on the fills and bassline subversions, they added to the chaos, energy and absurdity of the music. The fact it's so heavily inspired by the live and performative aspect is no coincidence, either. Jump-up has never lost sight of its primary objective.

"To make people lose their shit on the dancefloor!" exclaims Voltage, one-third of the Kings Of The Rollers and a solo artist who's spent the last 10 years joining dots between d&b subgenres with releases on labels from Low Down Deep to Metalheadz. "People aren't making jump-up to sit there and do a science experience. They're not like 'oooh this hi-hat needs to be perfect, I need to spend three weeks on a snare.' They just want to take a rave apart. There's this massive snobbery, you get people complaining about the mixdown or the technicalities, but you drop that record in a rave and watch thousands of people kicking off to it. That's why it will never die. It will evolve. And, just when people think it's getting tired or getting a bit formulaic, someone new will come along, add their own twist on it and it'll be hot again."

And this is the crux of why jump-up could never possibly die: it's never once lost its focus of who this music is made for: ravers who keep the scene alive with expendable income for tickets, merch and music... Unlike the older fans (who are also more likely to critique the newer sounds) who don't go out and support the scene half as much due to life commitments or forage further into the genre and settle into different, deeper, favourite styles. Jump-up is the first subgenre many people will have been exposed to, and it retains a youthful energy, both from the artist and fanbase perspective. "It's probably the only subgenre that truly evolves," ponders Voltage. "Other subgenres and labels stay very true to what they started out as. But jump-up is always changing with every generation who come into it."

Since the great XXL jump-up tsunami of the 2000s, new mavericks have indeed come through at key points and had huge influences on the sound. As the 2010s began artists such as Decimal Bass and Konichi (who later became Annix) introduced a much more

> **"**It's probably the only subgenre that truly evolves. Other subgenres and labels stay very true to what they started out as. But jump-up is always changing with every generation who come into it.**"**
>
> - Voltage

angular, technical and brutal funk to the sound. The late great DJ Dominator, Turno and Macky Gee all brought serious bounce and riffs back into the sound.

Acts like K Motionz, Kanine and Simula have set the benchmark in terms of versatility and refusing to be pigeonholed in any one sound while guys such as Serum and Voltage returned to their Bristol and V Recordings roots and reinterpreted the rolling, breakbeat-based sound for the modern age (currently known as 'the foghorn sound') Further afield, jump-up has also had its first significant international influence as a strain of jump-up associated with Belgium led to a whole series of triplet beats and high-frequency laser basslines.

"There's a passion and an energy here," explains DJ Premium, a UK artist who has such a strong following in Belgium he's moved there and has since launched a label - Exert Records - to help develop the local talent. "It's a new thing here, the kids go crazy. It's like a way of life. And a lot of them are now coming on to be new artists themselves. I'm including Austria in this as well; what we had in Belgium is now happening over there with a mad

loyal fanbase and crazy parties where they're really championing the new generation of the artists coming through. It's really exciting to see."

"We could feel this new generation a few years ago," agrees Jon from D*Minds not just from his perspective as an artist but also as one of the promoters behind one of Bristol's longest-running events RUN. "It's been a general movement of kids and new talent from all over Europe that's been unstoppable. And it's unsupported by any media or pushed by any of the big DJs, it's just grown very naturally and is unstoppable."

Jump-up has entered yet another new cycle and once again it's being driven by the new generation of artists, all putting their stamp on it and powering it themselves with the same DIY spirit every other jump-up generation has come through with. And that resonates with the youthful crowd it's always been made for.

"Jump up is the modern equivalent of jungle," says Nicky Blackmarket. "That's how I interpret it. It's the melting pot, it's 100% dancefloor focused. There have been times people have slagged it off, or it hasn't been accepted, but if anything it's thrived because of that and created the most loyal fanbase you'll get in this music. I can say this, being in the scene for as long as I have, jump-up will honestly never die."

DJ Premium

Voltage

BARS FOR YEARS

Words by: Tom Denton

IT'S 2019 AND, IN THE WORLD AT LARGE, MCS ARE HEADLINERS. THREE OF THE TOP TEN RICHEST MUSICIANS IN THE WORLD ARE RAPPERS. THE LIKES OF AKALA AND STORMZY ARE RESPECTED AS POLITICAL COMMENTATORS, WHILE DRILL LOOMS LARGE AS A MUSICAL BOGEYMAN FOR THE MORE ANXIOUS WING OF THE MEDIA.
BUT, ON OUR LITTLE ISLAND OF DRUM & BASS, THE DJ HAS TRADITIONALLY RULED THE ROOST. OLDER HEADS ARE WELL-USED TO SEEING MCS RELEGATED TO THE SMALLER FONT SIZES AT THE BOTTOM OF THE FLYER. RECENTLY, THOUGH, WE'VE SEEN THE EVOLUTION OF A NEW PHENOMENON: THE HEADLINER D&B MC.

We discussed this shift with Navigator, the four-decades-deep Godfather-status MC. He's been part of the journey since the days of acid house. Coming from a reggae soundsystem background though, he wasn't an immediate convert to dance music.

"I didn't identify with it at all," he tells us, "I was like, what the hell is this? It was 1991 or 1992 before I started hearing the influences that I identified with."

Early acid house was light on low end and heavy on electronic bleeps, worlds apart from the vibe and bass-weight Navi was used to. But the dance music scene offered new opportunities, as he explains:

"I came from a very big soundsystem in North East London, and we never really got a chance to express ourselves as artists because there was a lot of stuff going on around the soundsystem and we weren't getting the chance in the studio."

That "very big soundsystem" was the legendary Unity Sound, whose ranks also included a couple of mic men by the names of Flinty Badman and Deman Rocker, aka the Ragga Twins. They had also become dissatisfied with the lack of opportunities within Unity, and had begun making outside moves.

Blending their vocals with dance music, they set the template for the "ragga hardcore" style, as showcased on their landmark 1991 album, pointedly titled 'Reggae Owes Me Money'.

At that point, even the doubters could see the potential in this mash-up of reggae and rave music. The concept had been proven, and there was a ready-made army of clash-hardened soundsystem artists set to reconfigure their dancehall classics into jungle tear-outs and define a genre.

Navigator explains how the land lay: "When I came into the rave scene I hadn't really solidified myself as an artist yet, whereas General Levy, Top Cat, Tenor Fly, Sweetie Irie, Daddy Freddy, Tippa Irie, all these guys already had a catalogue."

That's the key word. Catalogue. It's the thread which connects the roots of d&b MCing to the state of the art form today. The OJ soundsystem crew knew it was all about catalogue, and the new breed of emcees know it too.

"If you haven't got the catalogue, you're not in the game", is how Navigator sums it up, "It's the only way forward... my whole thing was, for us to define ourselves as artists we have to be putting out our own content."

For a long time, though, that's not how d&b emcees did things. Understandably, making time to get in the studio wasn't top of the priority list. After all, these were predominantly young men, suddenly making a decent living out of going to raves... why would they want anything more?

Despite its scarcity of studio output, the mid-90s era of drum & bass MCing is pivotal in the history of UK music. And we can thank the tape pack for that, passed down from old skool junglists to a generation of younger siblings who took those influences and eventually gave them back to us in the form of grime.

We saw drum & bass emceeing take on a character of its own. The double-time from Det, Shabba, Fearless and Skibadee, the darkside one-liners of Bassman and the Shadow Demon click, the rave-hyping hooks of MC MC... flows and cadences that are still imitated 25 years on.

And, of course, we need to take a moment to discuss Stevie Hyper D. He's widely regarded as the greatest emcee our scene has produced. The reasons are technically complex, but can be summed up very simply: he could do it all. All of it.

He had the double-time, the hip-hop flows, the ragga chat and the melodic stuff. He spat conscious content alongside sing-alongs that we're still singing today. He wrote similes, metaphors and wordplay, showing us pen game before the term even existed.

He left a legacy beyond lyricism too. By bringing in Fatman D, one of the premier architects of the MC-DJ collective in d&b, he ensured the torch would be passed down the generations via New Breed to Biological Beats to Young Guns and beyond. And, even after he passed in 1998, Stevie was still setting levels. The posthumous LP 'The Next Step' was arguably the first MC-led d&b album.

But here's a question for the trainspotters: list all the d&b emcees who have, to date, scored a solo UK top forty hit. The smart-ass answers of Goldie and Rag 'n' Bone Man, of course, don't count because they were clearly ex-d&b emcees by the time they got their chart success. Navigator, Dynamite, General Levy and Tenor Fly are good guesses, but their credits are as featured artists or as parts of collectives. The real list, at time of writing, has just one name on it, and it's Tali.

"I got into hip-hop music initially", she told us, "I really loved the way that the people performing it were using it to tell the world about their world. I discovered

> "If you haven't got the catalogue, you're not in the game. It's the only way forward... to define ourselves as artists we have to be putting out our own content."
> – Navigator

more conscious rappers like Talib Kweli and Common, and how they were using their platform to talk about positivity and respecting women... I just loved the way you could use lyrics and music to move people."

Of course, the idea of conscious, even moving content would be well-familiar to the original soundsystem artists, but crowd hype and flow had become the priorities for most MCs around the turn of the millennium. The likes of Eksman, Flyte, Riddla and Kasha had elevated the levels of high-impact bar-spraying fireworks, and virtually every up-and-coming MC wanted to sound like them.

But there were other developments as the 90s continued too. Conrad and DRS were working with a whole different style of lyricism: less aggression, more emotion, perfectly adapted for the atmospheric Good Looking style of d&b they were associated with. Cleveland Watkiss, Fats and Stamina brought jazz and soul melodies into the mix. The likes of Chickaboo, Lady MC and Deeizm secured the position of female lyricists in the scene, an important step in making the genre inclusive and representative.

"If you don't see yourself reflected in the thing that you love," Tali tells us, "you don't feel like there's a place for you. If you don't see other women MCing and totally killing it then unconsciously you'll think that there isn't a place for you."

> **"There's certainly a change in the wind for d&b vocalism. Now that more MCs are featuring on tracks, I certainly feel there's a vocal revolution happening in the genre."**
> - Degs

Since then, we've seen Miss Melody, Starz, the Girls Take Action crew and others come through to the main stages and demonstrate that the role of d&b MC is becoming a viable and visible option for young women. It's also, slowly but surely, becoming a viable option for those who want to go beyond the conventional crowd hype and clash bars.

"The shit that people will come up to me and say they really loved, is they'll say, oh my god, I loved that freestyle you did over that track when you were talking about the planets, or you were talking about past lives," Tali tells us. "You do have to dig deep, and you have to be quite vulnerable and transparent. You have to divulge a certain sense of honesty."

These are not the words of the stereotypical drum & bass MC. But, then again, as is usually the case, maybe the stereotype doesn't tell the full story. You see, social media has changed the game. There are no gatekeepers, no-one to stop anyone with the motivation from making a track or shooting a video and posting it for the world to see. For the first time, we have a whole generation of up-and-coming artists for whom creating content is just everyday life.

Additionally, new artists have unprecedented access to thousands of rap battles, freestyles, mixtapes and

Tali

Degs

hear what he's doing. Little expletives coming in, little adjectives and little words... Moose always used to do that. He used to say one word, and it would describe the thing perfectly. I'd be like, how the fuck is he picking that out of the sky like that?"

And, as if to demonstrate that the student has become the master, Navi sums up the art of hosting in eleven perfectly-selected words: "You listen to the DJ and you wait for the spaces."

You see, decades of craft and creativity have gone into all aspects of the drum & bass MCs art. Surely things can only develop so far before we see one of our own catch the zeitgeist and become a bonafide daytime-airplay-level star.

If any of the current crop are capable of such a feat, Degs is definitely in with a shout. Combining soulful vocals with pen game, and with the mighty Hospital Records empire at his back, he's proved himself to be a crowd favourite ever since he was dramatically propelled into the spotlight just over a year ago.

We asked Degs his view on the chances of a d&b MC crossing over into the mainstream. "There's certainly a change in the wind for d&b vocalism," he suggests, "Why isn't that a target we should all try and reach? Now that more MCs are featuring on tracks, I certainly feel there's a vocal revolution happening in the genre."

Building on decades of influence, technique and study, drum & bass MCing has come of age in recent years. As the founding fathers like Navigator knew from the beginning, it's all about catalogue, and the current generation agrees wholeheartedly.

To echo Degs, drum & bass is experiencing a vocal revolution, 30 years in the making, and we're about to witness the levels our mic men and women can really hit.

albums to study, meaning the levels of technical ability have rocketed. Ten years ago you'd be lucky to find a handful of d&b MCs who thought about their bars in terms of punchlines, multis and schemes. Now those elements are basic training.

So, we have people like Decoy, Comma-Dee, Haribo and Duskee: content-focused lyricists who are as interested in saying something clever and meaningful as they are in hyping up a roomful of ravers. And, crucially, they're just as interested in releasing music.

"I've got to write music with a purpose", Duskee told us, "I want people to feel the music, and I want it to resonate with people... Some people like just going and spitting bars and getting gassed on the weekend, which is fair enough. But if you want to make a scene change and grow, and you want to be part of something and make an impact in music you have to release things, you have to spread your thoughts."

That's the new skool mentality. Or, more accurately,

"You do have to dig deep, and you have to be quite vulnerable and transparent. You have to divulge a certain sense of honesty."

- Tali

it's the old skool soundsystem mentality reborn, and it's seen a swathe of MC-led music, even full artist albums, over the last few years.

We've seen elegantly snarling introspection from Sense, the hype and hopefulness of Inja, cross-genre poetics from DRS, carnality and conspiracy from Mr Traumatik, New York hip-hop vibes from T.R.A.C... the depth and breadth is astonishing.

But d&b MCing isn't all about bars. Alongside the lyricists, there's that other elite group: the top tier hosts. We're talking the likes of GQ, Moose, SP, Rage and Blackeye, people who can manipulate the vibe of the dance with just a few precision-tooled words.

Navigator lifts the curtain: "I learned this lesson from my good friend MC Moose a long time ago. He was the first MC to school me on how to host on jungle properly. There are a couple of rules. Don't chat over a vocal. Do not roast the mix. Let the mix breathe, let the DJ

Duskee

Marc Mac & Dego

WORLD 2 WORLD

Words by: Oli Warwick

IN MUSICAL TERMS, IT'S HARD TO IMAGINE HOW AN ERA LIKE THE EARLY 90S COULD BE REPEATED NOW. THE RAPID ACCELERATION OF TECHNOLOGY AND A FEW DECADES OF DANCE MUSIC CULTURE COLLIDED SO POWERFULLY THAT, FOR A FEW YEARS, NO ONE COULD REALLY TELL WHAT WAS WHAT. TEMPOS SHIFTED WILDLY, METHODS OF PRODUCTION BENT TO THE SINGLE-MINDED WHIMS OF BEDROOM PRODUCERS WORLDWIDE, AND DEEP-ROOTED INFLUENCES ALL FED INTO THE CHURN OF CREATIVE POSSIBILITIES.

Marc Mac was among those blazing the trail others followed. Alongside Dego, Gus Lawrence and Iain Bardouille, he formed 4hero and helped define the early hardcore and jungle sound with a frankly intimidating number of seminal releases and the mammoth Reinforced Records. The combined force of their musical impact helped shape electronic music in the UK, and they pressed continually forwards from the gnarly, DIY rave era to ever more accomplished musicality, major label stints and myriad avenues of inspiration that continue to bear fruit to this day. But among the jewels in their catalogue is a cult record credited to Nu Era.

Beyond Gravity, released in 1994 on Reinforced sublabel Reflective, sticks out like a sore thumb amongst the other 4hero-related releases of the time. Compared to the ragged, sample-heavy sound of jungle, this was a purist exploration of machine soul clearly indebted to Detroit techno. However, it shivered with its own unique, restless energy, which explains why original copies of the relatively rare record still fetch astronomical prices.

By 1994 the lines had been drawn in terms of electronic dance music, and it wasn't that common for artists to flit around between styles when business was booming. From the outside looking in, jungle titans 4hero suddenly took a diversion into a genre they'd never been anywhere near before, but the reality tells a different story.

"When soul music started to have drum machines, I started to play those drum machine records," explains Mac, looking back to his early days on the Solar Zone sound system in the 80s. "Out of that, you had the house stuff that was coming in from Chicago, especially labels like Trax, and then soon after the stuff from Detroit. The Chicago music was more accessible with vocals, but the Detroit stuff was more about the technology. Hearing the way those guys were using those instruments and doing things from a technical perspective was what drew us into the techno even more. We started to hear instruments speaking to us rather than hearing the musicians.

"On the early 4hero and Reinforced stuff you can hear our obsession with synthesised strings," he continues. "At that point in time, we didn't go for the [Roland TR]909 or the [Roland TR]808 'cause we were into breakbeats. We took breakbeats from funk and hip-hop, we took reggae and ragga samples, and from Detroit techno we took those deep, orchestral string sounds. It was the Detroit sound that allowed us to take our minds to outer space and away from reality. Galaxy to galaxy, world to world!"

> "It was the Detroit sound that allowed us to take our minds to outer space and away from reality. Galaxy to galaxy, world to world!"
> - Marc Mac

Mac is keen to point out the significance of the escapism loaded into the Detroit techno narrative, and how it mirrored the escapism many of the hardcore and jungle pioneers were striving for in their own wildly futuristic music. "You only have to listen to stuff like the *Journey to The Light EP* or *Internal Affairs*. We were definitely trying to break away and escape from normality, and I think that's a link we have with Detroit."

"When we went over to Detroit and met Mad Mike and Underground Resistance for the first time," he adds, "we walked in the room and [Mike] looked at Iain and said, 'look, you could be my brother.' They looked really similar, but it also felt like, 'I don't know you, you're miles away, but we're doing exactly the same thing, there's a connection.'"

Techno pioneer Kevin Saunderson was the instigator of a connection between the Detroit scene and the UK hardcore and jungle community. After hearing the sounds 4hero and their peers were making while on tour, he approached them about releasing a record on his label, KMS. After getting past their initial disbelief at the offer, Mac and the others saw it as validation for the connection they felt to Detroit techno - that Saunderson and his fellow Motor City alumni were also hearing what was happening in the UK and sensing the connection too.

"The connection was deep enough that Kevin invited us over to Detroit," Mac explains. "He introduced us to practically all the cats. That trip we met Theo Parrish for the first time, Claude Young, Underground Resistance. We were sitting in Kevin's living room watching TV. It wasn't like getting invited to a venue and a hotel. It was more personal. It was more like family."

Saunderson was the most visibly engaged with the hardcore and jungle scenes - his Reese alias sired one of the genres most iconic bass sounds after all - but when they visited Detroit, Mac could hear the music being played everywhere, by everyone. From Claude Young pushing the pitch control and cutting up hardcore records to blend them with faster strains of techno, to hearing jungle tearing out over the shop system in Submerge Records, their music had found a true foothold in Detroit.

"As Kevin introduced us to the cats out there we realised they all knew what was going on with the jungle thing," Mac explains. "As soon as you started to speak to them, they could reel off all the tracks. They'd talk about different samples. I bumped into people I sampled without realising who they were. They'd say, 'Yeah, you sampled me on blah blah blah, that was cool.'"

You could even hear the influence of hardcore creeping into the music coming out of Detroit. DJ Tone's *Insanity 12"* on KMS was undeniably a rave-inspired track. Years later, Carl Craig's *Bug In The Bassbin* was a celebratory chop-up of drum samples in the jungle tradition, while Underground Resistance's *Something Happened On Dollis Hill* was an explicit nod to the area of London where 4hero's early music was recorded.

But back in the early 90s, amid a rapidly evolving hardcore and jungle scene they had helped catalyse, Mac and Dego set up a Reinforced sub label called Reflective and released a handful of singles and compilations, and Nu Era's *Beyond Gravity LP*. The contemporary techno they'd been hearing on the European gig circuit had mainly been the tougher, straighter, whiter stuff coming out of Germany and Belgium, which mostly left them uninspired, but things felt different after forging their US connections.

"After the trip to Detroit and meeting what I felt was the real techno, it felt more comfortable that this is music we should be making," Mac explains. "It almost felt like we'd been invited to be part of it. We went to all the different studios and came back with stacks of records. Hearing how adventurous, experimental and soulful they were, we wanted to do something like that. We said, 'right, let's escape from what's happening with the hardcore scene,' and me and Dego locked ourselves in the studio over one weekend and recorded *Beyond Gravity*."

A vast majority of the early 4hero material was the product of Mac and Dego working individually. While they would have discussions about the direction they were working in or perhaps lend some input in the latter stages of the production process, it was more common they worked on tracks on their own, but it was different with *Beyond Gravity*.

"The record myself and Dego collaborated most together on was *Beyond Gravity*. That was the one where we hired loads of equipment in and locked the door. We had our backs to each other as the DAT was rolling, getting the stuff down onto the tape. Some of the stuff was just going down live, and we did some live EQ on the desk and live drum machine programming... it wasn't all set in a sequencer."

While they were both brimming with inspiration from their trip to Detroit, Mac and Dego weren't consciously trying to clone the Detroit sound. Instead, they were striving to create their own interpretation of techno. Mac admits the Juno chords on *Mono Concentrate* were influenced by Mad Mike's approach on the more house-oriented Happy Records releases like Davina's *Don't You Want It*, but that's where the direct parallels end.

"There was something individual about *Beyond Gravity*," Mac considers, "and I think that's why it's still sought after at the moment, because it has its own little space within techno. I never wanted it to be generic techno."

Reflective was a short-lived enterprise. After *Beyond Gravity* there were two volumes of The *Deepest Shade Of Techno* which equally serve as vital portals into some of the most forward-thinking, soul-enriched machine music of the mid-90s, but then the label stopped as quickly as it

> **"**You only have to listen to stuff like the *Journey to The Light* EP or *Internal Affairs*. We were definitely trying to break away and escape from normality, and I think that's a link we have with Detroit.**"**
>
> – Marc Mac

had started. Mac credits this to signing to a major label – something which happened to the likes of Goldie, Photek, Roni Size and plenty of others. Suddenly some of the biggest pioneers in jungle were locked away in the studio working on albums instead of firing experimental 12"s out into the scene.

The Detroit connection remained strong, though. A few years after *Beyond Gravity*, Mac had an unexpected visitor at the 4hero studio.

"There was a ring on the buzzer, and some guy down there said, 'It's Juan.' And I thought, 'Juan who?' I didn't buzz him in. I went downstairs to see, 'who's this cat at the door?' This guy was standing there in a black leather jacket, jeans and white trainers, looked like any of the guys in the neighbourhood, and he goes, 'Juan. I wanna make some tunes.' 'Cause he had the American accent, the penny dropped, and he goes, 'Juan Atkins.' That was one of the strangest sessions I've ever had in my life. We probably said about 10 words for about three hours. We just started to make these tracks – it was this hybrid of jungle and techno, and as he started to play, I thought, 'yeah, this is Juan.' From there we just took flight and made two tracks in about three hours. One went on our Jacob's Optical Stairway album, and one went on one of his compilations or something."

After 4hero went through the experience of a major label deal with Talkin' Loud / Mercury and came out the other side, Mac and Dego were freer to explore their more experimental sides again. Dego went deep into broken beat with his 2000 Black project (amongst many others), and Mac was able to return to Nu Era, this time as a solo venture.

"I just couldn't leave the techno thing," Mac admits. "Me and Dego did speak a few times about doing more Nu Era stuff together, but at that point, he was really focused on building on 2000 Black, so I just continued doing it on my own. At the time, I was hybriding it with broken beat, so the beats were changing as well. I was always into fusing different styles together, and it's still somehow evolving into something... I don't quite know what it is yet."

And so Nu Era continues – albums in 2013 and 2014 came out on Mac's Omniverse label, and after a five-year wait *Evolve* dropped in Autumn 2019. It's a fitting title for a project which embodies the pioneering spirit of electronic music, from those first soul records with drum machines through the Detroit tidal wave to the hardcore explosion.

"There was someone online just last week that had a post saying, 'are there any other acts out there making techno music a bit like Nu Era?'" Mac recalls. "There was a thread going on, and most people were saying, 'well no, not really.' And that's the way I like it."

Juan Atkins, Derrick May & Kevin Saunderson

HAS NEURO FUNKED ITSELF?

Words by: Layla Marino

Black Sun Empire

BY THIS STAGE IN THE GAME, MOST OF THE D&B SUBGENRES HAVE BECOME LITTLE MORE THAN MEMES OF THEMSELVES, FURIOUSLY DEBATED OVER BY KEYBOARD WARRIORS BUT NO LONGER EASILY DEFINED, ASIDE FROM THE TYPES OF PEOPLE WHO LISTEN TO THEM.

NEUROFUNK, A STYLE OF D&B WHICH INITIALLY BEGAN OUT OF TWO OTHER VAGUE SUBGENRES, TECHSTEP AND DARKSTEP, HAS BOTH EVOLVED INTO SOME OF THE MOST TECHNICAL AND EXPERIMENTAL WORK BASS MUSIC HAS EVER SEEN AND DEVOLVED INTO A SNOOTY, ANGRY CARICATURE OF ITSELF THANKS TO THE WAY EDM HAS DEVELOPED IN GENERAL.

Ed Rush & Optical

How did neurofunk get to where it is now? Does it resemble what it originally was in any way? Does it matter what it resembles anymore? Has all this defining and neuro nationalism done more harm than good? And finally, where can it go from here? Has neuro "funked" itself and can it "un-funk", as it were?

With Kmag itself having been a compendium of neurofunk's journey, we've consulted some of the progenitors, innovators, and present neuro warriors who've grown the style into what it is today about where neuro came from, where it is now and where it's going.

A form of neurofunk has existed almost since the beginning of drum & bass. The unique kick drum that loosely defined d&b as being different from jungle around 1994 and 1995 seems to have instantly lent itself to dark bass, metallic clangy noises and a jazzy groove. Darkstep and techstep ruled the more aggressive side of d&b from 1996 and included classics like Bad Company's "The Nine", "Whiplash" by Future Cut, anything by Dillinja, Bad Company or Ed Rush & Optical. The list goes on throughout the 90s, and hard d&b comprises a big part of the genre's pull.

Unbeknownst to most neuro chads nowadays, the term "neurofunk" was originally created as a not very nice descriptor, according to Matt Optical.

"The term was coined by Simon Reynolds in his essay ("On the Hardcore Continuum #5: Neurofunk Drum' n' Bass versus Speed Garage" or "2 Steps Back" in The Wire Magazine) in 1997 and was not very complimentary or particularly accurate in my opinion as he said we were 'fun free' in our approach to making music. Actually, we were dancing around like mad people with huge grins on our faces most of the time in our studio."

Indeed from the outside with all its minor keys, glitchy synths and, yes, foghorns, neurofunk may have seemed a bit joyless compared to the also emerging liquid or jump-up d&b subgenres but, with this term, Reynolds hit upon a part of drum & bass that was both cerebral and groovy in its technique and construction and which garnered an almost rabid following. Other progenitor artists were just as bewildered by the term at the time.

"We were just making drum & bass, and the term neurofunk was coined as an observation of what we and a few others were doing at the time," Vegas of Bad Company muses. There were a few tracks we did that other labels and producers based their musical journey on, so I guess our energy spread into the mindset of future producers and the sound of d&b for the next 20 years through this neurofunk vein."

A lot of the supposed creators of neurofunk did realise something new was going on at this time in d&b, despite the naming of the subgenre being little more than poetic license from an overly wordy journalist (of course, none of us here at Kmag can relate). Skynet of the neuro power duo Stakka & Skynet certainly felt it.

"None of us thought of ourselves as being the sole creators of a genre. I think there were a few of us that were really pushing things at that time and it was a very inspiring time to be involved in music. I think for us, it was partly due to being brave enough to take risks and

Vegas

Phace

follow our feelings rather than a business model for the labels or follow what was trending. That's a great business model, but it's not easy running a profitable record label while trying to break new ground."

Record labels did profit from neurofunk even before it was neurofunk, however. Ed Rush & Optical started Virus, Renegade Hardware notably took up the mantle of neuro in a big way, and by 2001 even RAM and V Recordings had curated some of the biggest techy and ostensibly neurofunk tracks in

drum & bass to date in those formative years. From there, however, things got even more funky (or "neuro-y", depending on who you talk to).

As this book goes to print, Noisia, the group who, along with others like Black Sun Empire, Phace & Misanthrop, Current Value and a litany of others artists many believe are responsible for building neurofunk into what it is, have announced their split after 20 years of working together. When this group of largely European artists first crashed through into

techstep and neurofunk, it changed the game once again. Noisia, BSE and the like began to really focus on the "neuro" side of neurofunk, using sound design and some of the new technology available at the time to really amplify the technical potential of neurofunk.

Rene Verdult from Black Sun Empire thinks the way their sound (and others on the continent developed) was because of UK artists like Konflict, Usual Suspects, Skynet, Ed Rush & Optical but also because of the way rave music developed quite differently in places like the Netherlands and Germany.

"When we started, there were some DJs and producers who were doing what we ended up doing, like Konflict, Ed Rush & Optical, Stakka & Skynet and Technical Itch. I think the sounds that we grew up with here in the Netherlands found their way into our drum & bass: a lot of techno, some hardcore, even a bit of trance when that was still darker."

He also feels that the idea that neurofunk is the most technical subgenre may be overblown, just as is the idea that European neuro is too formulaic.

"We love the harder sounds," he continues, "but also feel like the music needs to have some melodies and hooks. When producers concentrate on making the loudest snares and ridiculous bass, they sometimes forget that most people listen to other things as well and in fact need those things to really connect with the music. As technical as this style can be, it is still music, meant to communicate a feeling or vibe. I think that's what we listen for in other people's music and try to create ourselves."

For better or worse, however, from 2003 on neurofunk was largely seen as being driven by sound design and technique. The race was effectively on to create more and more perfect beats with Noisia, BSE and Neosignal leading the way. To this day, if you give a neurofunk track to a producer of any other genre, the first thing they'll say is "the sound design there is crazy". No one can touch it. Some proponents of the early neurofunk, however, felt the "funk" was summarily removed from the equation and that it had, in fact, become too much of an equation; too forumlaic. Skynet feels this was down to the technology in production.

"A lot of the "funk" back then came from timing which is very difficult to produce in these atomic timed, digital-based systems. The brain switches off when everything is locked to that grid. If you add some groove and movement into your timing, a little loosening of things, this is better, but then it's just repeated over and over, the song it's not interacting with the other instruments. Basically, every note throughout the whole song needs to be changing in timing by the smallest amount. It's a delicate balance. Some have tried to override this by adding crazy edits or 10 riffs in a song, switching up drums every 4-8 bars just to try and keep the attention of the brain. I'm sure not everyone cares for the funk element, but I love the swag and movement. I don't care for sample-accurate timing, it turns me off. So I tried to keep the funk in my production."

Vegas seems to have similar feelings, but with working in neurofunk and hard d&b through all its phases, he and Bad Company (BCUK) have decided to roll with the changes, and now he's created Bad Taste Records to work with and continue to further the sound.

"It's gained technology behind it; the computers and

> **"**I have no idea how trends will shift, but I also don't care too much. I just push forward with my own wonky taste in music.**"**
>
> - Jade

plugins have got better, so the quality of sound has got a lot better. At the same time, neurofunk has lost some of the funk. Things can be too rigid, empty, similar and copied, but it is gaining a lot in mixdown and sound clarity with certain producers getting it sounding next to perfect and making it go off nonetheless."

Other artists who came up in this second wave of neuro recognise that what they were making wasn't really neuro in its original form and even sought to distance themselves from that subgenre label. Misanthrop and Phace, for example, managed to skirt being saddled with the neuro sticker when they started Neodigital/Neosignal in 2008 despite having some to the tightest sound design on the line and being pretty techy in their compisition. They made it clear that their work was a different thing, as did other artists like Current Value, although it's yet to be determined that drum & bass at large agreed at the time. For those who missed it, Misanthrop clarifies:

"In the eastern parts of Europe, people picked up that subgenre name later and branded a style with it that has nothing really in common with the original idea. Neurofunk from the early days was about producing never before heard sounds with unusual grooves and funky elements in it; experimenting to produce something new. Of course, things change, and I like change. But when music changes in a way that it should just 'work on the dancefloor', the pioneering idea is dead and so is the genre, in my opinion."

From the artist perspective, no one really wanted neurofunk or any d&b subgenre to lose that pioneering spirit, but fans can drive the music almost as much as the artists do. For a while in neurofunk it felt like only the tightest sound design, a certain tempo and a certain amount of metallic, robot-like synths were acceptable or made their way to the top spots in the charts or in festivals. As almost always happens when a style gets really popular, some people would only listen to certain artists and only if they sounded the same as they did when they came out.

As the genre drew closer to the present, hard drum & bass grew so big it fractionated itself into other sub-sub genres like halftime and the darker parts of dubstep. Noisia even started a new label, Division, to focus on slower, deeper cuts inspired by the likes of Ivy Lab and Shades, a new project Alix Perez created. Phace and Misanthrop started NËU to highlight new artists of any genre and labels like MethLab, Vale and Korsakov's new label rolled out of the neurofog as being all-inclusive bass music with a hard edge.

At the same time, labels like Eatbrain, Vision, Virus and Blackout still carried the neuro flag proudly, declaring with their releases that neurofunk could still be innovative and embrace any and all styles. Shock of all shocks, Jade didn't even know the term "neurofunk" when he founded Eatbrain:

"When I founded the label, I hadn't even heard the term neuro. It wasn't until two years later when I first encountered it. I wanted to do quality drum & bass, no subgenres excepted. Of course, I signed to my taste; that was high octane, dark d&b. Later I heard people calling it neurofunk, and I just went with it. I never enforced anything subgenre specific on the artists, I just signed what clicked with me and we ended up becoming one of the flagships of the style. It was never the goal."

Almost every Eatbrain release, despite its fans expecting straight-up neurofunk from it, has at least one track that is categorically not neurofunk and sometimes not even d&b. Artists like Teddy Killerz and Joe Ford have done techno and breaks on the label. Jade himself even caused a major stir in 2018 with his seminal "Man Eating Lizard Dragon" track which combined techno, gabber, dub and drum & bass in a beautiful mélange of all the things hard bass music is capable of. To say there was a mixed reception from fans was an understatement and Jade eventually made a more straight-up-and-down d&b VIP. He mirrors the sentiments of a lot of producers throughout the history of not just neurofunk but all of d&b:

"It's a tough one because fans can be elitist sometimes and it's not always welcome when we come out with something different. But I'm all about every kind of quality music and tunnel vision doesn't help you grow, so I always encourage everyone to make different tunes for their releases. Interestingly enough, many producers don't jump on the opportunity but

Skynet

the ones who do come up with the most impressive techno, breakbeat, liquid and minimal d&b tunes and sometimes even music that doesn't fit any boxes."

In a way, Jade's singular experience represents where neurofunk and all the subgenres are at the moment. Around 2017, many of the labels took on the idea that these classifications were getting out of hand. In neurofunk the artists seemed to push against the formulaic expectations of the fans actively. Blackout signed several unexpected artists but stayed steadfast in continuing its own sound. Noisia did a big push on the halftime and soundsystem end of Division. Bad Taste is now on the leading edge of discovering new artists and sounds no matter what subgenre, as Eatbrain and Virus have always been. A new rash of Eastern European artists like Synergy, Billain, Gydra and Zombie Cats began making hard bass music on their own terms, and both the fans and the industry have been put on notice to expect more change.

To this end, none of the artists or label heads seem to regret the journey of neurofunk. Its genesis, evolution and current state seem to all have been necessary

"Music genres always have ups and downs. I think we had far too much of the same music out at the same time with the same line-ups on raves. Sometimes things have to downsize to get healthy again"
– Misanthrop

in creating the next steps in hard drum & bass. The pendulum must take a few swipes to the left and right before it settles and comes back into its own. Has it come full circle? It's certainly proved it has staying power, and while neurofunk may not look a lot like it used to, it's still very much about innovation and pushing boundaries so overall it hasn't "funked" itself at all and will likely keep pushing d&b into the future.

The final words on the future of neurofunk should belong to the artists themselves:

"We were a group of like-minded people who just wanted to put together all the best elements of the music we loved and mash it up to make something new. I don't think we invented the genre of neurofunk as it is known now, but we are part of a group of many incredible musicians and producers who have contributed to a really unique, boundary-pushing and endlessly creative part of the musical world." - Optical

"I have no idea how trends will shift, but I also don't care too much. I just push forward with my own wonky taste in music." - Jade

"Tracks get signed one at a time for being good in their own right, and I guess it's a natural taste thing as a lot of them fall into neurofunk. Going forward, I see

the label covering the whole spectrum of d&b as a lot of depth is held in the more melodic soundtracks, and a lot of vibes are on the dance floor, wherever that may be. I like the feeling of things being free to naturally develop and welcome change and new things." - Vegas

"We want more and more people to listen to the label (obviously) but don't want to compromise the sound of it. We will still be looking for things that jump out at you, but what that is exactly, that's up to the producers." - Rene (BSE)

"Music genres always have ups and downs. I think we had far too much of the same music out at the same time with the same line-ups on raves. Sometimes things have to downsize to get healthy again. I personally can say harder d&b is something I wanted to listen to in my younger years, but throughout my life, I realised I have to change. I would feel very uncomfortable to repeat myself over and over again. I'm grateful I have contributed something to it, but I have to move on. I'm not a fan of a revival of past genres; I want to hear new ideas and new music." - Misanthrop

"Things come and go in circles or waves; usually every five to ten years things come back from the past and get an update on style and sound. I don't really know what is going to come next, I actually don't really care. But I am always open to change, which I think is one of the most essential attitudes a producer or musician should have, not to stand still, Sit down and do something that follows your honest feeling and inspiration and stop thinking too much." – Phace

Jade

Misanthrop

PREMIUM EVENT & MUSIC PROMOTION

Concrete PR™

www.concretepr.co.uk

MUSIC • FASHION • EVENTS

FALLEN SOLDIERS

IN THE FIVE YEARS WE'VE BEEN AWAY MANY TALENTED ARTISTS HAVE SADLY PASSED AWAY. WE NEVER GOT OUR CHANCE TO PAY OUR RESPECTS, SO OVER THE NEXT FEW PAGES WE PAY TRIBUTE TO MARCUS INTALEX, SPIRIT, TENOR FLY, TANGO, ANDY SKOPES, STORMIN AND DOMINATOR.

Words by: Colin Steven

MARCUS INTALEX

Marcus Intalex was one of the biggest names and characters in drum & bass. He released drum & bass on the likes of Metalheadz, Exit and Signature but he also made house and techno as Trevino. He was the founder of the Soul:R, Revolve:R and Birdie labels and was also active as a DJ from 1991 until his untimely death in May 2017. Calibre worked with Marcus and ST Files as part of Mist:i:cal and toured with him regularly. Here he shares his memories of him.

I first became aware of Marcus when I heard Fabio play 'How You Make Me Feel'. Marcus later told me it was inspired by my track 'Feeling' on Creative Source but at the time, I remember being totally in awe of it. Fabio told me about this guy in Manchester, and eventually Marcus called me. From his music, I thought Marcus was a black dude, but when he called, I realised he wasn't as he had a very unique voice. We talked about music for a while, and I liked him instantly.

When I went to Manchester for the first time, I stayed on Ryebank Road, which is where they made How You Make Me Feel and all those other great tunes of that period. It was a good set-up, there were guys beneath them that worked on cars that didn't care about the noise. I just loved it. That's when we made the Mist:i:cal EP. We became good friends really quickly. We had mutual respect for each other that drove itself into other things later on in our relationship. I loved the guy, even when we fell out.

Sometimes Marcus would just let me go because I was fast and the tune would be there really quickly. After a while, Marcus felt he didn't really need to be there. Then he would come back and do the arrangement. The tunes we made together in his house in Manchester I have very fond memories of as well. Just sitting in his triangular studio that sounded really loud. I liked working with him because he loved what I

Nik Sinha, director of the Marcus Intalex Music Foundation, explains why he set up the foundation with a group of friends.

As friends, family and colleagues of Marcus, his passing was a very difficult loss to take. He meant so much to us all, but also to the people that didn't know him in those close personal circumstances but have been moved by his music. He would have genuinely been surprised at the outpouring of emotion from the whole world when he died. But this was Marcus, no airs or graces, a man that didn't give a shit about status and would talk to anyone on the same level.

With all of that said, it was also clear just how much Marcus had inspired and been supportive of emerging artists and young people aspiring to have careers in music - especially in Manchester. He taught, mentored and nurtured many on how to be self-sufficient and navigate the industry. Knowledge that artists like Dub Phizix, MC DRS or Chimpo valued greatly.

In October 2018, myself and close friends set up the Marcus Intalex Music Foundation. We wanted to continue that legacy and ensure some of those opportunities and the knowledge that Marcus offered could continue in some capacity. We've already delivered some amazing projects which have seen many of Marcus' close friends and collaborators come together, offering their wealth of musical talent and advice to the next generation.

We've since had young people learning music skills from the likes of Martyn, D-Bridge, Dub Phizix, Jenna G, Ndagga Rhythm Force, Floating Points and many more... this is invaluable. Marcus' mum Pat and partner Ayumi have also given us their blessing which means a lot. We want to keep doing this and honour Marcus as the great person he was to us all, as well as how much he has contributed to music throughout his life. **Find out more at mi-mf.com**

did. Whenever I was doing something, he'd just sit there going "Yeah, yeah!" Whenever you get encouragement and love like that in the studio, it's easy.

He was always very driven and he had a great sense of music. I think it was through observation and a love of different types of music as well. We tried to get organised and got a studio in Ardwick. The guy that owned the place was a complete alcoholic and would just let us go in there and bang away making music in this really rough area. But then Marcus started going on the road a bit more, and Lee [ST Files] and I would be left in the studio. That changed the dynamic of the relationship between us all. Marcus felt like he wanted to do his own thing, he just followed what he loved, and I admired that about him. He really believed in what he was doing.

I only have really good memories of him, and even when he had to put up with my silly bullshit on tour when I was drinking too much, he was always really nice about it. It's only when you travel for long periods of time with someone that you really get to know them.

There was a period in his life when Marcus was up for a party, but then I guess he became a bit more serious and on the job and tried to maintain his fitness. I remember being on the road with him a long time ago and realising that he wasn't well. He was always affected by travelling. He was so driven as well, and he never stopped, he just kept going and going. He didn't sleep well either, so he was constantly tired.

The thing about being a DJ that people don't realise is that it's really hard physically sometimes: constantly flying, playing late, not much sleep and early rises. I remember one time he stood up at an airport in North Carolina and shouted: "I bloody hate this country!" Everyone was open-mouthed, but he was really pissed off with being in America at that time.

Mark from ESP Agency broke the news to me when he died. I was really cut up about it. I had to take time off DJing because a whole bunch of things happened in a series. I had two years of emotional turmoil, and Marcus' death kicked it off. It really shocked me, it took me a long time to come to terms with.

We were actually talking about getting back together to do more stuff. Marcus and Lee had made up and were going to make music together as well. The last time I saw him alive was in Brighton, and he gave me a hug, and he never did that for all the years I knew him. He told me what a wonderful career I'd had and how proud he was of me. He'd never told me any of this before. He was so warm, and it really surprised me, but then a week or two later he died.

I think Marcus' talent was so great yet underrated. He had a really unique sound, and nobody sounded like Marcus. It was tough, it was soulful, it was in there, but it was different. His most powerful legacy is his music. A lot of people make that deeper soulful drum & bass now, and it's massive all over the world. Marcus took great pleasure in being able to make music that people loved, and that's what it comes down to really.

SPIRIT

Owner of Inneractive Music and co-founder of Phantom Audio, Duncan Busto aka Spirit also released quality underground drum & bass for over 20 years on the likes of Metalheadz, Shogun Audio, CIA, Renegade Hardware and Function. Here fellow Phantom Audio owner and long-time collaborator Digital pays tribute to Spirit.

....

Duncan and I are both from Ipswich. Around 1993 I got into rave music through a guy called Danny C, and I decided I wanted to start buying the music. I was a mainly reggae DJ before that. Spirit worked in Red Eye Records, our local record shop. Our taste in music was very similar and we hit it off. I mentioned how I wanted to make music and he told me he did too. He was practising at home at the time, and I was going around different studios. So we were both learning at the same time. Because of the record shop, we kept in touch. I started hearing what he was making and vice versa.

After I got a couple of releases under my belt, I started bringing him into a few projects. Eventually, we decided to start our own label Phantom Audio, but that was only because other record labels weren't interested in signing the music we were making. Luckily our first tune was Phantom Force, and that came good on our own label.

It was easy working with Spirit in the studio as we were both looking for the same end product and how we got there didn't matter. He was more technical than me, so I was on the keyboard doing my thing while he did his and we met in the middle.

I admired his talent, he was a genius. He was making bangers for 20 years consistently, not many people can say that. The same sort of thing with Marcus Intalex and Tango, they all made tunes that lots of people can relate to. That's what makes a big tune. His sound covered so many facets of drum & bass, and all of his tunes were so well done. Whether they were rowdy or on a liquid vibe, they were always complete tunes.

From day dot, he did exactly what he wanted to do. There's a Spirit section in the drum & bass world that nobody else can touch. He did Spirit from the start to the end, and he did it well. He might not have got all the plaudits that I think he deserved, but one thing I do know is that he stuck with his sound, he didn't try to be something else. Spirit's sound evolved over the years with technology, but it always had his heart.

TENOR FLY

Tenor Fly first made his name in the 80s as an MC on the reggae scene before moving into the dance scene in the 90s as part of The Freestylers and working with legendary jungle label Congo Natty. In 2003, he released 12 Years of Jungle with Rebel MC and Tenor Fly's second album was 2006's Two Veterans alongside Top Cat. Tenor had remained an active MC on the live circuit up until his death in June 2016. Fellow Freestylers MC Navigator remembers him.

....

I first met Tenor Fly around 1983/4 when he used to chat on a soundsystem called Sir Coxsone Outernational from Brixton. I was floating around on the north London circuit but hadn't joined Unity soundsystem yet. I remember seeing Tenor Fly at a party in south London. He came over and told me he rated me. I didn't really take it seriously as man would friend you up and you didn't really know what the motive was.

Then about two years after that, I saw him in north London outside a club. By this time I'd joined Unity and Tenor Fly had released Roughneck Fashion, and he was proper bigging me up again. You've got to understand that Tenor Fly had hits from back in the mid-80s. That's why he's such a huge monumental part of UK MC culture. It was a big deal for me that a man like that was telling someone who was still making his name that he rated them. I never forgot that.

I looked up to him. I remember one party at Upper Cut Club in Forest Gate about '85 or '86 when King Jammy's came over from Jamaica and brought Admiral Bailey and all these big artists. There were all these artists on stage from Jamaica doing their thing and then along came Tenor Fly, and he tore the place down performing Roughneck Fashion and smashed them all to shreds. That was a big moment for me. That made me realise I could do this too.

There were enough times when we used to chat on soundsystems together back in the day, but the main time I worked with him was when we did The Freestylers. In 1998 I got a call saying there was a band that needed a front man for a party called Fantazia at the G Mex centre in Manchester. So I went, and when I walked into the dressing room, there was Aston Harvey who had done a lot of the early Congo Natty programming, his production partner Matt Cantor, Jay Rock from Blapps Posse and Tenor Fly. I wasn't expecting that at all! They basically wanted me as a hype man. When I came off the stage the guy who ran their label offered me a deal for 30 tour dates.

So I was touring with Tenor for three years. That's when me and him became family. We were writing music together and sparring all the time. He was someone I'd always respected, but it wasn't until then that I actually got to know who he was as a person. We got on like a house on fire. He was a very funny guy. I give thanks for that because I have those memories of him now and it's a beautiful thing for me.

I admired his ability to write songs in a very short period of time. You could just fling any beat at him, and he'd just come up with something within seconds. A highly talented artist but he still had that rough edge and the swag. He maintained what we were about from the 80s, that soundboy edge. That's what I really admired about him. He also had a good stage presence, when he hit the stage you knew it was Tenor.

He was, and still is, a big part of UK MC culture. He was there right at the beginning and set the foundations for everything that's going on right now. You have to show respect to that legacy that he set. He was 35 years deep in the business, making music, having hits on many different levels. His music is his legacy, and people will always remember him for that. It spanned so many different generations of people. Nuff respect to Tenor Fly, his spirit and energy lives on.

TANGO

Tango burst onto the scene back in 1991 on DJ SS' Formation label with The Impact EP. 1992 saw further releases until 1993, which was arguably Tango's year. 'Future Followers' saw Tango gain maximum respect amongst his peers and ravers alike. A series of releases on various imprints followed until 1997, at which point he took a well-earned rest. He eventually returned in 2001 with longstanding partner DJ Ratty and continued where he left off. Pulse from Creative Wax also collaborated with Tango and he pays tribute to him here...

I first spoke to Jamie back in 1993 to ask him to do a remix for the label. He was the go-to producer at the time, every track he remixed was a killer. We met soon after. I drove up to the Midlands to the house he was living in at the time, which was literally in the middle of a field. His studio was in the corner of his bedroom. It was winter and the room was like a fridge, so cold we had to wear our coats to keep warm when working. I just remember thinking 'How is this guy able to make beats in this place?!'

His set-up also blew me away, just a small Allen & Heath mixer, a couple of basic effects units and an Akai S950. Yet what he was making sounded like it was coming out of a big studio. He knew the equipment inside out and got everything he could out of it, so technical, I was completely amazed that this quiet, unassuming guy was Tango.

We soon became good friends and would send each other music either by post or swap DATS via his best mate Ratty who we used to meet in various spots off the M40 when he came down to play in London.

I was always on at him to do a 12" for Creative Wax and then out the blue in about 1995 he gave me two tracks, Understanding and Spellbound. In true Jamie style, being a perfectionist, he talked them down and told me everything he thought was wrong with them. We were having none of it, and both tracks still get played to this day. The same year we collaborated on a Pulse and Tango release for Moving Shadow, one of many projects we worked on together.

Although Jamie took some years out from producing, he became a success with his career outside of music. The last time I saw Jamie was at his wedding just a few months before his untimely death, and he told me how proud he was to be marrying his wife Karen and how much joy his son Braden had brought into his life. He also told me he was ready to get into making some new music and was working hard on a release for Metalheadz, one of his biggest goals. For me one of the most underrated, sadly missed by us all - RIP Jamie.

ANDY SKOPES

Madcap & Andy Scopes

Andy started out working at the infamous Croydon record store Wax City back in the day. His first foray into producing was on local labels Jerona Fruits and Inperspective and Fizzy Beats. His affiliation with these labels and growing reputation helped him to begin DJing around the UK and Europe. Next came releases on heavyweight imprints such as Utopia Music, Dispatch, V Recordings, Good Looking, 31 Records and Metalheadz. Former collaborator Madcap remembers his good friend.

I was introduced to Andy back in 2003 through mutual friend Wilsh. We communicated through a d&b forum and swapped tunes using AIM - although it probably would have been quicker for me to drive down to his place in Croydon due to the slow internet speeds! I was impressed by Andy's production and even missed a turning driving to a radio show while listening to one of his crazy Amen break edits.

One of the first tunes I played out was 'Jah Jah Man', which we signed to a label I was co-running at the time called Uncertified Music. I loved this track and played it in all my sets. In the same year, I had a gig in London at Movement so invited Andy down to properly meet him. We got on really well, and this was the start of a great friendship.

That evening I remember asking him how he got his basslines sounding so good. He laughed and replied: "Come down to my place and I'll show you."

The results were 'These Sounds' and 'Hear Dis' which came out on Renegade and Immerse. Incidentally, this would be our first 12" vinyl together.

Away from the d&b scene, Andy worked hard as an occupational therapist. Originally based at Wexham Park Hospital, where he met his future wife Heidi. In 2015 it was an honour for my wife Mel and I to be invited to their wedding.

In 2017 we got back in the studio, but I then lost my dad. Andy showed great support during this time. A few months later he called and asked for me to take a seat and explained he'd been diagnosed with cancer. However, in true Skopes style, he switched up the conversation talking about his forthcoming Metalheadz release, a dream he aspired to. I was understandably shocked, wiping away tears. Andy remained unbelievably positive and kept focused on music in between therapy. We worked on about eight tracks which were signed and are due for release on Utopia Music and Dispatch.

At the start of 2019, Andy took a turn for the worse, losing his battle with cancer at the young age of 40. This was devastating news to his family, friends and fans. Andy was a gentleman with an infectious laugh, friendly, caring to all. He will be forever in our thoughts, and his music will live on forever. RIP.

STORMIN

Stormin grew up as a fan of jungle music, but found his way into the emerging grime scene via his hugely energetic live performances. He was an original member of N.A.S.T.Y Crew, one of the founding grime collectives. He later working in drum & bass and won awards for Best Crowd Hype D&B MC and Best D&B Group with SaSaSaS at the 2016 Drum & Bass Awards. Phantasy, who worked with as part of SaSaSaS, pays tribute.

....

I first met Stormin through Shabba as they were really good friends. He originally came from the grime scene and the craft he mastered there added another flavour to our scene when he came to drum & bass. He used to come out with Shabba and just jump on the mic for the love of it, try and get his name out there. I really remember his energy, he was so hyped on the set that he quickly became known as The Hypemaster!

I felt that drum & bass needed artists like him at that time. His energy was so infectious, and I just wanted to help him get his name out in our scene, so I put him on a few gigs. I told him that he could do really well in drum & bass, but he needed to understand that nothing happens overnight.

He had an amazing ability to make a lyric out of anything going on around him, and when he became part of SaSaSaS he would keep us entertained on those long road trips with his fantastic ability to make a lyric and freestyle about anything going on around him.

While hosting a stage at One Dance Festival I remember watching him on the closing set. He was surrounded by some of the best MCs from different genres, and he was in his element, as he loved performing and entertaining people.

You hear stories of people battling cancer and Stormin really battled it, he fought it for two years. He was a fighter and would never give up. He was an exceptional person. During a chat we had, he told me that he never wanted anyone to forget his name and I promised him that I will make sure that no one does.

DOMINATOR

Dominator was a producer who rose rapidly in the jump-up d&b scene thanks to productions for Biological Beats, Low Down Deep and his own D-Stortion imprint. He was renowned for his high impact sets and unique production techniques of orchestral intros, hard drums, heavy frequencies and dirty dancefloor basslines. Phantasy, who signed him to his management company, remembers the young talent.

....

Dom was one of the nicest people you could ever meet, so humble. What's so heart wrenching is that if he was still here now, he'd be one of the top DJs in the scene, guaranteed. He was on the way up. I told him he was going to be massive as he was doing everything right and really understood the business. He was young, hungry and talented. I still play songs of his in my sets today. I play songs of his, and Stormin's for that matter, as I don't want people to forget them. Everybody loved Dominator, he was such a warm character.

I said to him one day that I'd never heard him say anything bad about anyone and he just said he didn't have any time for that. He was a beautiful soul. As competitive a business as it is, you do make good friends as you go along and what makes the scene bearable is meeting people like Dominator.

We have a management company, and it took me over a year to get him under our wing as he was working with Logan D and was so loyal to him. I believed in him so much and wanted him to join us so badly that I did a deal with Logan so it was all above board and I wasn't stealing him. I didn't want that bad vibe. That's how much I believed in Dom.

The last time I see Dominator was at a show where TNA was supporting SaSaSaS, and it was so lovely seeing him so happy to be doing the job he loved so much and had dreamt about for years. That following week Skiba called me and told me Dom was in the hospital, so I texted him to find out what was going on. He replied saying he wasn't well, but he would be OK as the doctors were sorting it out.

We kept in contact while he was in hospital, but when I was in Australia, he messaged me to call this number. I called the number straight away and spoke with his partner, who gave me the terrible news about what the doctors had found. I was devastated. I never got to see him again as he was gone within weeks, it was tragic.

FOREVER AND EVER AMEN

Words by: Joe Madden

KMAG
DEC
2004

KNOWLEDGE CASTS AN AFFECTIONATE EYE OVER THE HISTORY OF THE UNDISPUTED KING OF THE BEATS - THE MIGHTY AMEN...

All junglists have had that moment. You're in a crowded club and the sound system's firing on all cylinders, with the best tune of the night so far tearing through the crowd on a wave of rudeboy bass and militant two-step drums.

Suddenly, the track breaks down, and starts slowly, slowly building again for a second drop. There's a split second of silence, and then the whole shebang smashes back in again, this time with a firing Amen loop in tow. The crowd roars, the energy levels double and everyone goes apeshit.

Probably for not the first or last time that night, Amen has reared its gloriously ugly head and sent the whole place into orbit.

Since its birth, jungle has always had a handful of sonic elements on standby that have never gone out of fashion. There's the sick whine of Mentasm, for example, or the menacing growl of the Reese bass sound. But no other sound tool has been as rinsed out by d&b producers as much as Amen has.

It's been used to add bouncy, bug-eyed energy to jump-up tunes; it's provided a graceful, rolling undercurrent to slinky liquid tracks; it's rattled abstractly over ragga and hip-hop samples; and it's given darkside tunes a threatening, feral edge.

It's not just drum & bass producers who have harnessed Amen's wildstyle energy. Its metallic roll can be heard crashing through hip-hop tunes, gabba tracks, TV theme tunes (Futurama) and even pop records - listen closely to Whigfield's super-cheesy 90s pop-dance hit 'Saturday Night' and you'll hear Amen rolling away in the background.

It's fair to say, though, that no other genre has taken the break to its heart in the way that d&b has. "I love Amen," says veteran break-spotter Equinox. "It's the king of the beats. I've been hunting for years to find a break that has the same impact as Amen; some have

come close, but nothing can touch it."

Amen first found its way onto vinyl in 1969, as the four-bar breakdown on 'Amen Brother', the B-side of six-piece funk group The Winstons' single 'Color Him Father'. A man by the name of G.C. Coleman was the genius on the drum stool.

Little information is available on the group, and if it weren't for the adoption of 'Amen Brother' as the junglists break of choice, they'd probably have remained sadly forgotten outside of funk trainspotter circles. Were they able to claim for royalties for the many thousands of times that 'Amen Brother' has been sampled, they'd undoubtedly be made far richer than they ever were through their own recorded output. As music publishing law currently stands, however, you cannot, unfortunately, copyright a drum break.

It wasn't until 1988 that The Winstons made a real impact on the public consciousness, when the crushing drums of 'Amen Brother' found their way onto two of the year's key hip-hop tunes.

Recognising the thugged-out power of the break, then-fledgling producer Dr Dre sampled it for use on 'Straight Outta Compton', the fierce, fiery calling card by gangsta rap pioneers NWA.

Perhaps even more important in terms of junglist history, however, was 'King Of The Beats' by Mantronix. A siren-powered monster of an instrumental hip-hop track, it boasted the first example of the Amen break being 'chopped' - crudely so by today's standards, perhaps, but chopped nonetheless.

It was during the hardcore/rave era of the (very) early 90s that Amen really started to come into its own, however. As a new generation of producers began to move away from the dreamy, four-four pulse that had characterised the acid house movement of the late 80s, they looked to combine a much harsher palette

of sounds with pitched-up hip-hop and funk breaks for a bone-rattling, roughneck effect - and the super-compressed, ultra-grimy Amen break suited their needs perfectly.

A whole raft of Amen-powered hardcore tunes followed, including Lennie De Ice's 'We Are IE', 2 For Joy's 'Let The Bass Kick' and - probably the most celebrated of them all - LTJ Bukem's classic 1991 roller 'Demon's Theme'.

As the joyous rush of hardcore gave way to the minimal, often nightmarish stylings of darkcore and breakbeat, Amen remained the producer's break of choice. Tracks like DJ Distroi and Boykz's 'Darkside' used Amen more aggressively, and at greater speed, than it had ever been deployed before.

By 1993 this brave new sound had passed the 160bpm mark and become known as jungle, jungle techno or drum & bass by its followers, and Amen had cemented its position as the don gorgon, the daddy, the king of the pitched-up beats. Tracks such as 'Scottie' by Subnation, 'Warpdrive' by DJ Crystl and 'Terrorist' by Renegade (aka Ray Keith) were taking those ferocious drums into uncharted territories, making them tear, twist and roll as never before.

"I just stuck the break in the Akai sampler, processed it till it sounded better and then got a four-bar loop out of it," says Ray Keith of the aforementioned 'Terrorist'. "A lot of people were using Amen in the early days of jungle, but 'Renegade' was one of the first tunes to use it 'clean' - I took it off a breakbeat compilation, whereas a lot of people were lifting it from that Mantronix track ['King Of The Beats']. Then people started lifting it off 'Terrorist'. Now you can just drop it into Recycle or whatever and chop it into a hundred pieces, but in the early days we had to chop it manually."

> **"I love Amen. It's the king of the beats. I've been hunting for years to find a break that has the same impact as Amen; some have come close, but nothing can touch it."**
> – Equinox

Equinox

Rohan

Tech Itch

Ray Keith

HOW TO HANDLE AMEN
A few words of advice for those looking to take on the break to end all breaks...

"First of all," says Remarc, "you need to keep it tight. Secondly, experiment: with the amount of plug-ins now there's no end to the possibilities of what you can do. And, thirdly, if you're making proper twisted stuff, don't overdo it. I hear so many tunes that make no sense, that are the verge of just being noise. Remember, however chopped-to-fuck, a tune still needs to flow."

"You need to keep in control," agrees Ray Keith. "I always keep Amen running between 170-175bpm. Otherwise it'll just sound like bloody toy-town, and there's too much of that about already..."

Remarc

'Terrorist' remains one of the best examples of the sheer bruising power of an Amen loop when it's kept simple, thugged-out and rolling. Elsewhere, though, other producers were looking to see just how far they could twist, dice and bend the break before it became nonsensical.

For many, the king of the super-technical Amen mash-up sound of the mid-90s was Remarc (whose finest moments from the era can be found collated on 'Sound Murderer', a compilation released on Planet Mu). On tracks like 'Ricky', 'Thunderclap' and 'R.I.P.' he shattered Amen into a thousand pieces and then put it back together in utterly alien but weirdly instinctive new shapes.

"There was definitely an element of 'top that!' to my Amen programming at the time," says Remarc, "not to other producers, but to myself. If you listen to all of my tunes in chronological order that progression becomes obvious. I used to like it when people listened to 'em and went, 'What the fuck happened there?' That's when I knew the track was twisted enough!"

The arrival of Alex Reece's seminal 'Pulp Fiction' in 1995 signalled the point at which many producers left Amen - and breakbeats in general - behind in order to concentrate on clean, two-step drum patterns. Many of the leading lights of the techstep era that ushered in around this time still sought to harness the power of Amen in their super-harsh, futuristic productions, however.

"Amen's the best break in the world, provided it's processed, EQ-ed and used properly," says Technical Itch, the undisputed master of the skull-crushing darkside Amen pattern. "There are so many ways you can use it. It can be used as the main beat for a track, or just left running away in the background to give another break a more 'live' feel."

In recent times Amen's stock has been on the rise

"It's the power, the energy and the rhythm - no other break has it."
- Rohan, Bassbin

again, as a new generation of break fiends seeks to reinstate it as the king of the beats. Labels such as Bassbin and Inperspective, club nights such as Technicality and producers such as Breakage and Equinox have breathed post-millennial new life into The Winstons' finest moment.

"It's the power, the energy and the rhythm - no other break has it," says Rohan, head of Ireland's Bassbin imprint. "Jungle was founded on breakbeats and the mixing of breaks to create energy, and the effect of Amen on top of other breaks creates a sound that just smashes it. Nobody wants to hear Amen all night, but dropped in the right place it just twists it up."

Equinox - whose 'Ital Tuff Lion Head' track on Intasound is one of the finest Amen workouts of recent times - concurs: "It's the energy of the break, man. It just hypes the dancefloor no matter what style of d&b is being played. Go to Metalheadz, Valve, Fabric, Technicality, One Nation or a Renegade Hardware event and you can see the crowd go proper lively when an Amen tune comes on."

So what does the future hold for the seemingly evergreen Amen? Will there ever come a day when it loses its impact and has to be put out to pasture?

"No," says Remarc, firmly. "I've heard so many producers say 'I ain't using Amen no more', but it

THEY ALSO SERVED...
Ten other breakbeats that have served their time at the drum & bass coalface...

Lynn Collins - Think (About It)
James Brown - Soul Pride
Dennis Coffey - Scorpio
Bobby Byrd - Hot Pants
Michael Viner's Incredible Bongo Band - Apache
The Commodores - Assembly Line
The Buena Vistas - Kick Back
James Brown - Cold Sweat
The Vibrettes - Humpty Dump
James Brown - Give It Up (Or Turn It Loose)

remains as strong and as important as ever."

Equinox: "Amen will always be there, no matter what happens. Even if the scene goes pure two-step, someone out there will be using Amen."

And for the final word on the matter, Ray Keith: "People will never get bored of it. It'll just keep changing with the times. It'll still be used long after we're all dead and buried."

To hear the Amen break in its original, unadulterated form, go to phatdrumloops.com/audio/acm/amen_brother.wav

"ESSENTIAL READING FOR ANYONE WHO IS INTERESTED NOT ONLY IN THE JUNGLE SCENE... BUT IN DANCE IN GENERAL, IN THE MUSIC INDUSTRY AS A WHOLE OR EVEN BRITISH SOCIETY AND ITS INFRASTRUCTURES."

DJ

A revised reissue of the acclaimed first-ever book-length investigation into the origins of jungle and drum & bass. Drawing on interviews with some of the key figures in the early years, the book explores the scene's social, cultural and musical roots.

ISBN 9781913231026

Buy your copy at **velocitypress.uk/books**

MEGA WHAT?

Words by: John Murray Hill

THE IMPORTANCE OF A GOOD DRUM & BASS SOUND SYSTEM IS PARAMOUNT. FOR THE SAKE OF THE CROWD, THE DJ... AND YOUR EARS.

No one is better qualified to comment on sonic set-ups than the architect of the only drum & bass sound system in the world - the man who puts the "OW" in "sound" - Karl Francis aka Dillinja. He built his own speaker rig as a direct response to the poor set-ups that plague clubs across the globe.

"I refuse to play on sound systems in other clubs because they are terrible," sighs Dillinja. "90% of venues have rubbish acoustics. The only reason that I play outside of the UK is for the people that come to see me. Clubs these days just don't understand the definition of a quality sound system. Most of the guys that open them just do it to make money, not to provide an experience to the public."

But don't club promoters realise that in order to make money, they require an excellent sound system? "They obviously don't!" laughs Karl. "There are rules to a good sound system. It needs to be powerful. It has to be able to express every frequency in the music as it was intended by the producer."

To clarify this - take your mind back to the drum & bass scene circa 1999. In that year, Dillinja released a four-track EP on Bryan Gee's Chronic label containing the track '30Hz'. 30Hz is the absolute lowest of audible frequencies (within the range of human hearing). In order for a club to harness these elusive sub-frequencies, it needs high-performance, 18-inch woofer-cones built into its speaker boxes, which are costly and difficult to configure properly.

"The amount of money the big clubs generate weekly means that they should all own expensive, professional sound systems. Ones that are full-range," he elaborates. "That means; from the high top-end to the low, deep bass, they can properly express all the frequencies and dynamics. But most clubs don't even bother."

Drum & bass is a phat, in-your-face type of music, which begs to be blasted from a heavyweight speaker stack. The origins of drum & bass lie back in the days of dub reggae, a genre that was broadcasted only on the biggest and most booming of sound rigs. The parallels between these two genres demand that the former is brought up to its ancestor's sub-laden standards, for crowds to enjoy. Sanjeev Bhardwaj, the chief sound engineer of Farringdon super-club Fabric, agrees.

"Some of the more bass-driven dance music deserves to be felt, as well as heard. We've taken this into account in Fabric, so our dance floor features sixteen 18-inch drivers - WSX subs from Martin Audio that face you as you look out from our DJ booth. We also have a 'line array' system by Martin Audio - a concert PA with ridiculous crystal-clear quality that no other club in the world has. And last but not least, we have the body-sonic floor," he beams.

"We're the only club ever to be featured on 'Tomorrow's World', where we demonstrated the body-sonic floor. There are three panels on the main dance floor. In the panels are 150 inducers - mini speaker-like components. They vibrate to build up a sensation of bass in your body. They are actually lifting the floor and you with it. So in all, you have bass coming from above, the side and below, which provides an all-encompassing feeling. It is not so much about the loudness, but about the clarity, and hitting the right frequencies.

"In general, the loudness and clarity are more important than anything else in Fabric nightclub. At the end of the day," he stresses, "we don't want anyone walking out of this club with their ears ringing. Loudness-wise we can take it really, really high but the clarity ensures that it is never painful. So these clubs claiming that they have 90 million watts or whatever means nothing unless their sound is clean.

"Near enough, I think we can hit down to about 18Hz in Fabric. I reckon we could actually jump-start someone's heart if we pushed it up hard enough. We've had people standing there saying that 'my heart is missing a beat' because of the subs. In the old days when we were testing the system out we did some mad things down there. On 'Tomorrow's World' we actually put a glass of water down on the body-sonic floor, and the water inside it was moving like it was in zero gravity."

Bearing in mind that an earthquake is made up of low-frequency sound waves travelling through the air at around 3Hz (3 cycles per second), the Fabric sound system isn't far off a full-scale natural disaster!

But Fabric is a one-in-a-thousand venue. The influential DJs on the circuit agree that the majority of other clubs take the piss when it comes to sound. Promoters, too, are being found guilty of not researching venues prior to renting them out. This isn't fair on the crowds, who pay to come and hear their favourite DJs play, not just to watch them. "I think a good speaker set-up makes all the difference in the world," says Klute of Commercial Suicide fame. "So many venues cut corners with their sound systems. It boggles my mind that someone would go into the business of club music and skimp in this department. It's the most important thing."

Paul Harding, one-third of the Pendulum trio, completely agrees. "A good sound set-up is everything," nods Paul. "A venue is nothing without a system to match, and I think people appreciate the music they're listening to a lot more if it's coming out of a well-designed, powerful one. As far as drum & bass goes, the Valve sound system does a lot of justice to the music, as do the set-ups at both Fabric and The End. But most other clubs pale in comparison."

And if this is how the DJs feel about it, just imagine what is going through the crowd's minds! "It's just shocking," says André Vladareanu, a Romanian drum & bass raver from West Kensington, "I don't go out as much as I used to because most of the time the music sounds underwhelming and tame."

To make matters even worse, DJs can't seem to unleash killer sets unless the sound systems they're gracing have the capacity to rile audiences into a frenzy. A performer can't be expected to get on a roll unless

> "I think a good speaker set-up makes all the difference in the world. So many venues cut corners with their sound systems.."
> - Klute

> "I reckon we could actually jump-start someone's heart if we pushed it up hard enough"
> - Sanjeev Bhardwaj, Fabric

Dillinja

DJ Fresh

Klute

Pendulum

their spectators are responding positively to their set. Therefore, a sound system is not only important in defining the clarity and loudness of music, but also how well a DJ presents it.

"Without a doubt, I play better on a powerful sound system that gets the crowd going," reveals Klute. "If the crowd can hear properly what you're playing the response is far greater. One of the best sets I've ever done is in the Flex club In Vienna, Austria. Their system is top notch - they've had the subs sunk into the foundations. The crowd always go nuts, which makes it an absolute pleasure to play there."

To a club-going audience, a 'good sound system' often refers to the PA speakers that surround the dance floor. But in truth, it means much more. A club can have the most formidable speaker rig in the world, but if it doesn't own a decent monitoring system to match, the DJ can't play for shit. The DJ needs an isolated booth away from the sonic quagmire of the dance floor, with excellent near-field monitoring speakers and a good stereo image, in order to hear what they are doing. Forcing a DJ to play in a bad monitoring environment is like sending a cricketer out to bat with a blindfold on.

"It just makes it really uncomfortable to play," grumbles Klute. "It can be disorientating. If you're struggling to concentrate it makes it harder to get into the groove and you're less likely to get into the zone. Bad monitoring is so common that no one venue particularly sticks out as being bad. These venues that host frequent, popular drum & bass nights should really invest some money into improved systems. It seems these days that most English venues are holding-pens for people to come and spend money on alcohol - sod anything else. I think this is a big reason why 'club culture' is dying.

"No one makes an effort to do anything special any more - it's gone full circle. We're back where we were before the rave revolution. Week in week out we're expected to enjoy ourselves on the same shitty sound systems in the same shitty venues with the same old DJs. Obviously, there are people that do care and are trying to make an effort within the confines, but if something doesn't change I think it's going to die altogether."

Fabric has taken a revolutionary step towards eliminating poor monitoring. The inconspicuous digital panels behind the decks in the main rooms are actually EQ memory-banks that store all the regular DJs favourite monitoring settings.

"We've got dozens of signature EQ settings stored specially for our DJs, on our sound-web system," explains Sanjeev, the Fabric sound engineer. "I'm here during the week, so if the DJs are willing to spend the time they are welcome to come and visit so that we can design them a custom EQ curve. Then they can mix to the best of their ability on the night. It's all programmed in, all you have to do is press a button and the saved settings pop up."

But in all honesty, a club doesn't need an expensive, heaving behemoth of a set-up to unleash a fearsome sound. Take London's Bar Rumba for example - a relatively small club that plays host to the legendary Movement sessions on a Thursday night. Its speakers are small but devastatingly loud and clear. What gives?

The answer lies in the acoustics. The environment in which music is played is more influential in creating a loud, clear sound than the quality of the speakers themselves. Lofty roofs, for example, make the music echo and blur.

The high-frequency sound waves (often referred to as 'treble') that are typically found in snare and hi-hat sounds suffer particularly badly from poor acoustics. These parts of the sonic spectrum play an important role in the definition and clarity of what is audible (and therefore how easy it is to mix). High frequencies reflect off walls and hard surfaces, and if these sound waves bounce back onto themselves at the same angle, destructive interference occurs. The opposing frequencies of these waves cancel each other out completely - a bit like what happens to Agent Smith and Neo at the end of Matrix Revolutions. Therefore, some good-quality sound systems will sound muddy and unclear in a box-shaped room, but crisp and clear in an irregularly shaped venue with sloped ceilings.

But the speaker quality and acoustics count for nothing unless the crowd, and especially the DJ have good ears to decipher sound in the first place. A large percentage of people who work with music; DJs, producers and engineers, suffer from chronic hearing problems. Just look at what happened to DJ Fresh from Bad Company!

"My hearing is absolutely fucked," sighs Fresh. "If my hearing was a train, it would have crashed by now. I am horrified about it. I have a constant ringing in one ear and have only recently started using pro earplugs when DJing. All I can say to others who haven't experienced tinnitus yet is, 'you do not know how much it can fuck your life up... get earplugs now!'"

"That's terrible!" sympathises Sanjeev. "All my staff are provided with specially fitted earplugs. If sound is your living, and you often spend over two to three hours listening to loud music, then you should probably own a pair. It is not the loudness of the music that does the damage, but the quality."

"We at Dogsonacid.com," chips in Fresh "have just teamed up with the top manufacturer for DJ earplugs, who supply LTJ Bukem with his £1000, dual-use earplug/ monitor system. They do the full-range, full-cost plugs right down to the £20 temporaries. Soon we will have branded these earplugs with the DOA logo - so watch out for these on the Dogs On Acid site!"

An alternative to Fresh's recommended earplugs is the awesome ER15s, as owned by many of the industry's top names. These durable plugs are specially moulded to the shape of one's ear, at a clinic in London's Harley Street for around £160. They come in a variety of colours, and an appointment can be arranged with Capital Audiology for a fitting. If you have a career in music: DJing or producing, you are advised to purchase some.

So, what can you do to help improve drum & bass sound quality? Most importantly, demand more from your venue. Provide feedback to popular clubs with poor systems stating your thoughts on the matter. After all, the punter is the lifeblood of the business, and if enough of us articulate our concerns, they will listen. Also, new promoters - choose carefully in finding suitable venues for your nights. A good sound system is only effective if the club in which it is situated has suitable acoustics.

So, the next time you see a big promoter with eight or nine top-list DJs on their flyer, at a lame venue with a terrible sound system, ask yourself these questions. Do they really give a shit? Or are they content with cramming as many unwitting people as possible into their cattle pen, just to make their pockets fatter?

> "I refuse to play on sound systems in other clubs because they are terrible"
> - Dillinja

> "My hearing is absolutely fucked. If my hearing was a train, it would have crashed by now."
> - Fresh

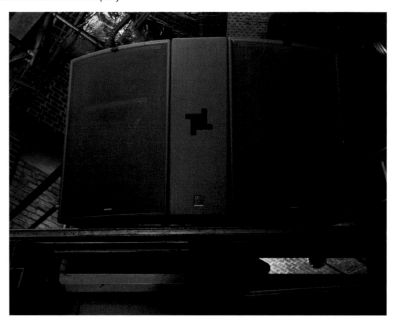

LIQUID ASSET

Words by: John Murray Hill

KMAG
JUL
2005

'LIQUID' IS THE BUZZWORD IN DRUM & BASS AT THE MOMENT. IS THIS TERM TO BE TAKEN WITH A PINCH OF SALT? OR DOES IT BEAR SERIOUS IMPLICATIONS FOR THE INDUSTRY? KNOWLEDGE HOOKED UP WITH THE SCENE'S BIG CATS TO FIND OUT...

Bryan Gee hasn't sustained his career for 15 years by being narrow-minded. He has always supported different styles of d&b – liquid being one of them. This receptive mindset obviously inspired him to start the Liquid V record label and club night. If anyone is qualified to comment on this new buzzword, it's him.

"I would say the phrase 'liquid' was invented by Fabio," Bryan ponders, "he coined it about the style of music he was playing at the time. It just worked and felt right. Before Fabio came up with that term, we referred to it as something else – usually in reference him! We used to say – 'yeah; it's like a Fabio tune!' He might not even have played it, but it made you think of him. But now, we've got a classification for it... and that can be equally good and bad for our scene. Good because it defines the music and makes it easily identifiable, but bad because it creates segregation."

And this is one of the "serious implications" that has come about through the rise of Liquid d&b - that it could create a divide amongst our community. Take the new Liquid V nights at Plan B in Brixton for example - the vibe there feels very different... almost separate from the typical d&b sessions at Fabric and The End.

"We don't want people to start breaking into factions and saying, 'I'm specifically into liquid' or 'I'm just into jump-up'," Bryan explains. "That would be worrying because we're like a big family and want to stick together. But on the flipside, I believe it's good that people outside of d&b culture can now easily identify something they like about it. As a community, we're always looking to attract new faces to d&b, and I definitely think liquid is encouraging people to get involved."

But why has liquid only now come to the fore? Fabio's pioneering album that supposedly coined the phrase liquid was released in 2000. Five years down the line, people are treating it like a 'new' genre all of a sudden. "Drum & bass is so massive now," Bryan explains, "that it's impossible for it to all fit under one roof. More producers are getting involved, and certain ones are sticking with one particular style... and making a name for themselves in the process!"

True - but Marcus Intalex and Calibre were making the same style of music three or four years ago, and back then it was just called 'drum & bass'. So why has liquid established a separate identity all of a sudden?

"As the music grows you pick up new fans along the way, and they become more demanding," explains Bryan. "You've got your big, heavy raves that will attract a certain clientele - for example, Breaking Science. The majority there will probably be a young crowd that demand a certain style of music, and specific DJs and MCs (like Andy C and Eksman). On the other hand, a DJ like Cleveland Watkiss would be better received by people who go to nights like Traffic and Liquid V."

This segregation is actually more beneficial to the scene than detrimental - the prominence of 'new' genres like liquid just goes to show that drum & bass music is thriving. Look at house music, for example. You can't advertise 'house music' on a flyer to describe an event's theme; it's got to be 'deep house', 'progressive' or 'funky' because the genre is so popular that it has many different subdivisions. Drum & bass music is becoming similarly diverse. This isn't to say that d&b hasn't had alternatives to the 'party' style for years, but it's only now that its other guises are being branded heavily into public consciousness. "I would love the music to get back to being one big family," admits

Bryan, "but at the moment it's not quite like that. We're all related, but it's branching in different directions."

It's not just the DJs that have a responsibility to nurture the fertile crop of liquid - it's MCs too. "I watch and analyse the MCs," Bryan begins, "and there is one gripe I have with them in particular, that [especially in the big raves] as soon as a liquid tune drops they slow their vibe down. MCs that can only interact when the music is banging are limited in skill. It annoys me when they suddenly look like they're having a fag or chatting to their mate when a liquid tune comes on. Considering that the crowds react off the MCs so much, this isn't good for our scene.

> **"We're always looking to attract new faces to d&b, and I definitely think liquid is encouraging people to get involved."**
> - Bryan Gee

"The MC is the first point of contact in a rave - the front end - so they have a responsibility to understand all the styles of music for the benefit of ravers who come to see them. Some MCs know how to switch it up and work with a DJ well, but others seem to get lost when you flip the script. They're like 'Ah! My trousers are falling down!' and they start grabbing at their belts and pretending to fasten them," Bryan jests. "As DJs we need the MCs' help! When we get good support from the MCs the crowd love it. DJs can also be guilty of not playing varied enough selections; so I'm not pointing the finger at anyone in particular. I'm just saying that it's important for our scene to have the best of the best on display - especially when impressionable, new faces are cropping up in a crowd. DJs, MCs and promoters have a responsibility to educate and push the music out there."

One lyricist who can undoubtedly claim to be versatile is MC SP. Whether it's a heaving event down in Milton Keynes or the sultry Plan B in Brixton, SP is more than capable of adapting to the situation. "I just try to adapt to individual situations, and give the

Bryan Gee

majority what they want to hear," SP explains. "For example, Faster at Islington Academy is a ravey type event, and there I feel I have to fire off a few more lyrics than at a liquid one. At something like Hospitality and Soul:r, therefore, my delivery is slightly different."

Does MC SP enjoy this new role he's adopted for liquid-specific events? "The new Liquid V night at Plan B was something I did recently," he remembers, "where I hosted the entire event. It was wicked because I was able to establish a vibe. This was in complete contrast to a typical hour-long set where you have to jump on the mic and just drill it off. Liquid events are less about high impact; more rolling out, holding it down and hosting."

But as SP explains, the idea of 'hosting' is not a new concept (and neither is the term 'liquid') "Yep - hosting has been going on for ages," SP explains. "At liquid events, the MC often plays second fiddle to the DJ - people are more into the tunes than the lyrics. This style of MCing has been going on for over a decade. Like at Blue Note, for example. Down there you used to get DJs and MCs like Watkiss and Justice. Yes, the sound was a little more aggressive, but the MC still held it down and generally hosted the proceedings, rather than running riot over the speakers. GQ also used to do that at AWOL, ten years ago. I think it's a valid point to say that 'hosting' is not a fresh concept; just a different style of MCing lending itself to the liquid sound that's now coming back into fashion."

D-Bridge

> **"People have now tried to pigeonhole me into the liquid market, but I want them to look further than that - to recognise my work as good drum & bass and nothing else."**
> - D-Bridge

So what does SP think about the notion of liquid turning into a breakaway genre? "It's hard to predict how things will turn out," admits SP. "I don't really call it 'liquid' - that's a debate in itself."

Who would you say are the pioneers of liquid, then? "I would say that a couple of years ago tunes sounded more liquidy. You had your Carlito and Addictions, your High Contrasts and Danny Byrds - that to me was liquid because it had a genuine distinction to everything else. Now the top dogs of the liquid scene are being stereotyped as Calibre and D-Bridge; but if you listen to their stuff you'll find it's pretty fucking weighty! It hurts the dance floor like a Dillinja tune... almost. 'Highlander' and 'Mr. Maverick' get reviewed as liquid tunes, but to me, they sound more like old Bristol rollers."

Perhaps the media just needs an easily digestible catchphrase in order to simplify the wild and uncharted subdivisions of drum & bass. "Exactly," agrees SP. "People need to call it something - you don't want to have a ten-day debate about it every time. It's just a tag, and what falls under it is much more than just liquid. The jump-up material in the D&B scene is very easy to categorise, as is the dark stuff; and supposedly anything else that's left over is liquid. But I don't think this is fair really, because the term liquid is too general to apply to all the great material out there."

So - the man mentions Calibre and D-Bridge as being the 'top dogs of liquid'; so it's quite fitting that we nabbed one of them for this interview. What with Calibre being so highly praised and worshipped throughout the industry, it's only fair that D-Bridge receives a bit of the limelight too. And besides, here is a man who embellishes both the dark and light sides of d&b simultaneously - something few can claim to have achieved. He is the Darth Vader of d&b.

"I'm trying to find an equilibrium in between liquid and dark," smiles D-Bridge. "If you look at my career, you'll see why I'm remembered for the harder things - because of the tracks I produced with Future Forces and Bad Company. I think that drum & bass has always had so-called 'splits' going on - for example with jump-up and tech-step. At the end of the day, they're all variations on the same thing. There's nothing that can be done about people who put it into brackets. I think people need to accept liquid for what it is - music, at the end of the day. We're just lucky that d&b can be expressed in so many ways."

It seems that D-Bridge would prefer it if liquid didn't seem so separate from the rest of the d&b industry... "Yeah, definitely," he nods. "There's good stuff on both sides, and I think it's a shame that some people feel the need to represent only one style. For me personally - back in 1997 - that was when d&b was in its heyday, in the sense that it matured into something that could be expressed in many different ways. If you went to Blue Note you would hear hard tracks mixed into softer ones, and nobody batted an eyelid. Liquid hadn't even been coined or defined yet. Would you class 'Pulp Fiction' as a liquid tune? On the same label as 'Pulp Fiction' Goldie put out harder stuff like Dillinja's 'Angel's Fell'. And that's what made Metalheadz such a great label - it wasn't pretentious - it just appreciated good music. I'd like it personally if people got away from this segregation and the emphasis was put solely on quality tracks."

So where does D-Bridge feel he stands amidst this quagmire of stereotyping and segregation? "My mission is to combine the two prominent styles of d&b together, getting that hard edge - the tough sickness and the twisted b-lines - combined with melodies. People have now tried to pigeonhole me into the liquid market, but I want them to look further than that - to recognise my work as good drum & bass and nothing else."

D-Bridge is no stranger to being stereotyped. His early work with Bad Company contributed to the media wrongly bracketing him as a 'dark' artist. "There's a sample I was going to use by Bruce Lee the other day," recalls D-Bridge, "where he's talking about different styles. When someone sticks with one style, they become crystallised. Lee's theory behind kung fu was about marrying different elements of it and keeping things moving. I'm on a similar tip. I got pigeonholed as being part of BC - having one style - so I moved away from that. And now they're trying to pigeonhole me for being solely a liquid artist - but that's not really what I'm about either. If you can all meet me in the middle, it's all good, because that's where I'm at!"

At the end of the day, the media can make their

> **"At liquid events, the MC often plays second fiddle to the DJ - people are more into the tunes than the lyrics."**
> - MC SP

MC SP

assumptions about liquid drum & bass; but we all know that it's part of a core genre and one that's definitely on the up... "I went into HMV the other day," beams D-Bridge, "and I noticed that they've re-racked the drum & bass section! It's quite cool - it made me think' you're showing us love again'. It seems that things are going in the right direction.

"I believe that if producers / DJs just continue what they're doing and collectively acknowledge their strengths and weaknesses, then everything will come good in the end. If you're a producer and you only make party anthems, for example, then there's absolutely no problem with that. There always seems to be this mentality of getting one-up over someone else in this scene, where people stick their noses up

at each other's styles. But I think we should forget about this. If you're not into what someone else is doing, then that's fair enough," D-Bridge chuckles. "Just do your thing - but recognise that an alternative needs to exist in order for you to be able to have your own distinction and progress as an artist."

"Yeah," Bryan Gee draws the proceedings to a close. "We're not trying to be better than anyone else. It's just drum & bass man, and we all complement each other well. We've got to stick together. You may not like all the tunes out there - but it's still all good, baby! We are all helping to push barriers and make the scene better in our own individual ways."

ENTER THE NUUM

Words by: Paul Sullivan

KMAG
JUL
2009

AROUND 2006, MUSIC CRITIC AND THEORIST SIMON REYNOLDS COINED A NEW PHRASE - THE HARDCORE CONTINUUM - TO DESCRIBE A LINEAGE OF UK URBAN MUSIC THAT INCLUDES RAVE, JUNGLE, UKG, SPEED GARAGE, 2STEP, DUBSTEP AND GRIME. PAUL SULLIVAN FINDS OUT MORE.

The Hardcore Continuum, or 'nuum' for short, is a term coined by music critic Simon Reynolds (author of legendary jungle / rave tome Energy Flash and recent post-punk book Rip It Up & Start Again among others) while penning a series of articles on everything from jungle to 2step, UKG and grime for experimental / avant-garde music magazine The Wire.

On 11 February 2009 at Liverpool's FACT centre, Reynolds spent a couple of hours explaining to an assembled audience the basic premises of the nuum, which describes and supports the connections between these UK urban scenes in terms of factors such as continuity of infrastructure, population, rituals, musical influences, broadcast mediums and personnel.

He explained why it's called 'Hardcore' ("because the tradition started to take shape circa 1990 with what people called Hardcore Techno or Hardcore Rave") and how the nuum has its roots in the groundbreaking collision of four main musical elements - house, hip hop, reggae and techno – in late 80s Britain.

"What really alerted me to the "continuum" idea was that with speed garage and 2step you had all these tracks that were remaking hardcore rave anthems, and lots of samples from classic hardcore and jungle tunes," he says via email.

"So it was like the scene was paying homage to its own ancestry and consciously emphasising the continuity. And that's carried on to this day, you have

things like dubsteppers Caspa & Rusko and Hijack remixing Lennie D'Ice's "We Are I.E." which was a hardcore rave classic, I think it actually came out in 1991, when Caspa was nine years old!"

The basics of the nuum – that the urban genres mentioned above share intimate and visible connections - are difficult to refute. Aside from sounds, locations and other overlapping factors (from economic infrastructures and pirate stations to record shops and rewinds), there's the visible crossover of personnel.

From the multitude of DJ/ producers – Nico, Jonny L, MJ Cole, Grant Nelson to name just a few – that have moved fluidly from the rave through to garage, 2step, and even dubstep and funky, to pirate stations like Rinse FM that have mirrored the scene's permutations and the links between Grime MCs and their jungle counterparts, the connections are generally highly visible.

"Jungle was definitely the one that started me off,"

> **"**Jungle in many ways was the UK's answer to hip hop, as opposed to the actual Brit rap scene, which despite its best efforts tended to be more straightly imitative of America.**"**
> - Simon Reynolds

says MC Sway. "Loxy and Ink are my older cousins so they switched me on to that side of music. I used to go to Under 18 raves and see the reaction people like Shabba D got from the crowd - it was crazy! It opened my eyes to the power of the music.

"I started freestyling to the music and it grew from there. One of the most exciting developments was the success of garage and 2step - it showed there was potential to make credible music that could commercially crossover and get in the charts. That encouraged me professionally too."

"I like the way Reynolds has shown the links between what some might think are disparate, disconnected scenes," agrees Heatwave founder, DJ / producer Gabriel Myddleton.

"Loads of kids who were into jungle when I was at school were going to garage raves by the time we were at sixth form. Many garage or drum & bass DJs and producers I knew at university went on to become big in grime and dubstep. As Simon Reynolds

Simon Reynolds

says himself, it's less of a theory than an observation of fact: the progressions and connections are clear."

Yet the nuum has inspired intense debate, mostly on the blogosphere but also via organized panels like "The Hardcore Continuum? A discussion" where a group of speakers ranging from Mark Fisher (K-Punk), Steve Goodman (Kode 9), Lisa Blanning (The Wire) and Kodwo Eshun (author and critic) sat together in the University of East London and asked questions like 'what is the value of the concept?' 'Does it still usefully describe the context from which dynamic new beat musics emerge?' 'Can the conditions of creativity in the 1990s be replicated in the era of web 2.0?'

Blackdown's Martin Clark was among those in the audience. "The talks were designed to address the concerns some writers had that the theory was at best out of date or at worst, broken" he says. "Clear outcomes are hard to pin down, but it certainly raised the points that the new house mutation funky was being badly dealt with. Wonky, a theme running through several genres I proposed last year, caused lots of discussion, mostly when other people used it as a genre.

"Kode9 and Kodwo Eshun proposed a very elaborate and creative paper that highlighted a separate thread, of how you could trace a link back from Joker and Terror Danjah through G Funk to the Ohio Players and Roger Troutman. Pretty funky stuff. Best of all it got all of the main writers and bloggers debating the issue, including Simon Reynolds himself."

Certain aspects of the nuum have indeed been open to criticism and / or misinterpretation. Reynolds has been quick to clarify certain points, namely that the 'nuum' is not a theory but "an actually existing, empirically verifiable (and abundantly verified) thing-in-the-world, like jazz or reggae or folk or metal" (though it can of course be theorised about).

That he uses the term 'continuum' because "it's another way of saying tradition, which I prefer because "tradition" has that folksy / rootsy whiff about it." And that the nuum is not about "what's in, what's out disputes".

That said, one of the main criticism towards the nuum is precisely that it doesn't include several genres that some would argue should be in there. One of the biggest controversies, as mentioned above, is that Reynolds does not consider funky part of the lineage.

"I kind of wish I liked funky more," he admits. "It has just one too many flavours in it that doesn't appeal to me. But as a scene, looked at objectively, it's a classic London "road" scene in terms of having the pirate radio link, the multiracial audience. I'm hoping it'll veer in a direction that's more my bag.

"One of the things that makes me doubtful about it is that of all the things to come of the continuum it's the one that's created the least buzz outside London. There's only a handful of international 'hardcore continuum' obsessives talking about it on the web and as far as I know nobody's attempted to do a club

Gabriel Heatwave

"I like the way Reynolds has shown the links between what some might think are disparate, disconnected scenes."

— Gabriel Myddleton

around it in New York. You probably get dubstep DJs here trying to work in a bit of it into their sets maybe. But it hasn't really captured the wider world's attention, which is what jungle, 2step grime, dubstep all managed to do to varying degrees."

"There's no doubt for me that funky is part of the lineage of London-centric dance music that includes hardcore, jungle, garage, grime and dubstep," says Myddleton. "From what I understand of Reynolds's theory, there are numerous aspects of funky that echo what he has outlined as being common threads tying together earlier scenes, such as chopped and re-pitched female vocals, sampled dancehall, heavy bass, and continuity of infrastructure in terms of radio stations like Rinse or Déjà vu and record shops like Blackmarket Records aka BM Soho. There's also continuity of personnel - countless key players in funky have histories in grime, dubstep, garage and jungle, for example Donaeo, Marcus Nasty, Geeneus, Perempay or Sami Sanchez. Big names from previous scenes are also getting involved, such as Scott Garcia, Boy Better Know, Lady Chann, Gappy Ranks, Maxwell D, Sticky, Wookie or Kode 9."

Other important and influential genres such as breaks, trip hop, broken beat, or even UK hip hop don't get much of a look in either, though as always Reynolds has reasons: "Jungle in many ways was the UK's answer to hip hop," he states, "as opposed to the actual Brit rap scene, which despite its best efforts tended to be more straightly imitative of America. Trip hop produced lots of great stuff early on especially but really it's a separate lineage I think. It's much less about dancing and rave energy, more about the head-nod. It's smoker's music, but it does have similar sources in terms of hip hop and reggae.

"Nu skool breaks is an odd one, I guess there is a relationship to hardcore, Rennie Pilgrem worked with one of the big rave outfits Rhythm Section. But overall breaks feels like it's branched off to be its own entity. I could be letting my personal lack of enthusiasm for the sound colour my judgment here though. Broken beat is a bit like trip hop I think, it's a much more a mellow dancing or head music type thing. It doesn't have that sort of rude-boy aspect that runs through most of the continuum, nor the continuum's other side, which is a sort of fearless cheesiness and poppiness, i.e. lots of cheeky samples from chart hits. But of course certain key figures from jungle moved into broken beat like 4 Hero."

"The hardcore continuum by definition doesn't try and include all UK genres, just what comes out of the urban multicultural working class areas," defends Clark. "So with breaks you could say it makes an appearance when Zinc's "138 Trek" becomes the biggest record in UK garage circa 2000 but the current breaks scene, which has minimal presence in urban London or through the pirates, isn't. Similarly when jungle was, ahem, massive in Hackney it's a core part of the continuum. But when Pendulum are touring international rock stadiums, it isn't. Trying to force Pendulum's stadium rock to fit into the continuum is to miss what the continuum is about."

Myddleton, for one, would like to see the nuum stretched to include the larger and longer line of soundsystem culture originating in Jamaica. "The likes of John Eden and Dave Stelfox have written about this, and the compilation An England Story that I compiled for Soul Jazz Records explores those JA/UK links as well," he says. "Obviously, hardcore is the beginning of a new chapter in that it blended Jamaican soundsystem influences with UK/US rave music, but seeing it in a deeper historical context seems to make sense. The way grime and funky interact with Jamaican music, culture and language is not dissimilar to the relationships between English dancehall MCs and their Jamaican counterparts in the 1980s."

"Music and culture is messy, so when I talk about these big patterns it's really general outlines and broad trends," states Reynolds. "Naturally there are always exceptions and overlaps and so forth. I don't think any of the various nits that can picked undermine the central argument which is that in the early 90s when house music and techno collided with hip hop and reggae influences in London and a few other multiracial cities in the UK, something remarkable happened - there was a surge of cultural energy, partly fuelled by ecstasy's ability to melt social barriers and open people's minds to strange mind-bending sounds and also just get everyone buzzing with belief. That energy-surge then played out through successive mutations in a context of raves and rave-like clubs and most crucially pirate radio. You have various hallmarks of the continuum that make its vibe drastically different from traditional house and techno, the role of the MC, rituals like the rewind, the use of dubplates. It's the most amazing cultural phenomenon I've ever witnessed with my own eyes and ears."

In the end it seems the nuum's most applicable aspects are its most obvious ones: that it accurately describes the connections - musical ideas, broadcast medium, rituals, influences, personnel etc. – that run through much of our beloved UK urban scene, As Martin Clark points out, "it shows that root causes are connected and that key elements are retained. It explains that when drum & bass became too tech-steppy, UK garage arrived to accommodate all the women in inner city areas that didn't want to rave to dark machine music. Or when grime became a serious concert based around aggressive male reputation and conflict, it explains the rise of funky - music you can dance and have fun to. This is because it seems that there are a bunch of balanced musical elements in a lot of these genres and history shows if you unbalance them, the continuum mutates to re-accommodate them."

Which begs the question: what's next? "I'm not a big one for predicting what's going to happen, though I suppose it's usually a safe bet to predict some kind of cycle," says Myddleton. "So a retreat from fun, party music to something darker is probably round the corner at some point. I've seen this happen a few times in the decade or so that I've been listening to Jamaican music, from the grimey, minimal Ward 21 productions, which dominated the late 90s and early 00s to the fun, over the top jiggy/dancing tunes popularised by the likes of Elephant Man in the mid 00s. What I'm particularly excited about at the moment are the possibilities for musical collaboration between Jamaica and the UK. It seems like bashment and funky are made for each other, sharing vocal styles, tempos, drum patterns, certain production qualities and a fun, dancefloor-focused philosophy. I think we're looking at some fertile years for creativity, innovation and interesting connections."

"All kinds of scenarios are imaginable," reckons Reynolds. "One is that the continuum tradition has used up all its resources, musically, in terms of that matrix of house/techno/reggae/hip hop. And to get fresh renewing "vibe" it will have to siphon more and more ideas from elsewhere - from different elsewheres - which will cause it to fragment, with different bits joining up with other genres. That maybe what's happening with funky, that to keep a fresh vibe in the mix it's pulled all these sounds from tribal house and broken beats and soca. That in turn expands its demographic reach maybe.

"A similar possibility in terms of demographic changes in the crowd actually changing the sound is dubstep. It seems to have become something else, this party-hard sound, it's come a long way from where it started. The UK garage roots of it are almost gone, and quite a lot of the reggae element too. It's become this bombastic hard-riffing thing, which appeals to a different crowd - students, former drum & bass people, free party crusty types even. It's becoming a populist sound and in a bizarre way, more of a ravey scene, even though it's slow in tempo. A sound for munters. The original dubstepheads are fleeing for the exits, they hate it. It could become something absolutely grim, or something interestingly extreme, like slowed-down gabba."

> **"The hardcore continuum by definition doesn't try and include all UK genres, just what comes out of the urban multicultural working class areas."**
> - Martin Clark

Martin Clark

Reprazent

STATE OF BASS

Words by: Martin James

VETERAN MUSIC JOURNALIST MARTIN JAMES WROTE THE FIRST BOOK ON JUNGLE/DRUM & BASS BACK IN 1997. ENTITLED *STATE OF BASS: JUNGLE - THE STORY SO FAR*, IT HAD SOLD OUT BY 1998 AND HAS NEVER BEEN REPRINTED. UNTIL NOW. A REVISED REISSUE ENTITLED STATE OF BASS: *THE ORIGINS OF JUNGLE/ DRUM & BASS* WILL BE PUBLISHED IN APRIL 2020.

THE UPDATED VERSION EXTENDS THE ORIGINAL TEXT TO INCLUDE THE AWARD OF THE MERCURY PRIZE TO REPRAZENT AND PREVIOUSLY UNPUBLISHED INTERVIEWS WITH RONI SIZE, GOLDIE, LTJ BUKEM, FABIO, SHY FX AND OTHER KEY PLAYERS FROM THE EARLY YEARS OF THE SCENE. HERE MARTIN JAMES REFLECTS ON THE CULTURAL ROOTS OF JUNGLE/ DRUM & BASS AND ITS RELATIONSHIP WITH THE MAINSTREAM MEDIA IN THE 90S...

When Roni Size & Reprazent beat competition from The Prodigy and Radiohead to win the Mercury Prize for the 1997 album *New Forms* it seemed like mainstream culture fell over itself to try and understand both the album and the scene it came from.

Milled in the ferment of the uniquely British underground phenomenon of jungle and drum & bass, *New Forms* sounded simultaneously classic and future bound. It drew its hooks from the multicultural hues of urban Britain and linked them through the historical lines of reggae, dub, jazz, soul, funk, rare groove, acid house, bleep and hardcore.

It was a sound woven along the threads of the misunderstood fault lines of post-Windrush Britain where the progeny of the earliest arrivals soaked up British cultural influences and in return provided a deep influence to UK popular culture. The cultural roots of soundsystems, blues parties and shabeens spread to newfound friends and changed our music, our art... our lives forever. *New Forms* then was an expression of the post-Windrush British experience of a range of popular culture expressions, from Jamaican heritage sounds to daytime TV; US soul and jazz to UK rave.

New Forms was also the sound of the impact of that Windrush experience on white British youth. It comes as no surprise that the album was birthed in Bristol, a city steeped in not only the history of slavery but also one of the UK's first cities of music cultural fusion. Bristol's St Paul's was famed for its soundsystems and blues parties, just as the broader area of the Avon was notorious for the free parties of the traveller movement and, later, the renegade countryside takeovers of the urban ravers.

Roni Size and his collaborators may have been extending the rich lineage of black British music, but

> "ITV news wanted to know if giving the Mercury Award to an album from the drum & bass scene was in some way supporting the drug culture associated with raves."

they were simultaneously an extension of Bristol's multicultural punk, post-punk, hip hop and club scenes that produced genre contortionists such the Pop Group, Rip Rig and Panic, Neneh Cherry, Massive Attack and Tricky. Journalists and critics who later tried to differentiate jungle and drum & bass along the racial lines of blackness and whiteness missed the point by an inner city mile.

What *New Forms* represented then was the true sound of British urban youth at the end of the twentieth century. Coverage in underground dance music magazines was a given. The album also captured the imaginations of the glossy dance press, the rock and indie-heavy weekly music newspapers, the style magazines, the serious daily newspapers and the wider mainstream media. This wasn't a surprise. Many journalists from these publications and media outlets had been all over jungle and drum & bass from the start.

It's worth noting that the first serious mainstream article on jungle in the national press was in *The Times* newspaper and not the music press. Reviews of jungle raves and drum & bass clubs would become regular fare in newspapers like *The Guardian*, *The Independent* and even the right-leaning *Daily Express*. Far from being ahead of the pack, the national dance press emerged alongside *NME* and *Melody Maker* who too were quickly onto the scene.

Mainstream radio had also been unusually quick to pick up on the buzz. Responding to the wall-to-wall pirate pressure and Kiss FM's early support, Radio 1 even hosted a short series of special shows called *One in the Jungle* in 1995. These newspaper features, magazine articles and radio shows were driven by journalists, critics and producers who were former, or active ravers. They understood the significance of the music and its subculture. They were the friends within.

Hours after the Mercury was awarded I found myself being chauffeured across London to a series of the capital's new rooms. Sky News wanted to know what on earth drum & bass was. BBC News 24 asked about Bristol and managed to link their questions to the St Paul's riots of 1980. ITV news wanted to know if giving the Mercury Award to an album from the drum & bass scene was in some way supporting the drug culture associated with raves.

Channel 4 were more interested in finding out about the cultural significance of the jungle and drum & bass scenes. When I said it was the most important British phenomenon since punk rock in 1976/77 Channel 4 News seemed delighted. I'd given them a hook their viewers would recognise. For the record, I'd also described *New Forms* as 'this generation's *Sgt Peppers Lonely Hearts Club Band*' in weekly music paper *Melody Maker*. I don't think either was entirely accurate, but the aim was to show older music fans of The Beatles and punk that Roni Size's album had a huge cultural significance that couldn't be ignored.

One thing unified all of these news channels though - a look of disappointment when a home-counties raised white guy in his mid-thirties walked onto the set and not the young kid of blended parentage from one of London's urban ghettos that they'd hoped for. I'd been invited into these newsrooms because earlier that year I'd published *State of Bass: Jungle – The Story So Far*, the first serious book-length investigation into the jungle and drum & bass nexus.

Sadly, who I was didn't support stereotypical ideas of authentic breakbeat science or scientists. Not that I ever claimed to be a part of the scene. Indeed, in the introduction to the original book, I admitted that I was never a junglist, rather I was someone drawn to the music and the scene by its unadulterated power.

This admission alone was enough for at least one UK national music magazine to slate both me and the book in an unprecedented full-page review. I wasn't authentic enough to be writing about this music! I was too white, too middle class, too suburban - the antithesis of the jungle/drum & bass movement that was being defined by the media along the lines of race, class and location.

This idea that journalists writing about so-called urban scenes like jungle/drum & bass were expected to be 'from the scene' in order to retain an authentic voice was out of step with an egalitarian post-rave culture

Goldie

that celebrated the experience over the star. Magazines like *NME, Q, Mojo* etc. remained obsessed with long rejected ideas about subculture and authenticity.

They clung to the approaches of 'golden age' journalists who celebrated stars. They produced lists of essential albums made by people who were mainly representations of themselves - middle-class white men. They pretended to be free from commercial constraints, untouched by the industry, yet they colluded with the industry to create cover stars in order to increase advertising revenue and sell more copies of their magazines in a deal with the music industries that ignored the fact that they were complicit in the process of selling product to consumers. My face simply wouldn't do that for them.

No one from the scene ever said this to me though. Most people were extremely supportive and got the fact that I loved the music and didn't claim to be from the scene. They appreciated my honesty. Although the following year, Goldie would adopt that reviewer's confrontational stance when I asked him a question about the scene during an interview in support of his 1998 album *Saturnz Return*. Goldie took offence, jabbed me in the stomach and said he was 'sick of middle class white guys telling me how things were in the scene'. 'Where were you back in the day?' he demanded. My reply was simple, I was there on the frontline observing, writing and capturing the moment. It wasn't my moment to claim, but it was important to document. He was complimentary about my Stussy bench coat though!

To be a junglist was to live and breathe the scene, the sounds and the style. It was all about being there, a face in the crowd at the clubs and raves, nodding with approval as the DJ dropped the latest upfront dubplate or cued up a tune straight from the studio on DAT. It was all about the subconscious sharing of those collective threads of knowledge and experience that tied people into the greater fabric of culture and community. It was about family and a sense of belonging. A junglist diaspora.

As I've already said, I could hardly have called myself a junglist, but I loved the music, the style, the raves. I had done since I first stumbled upon 'Eye Memory' by Nebula II on Reinforced Records at a rave in Nottingham's Marcus Garvey Centre. A dark and brooding slice of post-hardcore psychosis, its breaks seemed to snap at the synapses, sending my already fried brain cells reeling in unadulterated frenzy.

Nebula II were a local crew who had honed their craft in the city where house music was first played by Graeme Park at a funk all-dayer in the unlikely surroundings of the Rock City nightclub. House quickly became a staple of his sets at The Garage club before he shared his tunes with the Hacienda in Manchester.

Nottingham's central role in the creation of a UK house scene has almost been written out of history in favour of Manchester and London. Back then though Nottingham, the Queen of the Midlands, was rave central. Little surprise then that the darkcore sounds of Nebula II were at the forefront of a UK post-hardcore breaks explosion that was just on the horizon.

The progression through dark, jungle tekno and drum & bass was as exciting a time in British club culture as had ever been witnessed. In recent years we'd raved while the rest of the world went through epoch-defining political change. Communism had collapsed across Europe, the Berlin Wall was dismantled, a lone figure held up a fleet of tanks in a student uprising in China's Tiananmen Square. In the USA President George H. W. Bush reneged on election promises and increased taxes to fund a war in the Gulf of Iran. The UK had just lived through ten years of Thatcherism, which brought destruction of the unions, poll tax riots and a rise in the underclass via poverty on a huge scale. The world seemed to be in a state of disarray, history was collapsing.

The jungle/drum & bass nexus was the sound of that collapse. It captured the emergence of accelerated culture as we started the race towards the end of the millennium. It was a sound that fed on music history and spat out high speed, cut and paste montages of sound. It was a collision of the be-bop of the jazz pioneers, the deepest dub cuts of the soundsystems, the crystal clarity of Kraftwerk's electronica, hooks from the electropop of Gary Numan and Japan, electro's body-popping twists, house music's soul, techno's pulse, the breaks and beats of funk, hip hop's ingenuity and the electro-acoustic mood boards of the film scores that had shaped the imaginations of the generation.

The scene, the sounds, the style were a mash-up of cultures all responding to the anger, the joy and the high-speed chaos of the times. It was also a scene driven by cheap technology. This was the period that saw the emergence of the games console as a core element in youth culture, the home computer wasn't unusual, the mobile phone was increasingly commonplace, and sampling equipment and sequencing software become cheap enough for a wide range of people to get hold of. No longer was it just for the wealthy.

State of Bass: The Origins of Jungle/Drum & Bass is a reworking of the original text to include further insight into the cultural significance of that period. Historically it extends to the phase when Roni Size won that Mercury and Goldie's second album *Saturnz Return*. This is in part because I've always felt that the original book came too soon. It charted the rise before any mass cultural peak had been witnessed. The Mercury Prize was that moment.

Saturnz Return, on the other hand, represents the period when the mainstream cultural industries lost interest in their investment. Jungle and drum & bass simply didn't translate to huge income for them and as the sound of poor reviews for Goldie's second album resounded everywhere so too did the cacophony of mainstream industries running towards 'the next big thing'.

In the wake of the mainstream's retreat jungle/drum & bass was restored as an underground phenomenon where it has existed as an ever more powerful presence ever since. The Prodigy's Liam Howlett once described it as 'the UK's only true underground'. He was right. Its significance is immeasurable. *State of Bass: The Origins of Jungle/Drum & Bass* aims to make sense of this impact of Britain's urban underground by taking a fresh look at the period of the 90s that music journalists now often tell us was all about Britpop.

So often forgotten in the rewritten histories of the 1990s, jungle/ drum & bass lit the furnace of the urban British youth culture that surrounds us today. Put simply, it was the real cool Britannia.

For more information on State of Bass: The Origins of Jungle / Drum & Bass visit velocitypress.uk/ state-of-bass

> **"So often forgotten in the rewritten histories of the 1990s, jungle/drum & bass lit the furnace of the urban British youth culture that surrounds us today. "**

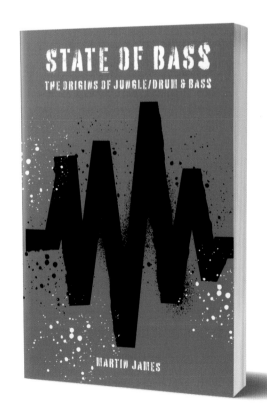

BLEEP, BASS & BREAKS: THE REAL ROOTS OF JUNGLE

Words by: Matt Anniss

Photography by: Vanya Balogh, David Bocking, Normski

IN THE EYES OF MANY COMMENTATORS, CRITICS AND CULTURAL HISTORIANS, THE EMERGENCE OF JUNGLE AND DRUM & BASS MARKED THE MOMENT WHEN BRITISH DANCE MUSIC FINALLY FOUND ITS VOICE. WHEN THE FIRST "PROTO-JUNGLE" AND "JUNGLE TECHNO" RECORDS EMERGED, MOSTLY FROM LONDON AND THE SOUTH EAST, IN THE VERY EARLY 1990S, THEY SOUNDED LIKE LITTLE THAT HAD COME BEFORE, MIXING HIGH TEMPO, FIERCELY CUT-UP SAMPLED BREAKBEATS WITH THE BOOMING BASS-WEIGHT OF JAMAICAN SOUNDSYSTEM CULTURE AND NODS TO THE REGGAE, RAGGA AND DANCEHALL RECORDS THAT HAD BEEN A FORMATIVE INFLUENCE ON MANY OF THE SCENE'S PIONEERS. JUNGLE WAS LOUD, EXTREME AND FORTHRIGHT, RIPPING UP THE RULEBOOK WHILE STICKING TWO FINGERS UP AT BRITISH DANCE MUSIC'S ESTABLISHED ORDER.

It was a key moment in the development of what would become British "bass music", a varied and nuanced collection of interconnected sub-genres born from the same sub-heavy blueprint. Be it UK garage, dubstep, grime, UK funky or bassline, the UK-pioneered styles that followed over subsequent decades all owe much to the sweaty, bassbin-bothering thrills of early jungle and drum & bass.

Yet jungle itself did not arrive fully formed. It was merely the most culturally significant step on a journey that had begun not in London, Essex or Bristol, but 200 miles north in Yorkshire. You see, the music you love may have been revolutionary, but the seeds of that revolution began not in Brixton, or on the dancefloor of Rage at Heaven, but in the spare bedroom of a terraced house in Bradford.

In late summer 1988, a DJ, a bedroom producer and an MC sat down to make a record in response to A Guy Called Gerald's peerless rave-era anthem "Voodoo Ray", the first house or techno of British origin to sound like it had been beamed down from another planet. Unlike the disco-influenced Chicago house records and sci-fi loving Detroit techno tracks that had come before it, "Voodoo Ray" was heavy, industrial, clanking and otherworldly, distilling the raw essence of the interconnected influences that had inspired its creator, Manchester jazz dancer and electro breakdancer turned soundsystem enthusiast turned bedroom producer Gerald Simpson.

The record was not particularly bass-heavy, but the space Simpson left around each of his intoxicating rhythmic and musical elements echoed the spaced-out aesthetic of the dub records he'd heard growing up in Moss Side, or at one of the many illicit, after-hours "blues parties" hosted within Manchester's Afro-Caribbean neighbourhoods.

The drumbeats he programmed popped with the swing of electro and the loose-limbed shuffle of jazz-funk, both sounds that had dominated underground dancefloors in the North of England. Yet like Chicago house, "Voodoo Ray" was also raw, sweaty and intoxicating, providing perfect fodder for the legions of serious dancers who spent their spare time heading to club nights and Sunday' all-dayer' parties in Yorkshire, the Midlands and the North West.

When those three men - part of a slightly larger crew of DJs and promoters known as Unique 3 - gathered in the Bradford bedroom to record their response, they were partly inspired by the man behind "Voodoo Ray". Like him, the members of Unique 3 were obsessed with hip-hop, house, techno, electro and Jamaican soundsystem culture. They had battled Gerald Simpson

> **"Warp should have been a pioneer in the jungle scene. It would have been if I was still there. But ours wouldn't have been dirty street music, it would have been accurately produced and very well mixed."**
> - Robert Gordon

A Guy Called Gerald

as breakdance rivals; if he could make a record that shifted the agenda, so could they.

And boy, did they. Released in its first white label form in October 1988, "The Theme" was even more shockingly revolutionary than the record that partially inspired it. Not only was it raw, stripped back and tough, with the same electro-inspired shuffle, but "The Theme" also boasted two unique elements that marked it out from everything that had come before: insanely heavy, distorted bass, rich in sub-bass frequencies, and sparse, ear-catching "bleep" sounds that could have come straight off a Kraftwerk record. This was

"Bradford bass", later to become "Yorkshire bass", "Sheffield bleep" and, ultimately, "bleep & bass".

Over the 24 months that followed the release of that first, bedroom-produced version of "The Theme" (it was later re-recorded and re-released on Virgin Records offshoot 10 Records), Bleep & bass became the first distinctively British style of dance music.

Significantly, it owed much to the dancefloor-focused "steppers" rhythm that was then popular within soundsystem culture, as well as the echoing, head-mangling effects of dub and the sheer bass-weight of reggae and its related genres. Combine this with the metallic clang of industrial music and the futuristic intent of Detroit techno, and you had a sound fully formed by its roots in Yorkshire's once-mighty post-industrial cities.

Bleep & bass first began to prick the public consciousness thanks to the work of Warp Records, a label established by two record shop owners (Rob Mitchell and Steve Beckett) and soundsystem-mad Sheffield producer Robert Gordon. The latter claims he was motivated by the idea of releasing records that united both his black and white friends in appreciation, fixing his love of heavy bass, steppers drums and the sounds of "future dub" to the glassy-eyed rush of the growing acid house movement.

Whatever his motivations, in the first 18 months of Warp Records he oversaw the signing, mixing and mastering of a string of initially Yorkshire-produced bleep classics: Nightmares on Wax's "Dextrous" and "Aftermath", LFO's chart-bothering "LFO" - the origin, perhaps, of jungle's obsession with the devastating sub-bass drop - Sweet Exorcist's "Testone" and Forgemasters' "Track With No Name", a cut Gordon co-produced with Sheffield DJ Winston Hazel and school friend Sean Maher.

While Warp's early releases were amongst the most popular and influential of all bleep & bass records, there were plenty of others that carried significant sub-bass and made an impact elsewhere in the country. Records such as Ability II's "Pressure", Ital Rockers' "Ital's Anthem" and Juno's "Soul Thunder" - all engineered and co-produced by a little-known figure called Martin Williams in a studio above a skateboard shop in the centre of Leeds - proved particularly popular elsewhere in the UK, first inspiring producers in the Midlands (see Rhythmatic, Demonik, Nexus 21 and Cyclone) before those in Hertfordshire, Essex and London began making their own bleeping, bass-heavy records in response.

Few were more inspired than the founders of Britain's breakbeat hardcore scene; DJs and producers such as Fabio & Grooverider, Jumpin' Jack Frost, Bryan Gee, 4 Hero, DJ Hype, Mark 'Ruff' Ryder, Romford's Boogie Times Records crew (later to found the hugely influential Suburban Base imprint), Paul Ibiza, Shut Up & Dance and James' Noise Factory' Stephens. Hooked on the sparse bleeps and booming sub-bass but keen on finding their own groove, the records they made in tribute replaced Detroit and Chicago influenced grooves with breakbeats sampled from rare groove and hip-hop records.

As has been previously pointed out, the club where

this gestation took place was Rage at Heaven, where resident DJs Fabio & Grooverider championed sparse, alien and insanely bass-heavy records whatever their origin. Initially, that meant tougher and more intense forms of mutant acid house and Detroit techno, as well as stomping, rave-friendly techno records from Belgium and Holland. "Fab and Groove" loved bleep & bass, too, turning weighty and intoxicating records from "up North" into anthems.

Yet their heart always lay in music with breakbeats, so it was the London and South-East centric "bleep & breaks" sound - early, often house-tempo breakbeat hardcore records that otherwise bear all the aural hallmarks of original bleep tracks - that helped shape their sound.

As these records began to get darker and tempos soared, some of their punters began referring to "jungle techno" and later "jungle". It was not a codified sound just yet, but rather a loose stylistic idea; something screamed out from the dancefloor when the two Rage residents dropped a particularly heavy, breakbeat-fuelled cut.

> "Fabio and Grooverider loved bleep & bass, too, turning weighty and intoxicating records from "up North" into anthems."

By 1992, bleep had all but died as a standalone genre, with its original pioneers either out of music entirely or making records that bore little stylistic similarity. Some were merely bored with the over-saturation of bleep sounds and the low quality of many of the records that had been made in tribute, while others had seen life - and the need to earn a living - take over.

Yet the enduring influence of the tracks they produced, and the bass-heavy blueprint they collectively crafted, remained hugely influential. After the natural full stop on the mass movement that was rave took place at Castlemorton Common in 1992, the hardcore scene split bitterly.

On one side stood the giddy over-excited ravers who wanted the rush-inducing piano riffs, sped-up vocal samples and mind-altering "hoover" noises of happy hardcore; on the other, the acolytes of Rage and the people who made records to be played there. They didn't want silliness, but darkness: the claustrophobic intensity of poverty and drug-induced paranoia coursing through soundsystems capable of rocking bodies to their very core.

This was darkcore, the style that pushed hardcore towards what would soon be described as jungle. Faster, moodier and more intense than anything that had come before, the earliest darkcore records mixed booming bass and elements from horror movies with blistering breakbeats and - in the case of some of the earliest examples - sneaky samples from bleep & bass records.

Many of those producers, DJs and labels who would become stars of the early jungle scene produced or released key darkcore cuts, including DJ Hype, 4 Hero and the Reinforced Records crew, Goldie/ Metalheadz, Rob Playford and Moving Shadow, Origin

Unique 3

Unknown, Boogie Times Tribe/ Suburban Base, and Noise Factory/Ibiza Records.

Then there was the man who arguably started it all, Gerald Simpson aka A Guy Called Gerald. After cutting his ties with major label CBS, Simpson left Manchester, headed to London and delivered a string of "proto-jungle" records on the Juice Box label. A

LFO

Forgemasters

Cabaret Voltaire

fanatical hip-hop head with a deep-rooted love of soundsystem culture - something shared by many of those within the formative jungle scene - Simpson not only embraced breakbeat hardcore and darkcore, but pushed it even further, offering up ragga and reggae-sampling cuts such as "28 Gun Badboy", "King of The Jungle" and "Free Africa"; tracks made in 1991 and '92 that would now be considered key early examples of the jungle sound.

He was not the only UK house and techno pioneer to embrace what would become jungle, either. Robert Gordon, the producer who did more to define the sound of bleep & bass than any other, was also a fan. While it would take years for his experiments in jungle and d&b to be released (see his 1996 debut album "Rob Gordon Projects"), the Warp co-founder was a keen advocate of both breakbeat hardcore and jungle.

He argues that many of the earliest jungle records simply sound like sped-up versions of the tracks contained on Warp's first compilation, Pioneers of the Hypnotic Groove, 'with added breakbeats'. He also says that had fellow founders Steve Beckett and Rob Mitchell not ousted him as a director of Warp Records in late 1990, the label would have eventually championed jungle. "Warp should have been a pioneer in the jungle scene," he told me in a 2018 interview. "It would have been if I was still there. But ours wouldn't have been dirty street music, it would have been accurately produced and very well mixed."

It's all conjecture, of course, but there's no denying that the roots of jungle lie just as much in the sparse, alien and sub-heavy sound of bleep & bass as they do in London's soundsystem scene, on the dancefloor at Rage or in the illegal raves that popped up around the M25 from 1989 onwards.

There were plenty of other things happening musically that fed into the development of what would become jungle, but little quite as significant as Britain's first fully homegrown, bass-heavy style of dance music. Perhaps it's time for drum & bass culture to recognise and celebrate this fact.

Matt Anniss is the author of Join The Future: Bleep Techno & The Birth of British Bass Music, which is out now on Velocity Press. For more information visit velocitypress. uk/join-the-future-book and jointhefuture.net

ALL CREWS CHRONICLES

Words by: Brian Belle-Fortune
Photography by: James Burns

BRIAN BELLE-FORTUNE'S ALL CREWS BOOK IS OVER TEN YEARS OF JOURNEYS THROUGH JUNGLE/DRUM & BASS MUSIC AND FEATURES INTERVIEWS WITH ALL THE TOP ARTISTS. INITIALLY PUBLISHED IN 1999 AS ALL CREW MUSS BIG UP, IT WAS CONSIDERED THE DEFINITIVE SNAPSHOT OF JUNGLE'S EARLIEST YEARS BUT QUICKLY WENT OUT OF PRINT AND BECAME CULT READING. REPRINTED IN 2004, ALL CREWS FEATURES NOT ONLY THE ORIGINAL TEXT BUT ALSO AN EXTENSIVE UPDATE (HEAD TO SHOP. ALLCREW.UK TO BUY A COPY). SINCE THEN IT'S BEEN TRANSLATED INTO RUSSIAN AND ITALIAN AND CONTINUES TO SELL WELL. ALL CREWS HAS TAKEN ON A NEW LEASE OF LIFE WITH ANNUAL APPEARANCES AT THE SUN & BASS FESTIVAL. HERE BRIAN EXPLAINS WHY AND BRINGS US UP TO SPEED WITH WHAT ELSE HAS BEEN ON HIS MIND RECENTLY.

La Cinta Beach, Sardinia 2017. Sun & Bass Festival. Backstage, the All Crews crew gather, wearing Nadine's green T-shirts. Our yellow dreadhead logo shines, bigging up all our chests. Up on stage right Calibre sits legs dangling. His set done, he's content to have played to a modest crowd, as the powdered sand sips Sardinia's emerald sea.

That crowd thickens as Tali's lyrics leave her lips. The bass lovin' crowd have flown in from Russia, New Zealand, America, Europe, Brazil - all points global. Amongst the babes in bikinis and junglettes glittering, boys in boxers, slides and bare feet, the headz drizzle between them.

Stage front, John B, his hair of crown of blond spikes shines like gold under a clear blue sky. Storm rests up on a wall, pulling deeply on a spliff. Grooverider, arms folded, leaning against a palm tree, has come to see what all the fuss is about. Bailey, who always checks our sets, is there with his beautiful wife Sunshine.

On stage, Blackeye introduces: "Right now we're

> "All Crews is about celebrating everyone's talents. So I opened things up adding three permanent members and a guest slot."

going to be rolling through with the All Crews family. First up, Brian Belle-Fortune... Selector!" Dillinja's Punk vinyl screams...

"I've had enough of this!
I've gotta clear my mind and then I'll break through.
Don't want to be a part of this!
I gonna tear you down...
And then I'll crush you!"

From the stage through the crowd, faces shout, "What Da Fuck!?!"

"All Crews in session!" raps Blackeye.

What follows goes down in Sun & Bass befuddled, head shakin' history. As Rude FM supremo DJ Staunch macerates the beach with Deadcode's absolute air strike tune Ratatata, there's fear in men's eyes.

In the breakdown, Blackeye cautions: "Breathe in. Breathe out... Breathe out, Breathe out..."

James Brown screaming, "Lord Have Mercy" is on speed dial. Four DJs. Four sets. No compromises. DJ Chef's hand slaps the deck spinning, "Everybody loves the sunshine." And All Crews' guest DJ Dexterous closes the set.

All the while, Dr DnB Chris sways and films, as the crew on stage party like they're Earth Wind & Fire meets Funkadelic. From P Boss' outstretched arms held heavenly high, to Queens Nadine, Josie and Adrianna's Chic Le Freak moves, to Greg and Yan's brethren inna dance grooves... they're havin' it.

JB weaves boxer-like through the throng. Producer Stretch stands arms folded at the rear of the stage as Stefano, Mr Sun & Bass himself, weaves through the throng shaking his head. He's never seen anything like this. Our eyes connect with that knowing look which says, 'This is a special moment'.

I'd been playing Sun & Bass, the world's most loved drum & bass festival, since 2012. It's one of those happy benefits to have come my way after having

All Crews in session at Sun & Bass 2017

Brian Belle-Fortune

written All Crews: Journeys Through Jungle Drum & Bass Culture. Author on the decks sort of thing. So I've been lucky enough to play in Milan, Berlin, Stockholm...

Though I have to say that the most memorable was the former nuclear bunker in St Petersburg. To think I lived through the Cold War in deepest fear of the annihilation of the human race. Sting sang, 'We share the same biology, regardless of ideology. Believe me, when I say to you, I hope the Russians love their children too...'

Of course they love their children. And I've lived to learn that the Russians love their beats too. One of the most amazing aspects of Sun & Bass is meeting, talking to and dancing with drum & bass heads from across the globe while hearing the best artists on the planet. But Sun & Bass also attracts artists who contribute something different to the festival.

The year after my first performance at the plush pool venue Bal Harbour, the organisers tried bringing beats to the beach. Playing vinyl, I was the first DJ to spin discs on that stage. Think of spinning discs, and you'll probably envisage a wind-assisted frisbee. The technicians were so worried about the wind carrying my discs into the distance that they built a bespoke cardboard shelter around the decks. A hilarious contraption, it did the job.

As it was a beach venue, I started playing ambient type tunes, but part way felt we needed more, more beats, more energy, more dancing. On went Odyssey, Peshay and Dillinja. The beach went mental. Laughing in shock, my mate Daniel cautioned, "Mate! You can't be playing beats like that on the beach in broad daylight!!"

La Cinta beach will always be a special place for me. A couple of years later Knowledge Mag and All Crews editor Colin Steven interviewed me, the book's designer Nadine Minagawa and Russian publisher Anna Sapegina on stage, broadcast to the beach and Bassdrive Radio to the world.

By then Nadine had been designing special All Crews Sun & Bass t-shirts. That year's colour was burgundy. As I refused to have my face on the shirts (my ego is not that big), Nadine based the logo on my dreads. It's a good look.

2015 was the last year I played Sun & Bass as our only DJ. It struck me that it was time to bring some other DJs in. "What?!" said an incredulous Nadine. "I've never heard of anyone giving up their slot. Never!"

I'd played Sun & Bass three times. Some All Crews members are excellent DJs who'll probably never get to play this festival. All Crews is about celebrating everyone's talents. So I opened things up adding three permanent members and a guest slot.

DJ Staunch is a powerhouse from my old station Rude FM. DJ Chef's experience is heavyweight. Aside from accumulating decades of deck time, he's played shows on the mighty Kool FM and teaches music technology. His mentorship has given us much strength.

Newest member Reese from Origin FM brings in that youthful, uncompromising energy. Over the years London From The Rooftops photographer and entertaining bedroom DJ JB has played a set, as well as the king of the jungle himself, DJ Dexterous. Opening up diversity, Romania's Ana Trif was the first woman to play for All Crews. Along the way, we've produced a podcast voiced by golden voice himself, MC Singin' Fats.

In 2019, we celebrated 20 years since All Crews was first published. Under the moniker May The 4th Be All Crews, that was a night to remember. We found a low ceiling canal-side joint in Camden. People flew in from Amsterdam, Berlin and Dublin. Alternating male and female DJs on the decks totally changed the energy on the dancefloor. Promoters take note, with more women on line-ups, you'll have more women dancing enthusiastically front and centre of your night.

Looking back over 20 years, I didn't know if All Crews would become the testament that it is. Of the scene in general, I'm unsurprised that jungle/drum & bass is still strong. I was surprised by (and then bored by) yet another article affirming, 'drum & bass is back!' Oh pa-leeese. It's never gone away.

Nowadays, I have to remind myself to notice which radio or TV advert is playing d&b. Andy C has rinsed Wembley Arena. Both Andy and Calibre have hosted sold-out legendary London residences at club XOYO. Of course, the nights to hit in London town are Bailey and Need For Mirrors' bi-monthly Soul in Motion and Mantra and Double O's Rupture, for which some punters fly in from abroad, craving a serious night of punishment. A real iron fist inna velvet glove stylee, it's London's top night. Rupture re-animated my love for jungle.

Our man, Shy FX still sneaks tunes into the charts with Roll The Dice featuring Stamina and Lily Allen on vocals. Chase & Status re-visit Original Nuttah to devastating effect. After years of sparse company on the shelves, All Crews is joined by Billy Daniel Bunter's Music Mondays. They've committed biographies by Uncle Dugs, Frost and Rap to print. There's more to come.

As some of us long in the game sprout grey hairs, our kids are well into drum & bass. Though I confess, I've been indoctrinating them since they dwelled in the womb. Nicky Blackmarket spins tunes at Raving Tots. And for us grown-ups, aside from Sun & Bass, Outlook and Hospitality On The Beach (and

in Finsbury Park) are major quality annual events. It brought tears to my eyes seeing my son Zyon dancing in the crowds at Sun & Bass.

Something which also brought tears to my eyes (but in a bad way) was the closure of more than half of London's clubs... More than half! Think about it. The roll call of clubs deceased is tragic. Sometimes slowly encroaching Crossrail is to blame. Sometimes as new money displaces the arty, all that's cool and trendy is erased. Once trendy underground Hackney, now has zero late night licences. It's an age-old pattern. Travelling from Tottenham to Vauxhall's club Fire yet again, felt like the authorities were rubbing salt in my wounds.

But, happily, the police report that the number of illegal raves in London between 2016 and 2017 doubled on the previous year to 133. Fabric fell foul of the law, temporarily losing its licence, only to be pardoned at the final hearing. We've witnessed the birth of The Steelyard, Printworks and FOLD near Canning Town boasting a 600-soul capacity, dashing down a brand spanking new 24-hour licence. Though, as Brexit looms again, I'm reminded that London loses out to Berlin when it comes to club culture.

I couldn't help feeling envious when Stormzy headlined Glastonbury 2019, wondering why drum

> **"Looking back over 20 years, I didn't know if All Crews would become the testament that it is. Of the scene in general, I'm unsurprised that jungle/drum & bass is still strong."**

& bass hasn't done as well. Grime has lyrics, visible artists and doesn't seem to suffer from the same insular infighting that affects pockets of our scene. But the thing about Glastonbury is that what goes down on The Pyramid stage and on camera isn't the whole story. My spies tell me that the festival oozed jungle from every pore.

While I'm on the subject of British born music, I'm tired of people forgetting to mention jungle/drum & bass. BBC 4's The People's History of Pop presented by Sara Cox was a perfect example. The program, filmed, produced and directed by Tamsin Curry, covers raves, house and hardcore then inexplicably jumps straight to UK Garage. Superfan Mr Brown states; "UK garage is the first truly home-grown music... Garage is the first time that we could see that this is multicultural." How these ill-informed comments made it on BBC TV beggars belief.

I prefer to drift back to that night in Summer 2014 when Goldie's Timeless was performed by the Heritage Orchestra. The staff at Southbank's Royal Festival Hall had never seen an audience like it, with people brukin' out in the aisles. And the music... From the first note, I was thinking, 'This must never end.' But end it did perfectly, with Kemistry. Unforgettable.

All Crews is celebrating its 20th anniversary with a limited update and a conversion into an audiobook. Unfortunately, our production schedule has been held up, but we'll remain striving positively for the scene and music we love, raising a glass or two since, as it was in the beginning, All Crews Muss Big Up.

Blackeye

MOSCH PIT

Words by: Andres Branco

FASHION AND MUSIC HAVE ALWAYS GONE HAND IN HAND, AND JUNGLE/DRUM & BASS IS NO DIFFERENT. IT SEEMS LIKE THINGS HAVE GONE FULL CYCLE RECENTLY WITH FASHION BRANDS REFERENCING AND REVIVING 90S STREETWEAR STYLE.

One brand is Wavey Garms and they recently collaborated with Chase & Status to produce an exclusive MA2 bomber for their RTRN II JUNGLE merchandise range. We asked Wavey Garms founder Andres Branco to chat with Saul Milton, aka Chase, about fashion, his Moschino collection and which designers he rates then and now.

Tell us about what you're wearing today...

I'm keeping it simple in my most regular outfit. I'm wearing a fitted black Ralph Lauren tracksuit with a white RTRN II JUNGLE T-shirt of ours, and I've got white Reebok classics on as a standard too. I also like to have accessories so am wearing a bespoke Cuban Links chaps and chain from jeweller Toby Mclellan and a 1991 gold Rolex Day Date. Smart tracksuits are definitely my outfit of choice and have been for many years.

Who are your favourite designers old and new?

Tough question because, as you know, my fashion really is still deeply rooted in the 90s and my youth. So Moschino, Versace, Iceberg, Ralph Lauren, Reebok etc. are still very prevalent in my life. These brands meant so much to me back then, they were like a medal of honour, a code, a uniform of the culture we were in and represented the music and social lives we lived. The fashion back then was a direct response to the social climate, and these brands were synonymous with jungle and garage - the two scenes that shaped so many of our lives.

Today I still wear all of the above, but I also have a more varied palette. It's not only Gucci loafers I wear but a lot of Gucci as a whole, and of course, I love their head to toe tracksuits for one. Moncler and Fendi are also brands I like very much, and they aren't new brands, but as you can see, that's the theme with me.

dancehall riddims that we made with some of our favourite dancehall artists new and old. We then had our own samples and treated them as such and turned them into the tracks that you hear on the LP.

We also released an EP – 'RTRN The Originals' which was the original dancehall tracks that we made. RTRN is more than just an album or some tracks, it celebrates the culture that we love so much and are from – jungle. We've put on a load of nights, raves, our own stage at Notting Hill Carnival two years in a row and we've been blessed to be able to bring along lots of heroes of ours and legends of the scene. There's plenty more in store from RTRN, check it all out at rtrniijungle.com

What tracks, producers and labels are you feeling at the moment?

There's a lot of great new producers out there at the moment and loads of wicked tracks too. D&B is in a great place right, and it's exciting to see. 'Shut The Front Door' by Benny L is one of my favourite dubs right now, wicked roller and works well in the mix. Dawn Wall are some of my favourite producers as of late. Skantia has a real distinct sound with a very high level of production and Traumatize has made some big tunes too.

What are your future plans?

We've 'RTRN Revisited' dropping at the end of the year, and we're already back in the studio working on new music for a new record. 2020 will also see the third instalment of our Super Sharp exhibition series which will display all 1500 pieces of my Moschino collection.

Would you say you're a collector?

I most certainly am a collector or, as some might put it, a hoarder. My Moschino collection is brimming at 1500 pieces, and I don't need to get into the other plethora of collections I have. Collecting lets you indulge your OCD and mine isn't about being neat – it's about repetition and doing the same thing in the same way over and over so everything I do/get into falls into that category. I guess the first collection I really had was vinyl and thankfully that obsession put me on the path to doing what I do today and I'm lucky to do something that I love very much for a living.

What's the rarest item of clothing you own?

That's a tough one, I've some mad pieces and shades and Chanel and Versace catwalk jewellery but if I had to choose it would be the Moschino 'Fried Egg' shirt. It took forever to source and is one of my most cherished pieces.

What's your favourite item of clothing?

On a practical level, it's one of my many plain, comfy tracksuits but in terms of Moschino, it's the moving images series. I have all colourways in all the pieces, so it's hard to choose, but one of the jackets probably clinches it. I also have a huge amount of women's Moschino in my collection which my wife can enjoy and

the Moschino leather jacket with the gold lions on the lapels with the chains a la a knocker on a front door is one of the standout pieces I own for sure.

What's your biggest fashion mistake?

1997 JNCO Jeans. If you don't know about it then Google it but don't hit me up after you've seen them – we all make mistakes!

Tell us more about the RTRN II JUNGLE project...

RTRN II JUNGLE is multi-faceted. The campaign began with two exhibitions, Super Sharp & Super Sharp Reloaded, showing and showcasing pieces of my Moschino collection at The London College Of Fashion and Selfridges respectively. RTRN II JUNGLE is exactly what it says on the tin, it's us strictly making jungle in 2019; going back to our roots and passions and the music and scene we love so dearly.

We didn't want just to make jungle that was straight out of 1994, we wanted to make it how we would envision it being made today. So we aren't just basking in nostalgia but updating it and putting a new spin on it. Rather than sample the same old tracks that have been sampled to death we decided to go to Jamaica for a week in 2018 and record a load of dancehall on

> **"My collection tells a tale of those raving years, finding yourself, growing up."**
> – Chase

HIGH FLYER

Words by: Colin Steven
Photography by: Rich DaCosta

BACK IN THE EARLY 90S, ONE MAN BOUGHT US ALL TOGETHER THROUGH HIS ARTWORK. HELTER SKELTER, RAINDANCE AND WORLD DANCE AND MANY MORE RAVE FLYERS WERE ALL TOUCHED BY THE AIRBRUSH OF STEVEN PERRY, AKA PEZ. BACK THEN, KNOWING WHICH PARTY ATTEND WAS OFTEN BASED ON WHAT THE FLYER LOOKED LIKE AS MUCH AS THE LINE-UP.
WE ALL ADORNED OUR BEDROOM WALLS WITH HIS FLYERS, NOW WE CELEBRATE THE MOST PROLIFIC RAVE FLYER ARTIST, PEZ. WHERE BETTER TO MEET HIM THAN AT THE RAVE THEMED SWEET HARMONY EXHIBITION AT LONDON'S SAATCHI GALLERY.

I read you were studying to become a lawyer originally.

Yes, I wanted to be a lawyer since I was a small boy. I was always good at arguing and thought I could help people. I did my A-Levels and realised that the law was more about who you know, and you needed a lot of money to get to the top. Fortunately, graffiti came along and distracted me. So graffiti took over, I finished my A-Levels and embarked on an art career.

How did you discover raving, and what was your first rave?

There was a big hip hop, rare groove and ragamuffin scene around '87/'88, and then I went to Hawaii for three months. I was spraying surfboards and doing art stuff out there. I came back, and the acid house scene was really kicking off. I just got sucked into it because a lot of people in Southend were involved in it.

My first night out was Elliots on the 127, then Slough Centre and Biology all in one night! A pretty crazy night and I never really looked back from there!

How did you get into designing flyers?

I remember coming out of Biology and being handed a couple of black and white photocopied flyers and thinking 'this is open!' Hip hop had already been done. Subway art - all those graffiti artists had their chance on trains, and some were household names by then.

It occurred to me in a lightbulb moment that my trains were going to be flyers. I'd found a vehicle which meant I could carry on my artwork, get paid and party! Fortunately for me, I already knew people organising parties as they also came from Southend.

Some of your very early work has a graffiti influence...

Yes, it was like, where are we going with this? The more I went out with my friends and got a feel for what we were a part of I realised I needed to speak to them.

As the parties went on, I found my voice and that was to be as crazy, messed up, psychedelic and surreal as possible!

Pretty soon it snowballed and you were working for nearly all the top promoters...

Yes, the peak was 1992 to 1993 for the number of different organisers I was working for. In 1989 there was Rage, Beyond Therapy, Fantastic Ibiza and Biology - they were like the 'intro' plus I started painting backdrops for parties too.

As 1990 dawned I started working with Raindance a lot and, by the end of that year, it just went crazy. I remember coming out of Rage in 1992 and out of the 14 flyers being handed out, ten of them were mine!

A lot of the designs were quite simple then. Ten years later, my work for Helter Skelter would take me a month to create. I was painting two flyers a week back then, sometimes more.

I did most of the work predominately, but I also worked with another artist from Southend called Antony 'H' Haylock just churning them out! We had a small shed at the bottom of my mum's garden and crammed in there we had satellite TV, bassbins, a drawing board and my brother with his drum machine!

Tell us more about your airbrushing style...

At that time Photoshop and computers weren't as powerful as they are now and you couldn't afford to do what I was doing on a computer. I was trying to create something that had a Sega game cover computer-generated look. To look futuristic, surreal and a bit twisted, off-key and disturbing. I knew what state the audience was going to be in after all.

Through the colours and products I used, I discovered that this particular paper, masking film and inks worked. So that lent itself with the materials, and the way I went about it gave it that style.

Did you work on canvas for the flyers?

No, they were done on Bristol board, a kind of heavy card paper, and Frisk film, which is discontinued now. I'd use a scalpel to cut out little sections, but you had to be careful when you peeled the Frisk off as you could peel the picture away. It was layers upon layers upon layers.

COACH.COM

Saturday 9th March 1996 all night 9 p.m. - 7 a.m.

HELTER SKELTER

At the Denbeigh Leisure Park, V7 Saxon Street, Bletchley, Milton Keynes

All Systems are Go as we streak ahead and prepare ourselves for The Voyage through 1996 and continue towards the next Millenium.   The Countdown Continues............

Est. 1989, 90, 91, 92, 93, 94, 95, 96.........

It was like printing, but you were painting.

A lot of the flyers were backgrounds of the sky which were freehand but then perhaps you'd mask off a face. The first ones were A4 size, but by the end, they got up to a metre square. As big as the board I could buy, but you can't buy that board any more.

You can purchase something called Bristol board, but it's not the same. I have to use canvas now if I want to produce a similar piece of work.

Did printers manage to reproduce your work faithfully?

Back then, I'd give the promoters my work, and it would disappear to some printer somewhere. When I'd finally see the flyer, sometimes it would look nothing like the way I wanted and other times it was spot on. You were at the behest of where they were getting it scanned and printed. In the end, I approached a good printer in Southend and delivered everyone to them, as I was tired of flyers not turning out properly.

What influenced your style?

Before the party scene, I was into art through graffiti. There was a publishing house called Paper Tiger who produced single artist books on people like Rodney Matthews who designed lots of great rock album covers. I'd collect those and use them as references.

Style and fashion magazines like Arena, The Face and Vogue too. A lot of the heads and figures in the flyers are famous models from magazines. The thought process was

like 'she'll look good over a city with a helter-skelter coming out of her body!'

How important was it not to reveal the meaning behind each artwork?

They were supposed to be a window in the world of Pez. So I wanted people to see it as a freeze-frame of a moving world and to wander around. So they got the flyer coming out of The Sanctuary, and they're in the car wondering what I'd done this week, looking for the little spider or other motifs. Let them go on a journey as they're in the right state of mind to be doing that.

Did promoters give you the direction, or did you just do what you want?

Sometimes, but it was infrequent that party promoters got involved. I'd often meet them at Rage, which was where I did most of my business. When it was finished I'd be under the arches at Heaven with my portfolio and promoters would come and have a look. I usually asked them what they didn't want rather than what they wanted. Then I had free rein to create a Pez flyer really.

However, sometimes I'd paint something that was so good I decided not to give it to them! I'd show that artwork to the organisations that really looked after me, and they'd have it. I'd then have to make another painting for the original promoter!

Which promoters did you work for?

The three main ones were Helter Skelter, Raindance and World Dance but

I've worked with pretty much all of them in one capacity or another: Biology, Sunrise, Fantastic Ibiza, Life Utopia, Telepathy, Dreamscape, Amnesia, Jungle Fever, Jungle Splash and Beyond Therapy. The only one I didn't work for was Fantazia as they had their own style. In 1994 I got married, and I reduced my client base down to Raindance, World Dance and Helter Skelter.

You moved to Taunton around this time, didn't you...

Yes, my wife's parents moved to Taunton, and we followed. We ran a restaurant, and that's how I got into the restaurant business, which is what I do now. We started a family, and my whole world changed. I decided I wanted to focus on my family. As I was only working for three promoters, it was nice to do one every other month.

How have your working practices changed over the years, particularly with the development of image manipulation technology?

I've learned Photoshop, obviously. I've only really used it to touch up old work that has deteriorated. Some of my originals are nearly 30 years old, and they're ink on paper. However, my recent campaign for Coach handbags, which was all over London on billboards was the first time I'd imported hand-painted images in Photoshop to create a work.

The reason being was they wanted it in so many different sizes and dimensions and they had to be six metres by four metres, so huge files. The only way to approach it was to paint every item separately, get them scanned in and do it. A lot of people think my work is

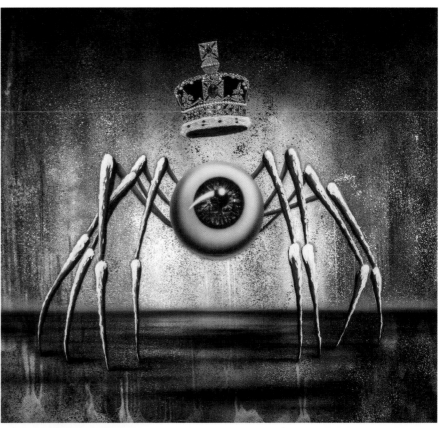

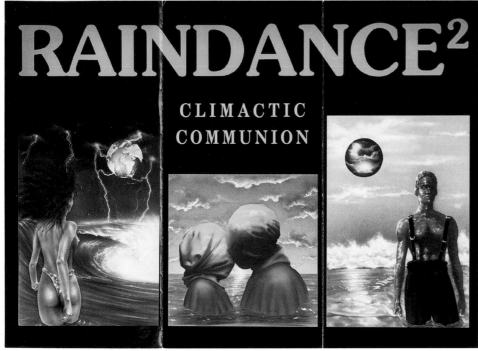

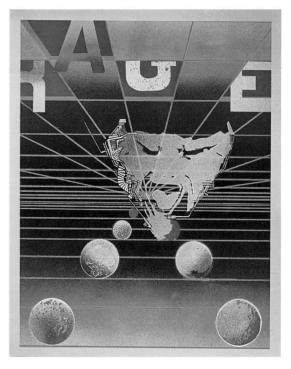

computerised, but it's not.

The fact that a brand like Coach is interested in dance music culture shows you how far we've come.

What other brands are you working with?

I'm collaborating with Wavey Garms, a clothing brand based in South London who actually introduced me to Coach. Also Cult to Culture, we're producing a scrapbook of Pez art for release in September.

You also have a merchandise range on your website...

Yes, go to pezlondon.com to buy canvases, clothing, mugs, backpacks and cushions. I've got a massive catalogue of images from way back, and the idea is to package it a bit differently. People used to have flyers all over their bedroom walls, they probably don't want Pez wallpaper, but they may want a cushion, painting or mug. It's done in a fun way and as a reminder of your misspent youth!

Are you surprised how collectable your flyers have become?

Yes, some of the rare ones are changing hands for silly money. A lot of people out there are mad collectors. There seem to be two types of people that appreciate my art from the scene. The ones that were there and the ones that were too young but got the flyers from the record shops and bought the tape packs and merchandise. They're probably more devoted to the genre because they took more interest in the designs. So when they started going out in the late-90s, they were already double keen.

Plans for the future?

I currently run three restaurants, so I'm busy with that, but I continue the artwork as something I enjoy. My youngest daughter encouraged me to start painting again three years ago after discovering a folder of the original artworks. So I have a studio now, and I only choose projects that I like.

I'm also putting together a pop-up exhibition in London around Christmas where you'll also be able to buy Pez original art, prints and merchandise, I'm just finalising a venue for that.

SLEEVE NOTES

Compiled by: Sarah Marshall & Colin Steven

WE ORIGINALLY RAN THE PROFILE ON DRUM & BASS SLEEVE DESIGN WAY BACK IN OUR TENTH-ANNIVERSARY ISSUE IN 2004. AT THE TIME WE SAID THAT DRUM & BASS SLEEVES HAD A DISTINCTIVE STYLE AND IDENTITY IN A SIMILAR VEIN TO BLUE NOTE JAZZ RELEASES. HOWEVER, WHILE THIS "SERIOUS" STYLE STILL EXISTS, IT'S NOW MUCH MORE DIVERSIFIED. HERE WE TAKE A RETROSPECTIVE LOOK AT DRUM & BASS ARTWORK FROM THE 90S RIGHT UP TO THE PRESENT DAY.

JON BLACK & SAM BENNETT

Jon Black landed his first job in 1992 at Rising High Records, working with artists such as Black Dog, Luke Vibert and The Hypnotist. Sam Bennett crafted his Photoshop skills at graphics company Green Ink, where he met Goldie. He worked on the 'Timeless' album sleeve, and the pair remained in close contact after the project had been completed.

Sam and Jon both worked together at Vinyl Distribution - a hub for drum & bass in the mid-90s. Here they designed sleeves for Metalheadz, Valve, Creative Source, Virus, Good Looking, Basement Records, 31 Records and many more. Sam also DJed for Metalheadz at the Blue Note and spun hip hop for Valve.

Contact:
jon@magnetstudio.com/ magnetstudio.com

ALEX REECE - PULP FICTION (1995)
Jon Black at Vinyl: "This was the first design I produced for Metalheadz. It's a simple tune, so I wanted to do something simple and iconic for the sleeve; it's a fusion of the logo and a speaker. This was also the first Metalheadz release to get its own dedicated sleeve."

RUFIGE KRU - TERMINATOR (1993)
Jon Black at Vinyl: "I think the concept for this is pretty obvious. For the original visual, I actually scanned an image from a magazine. Goldie liked the idea and supplied me with some photos of himself."

GOLDIE - ANGEL (1995) /
GOLDIE - INNER CITY LIFE (1995)
Sam Bennett at Green Ink: "The images used on these sleeves were screengrabs taken from the 'Inner City Life' video. Goldie already had a clear idea of what he wanted and directed me throughout; he came from a graffiti background and designed a lot of the early sleeves himself. Goldie drew the original skull head and had been using it for years. The pinks and reds on Inner City Life are also colours he regularly used in pieces. I knew his work from the book 'Spraycan Art' and respected the stuff he'd done. I owe a lot to Goldie; he took me under his wing and helped me develop my style."

ED RUSH - SKYLAB (1996)
Jon Black at Vinyl: "This image is of Detroit. I found it in a satellite photography book. The Metalheadz logo itself is slightly transparent to give the impression that it's floating above the city."

HIDDEN AGENDA - DISPATCHES (1996)
Jon Black at Vinyl: "These photographs were taken at a London airport. I asked a photography friend to take some pictures for me. He came back with these, and I scanned the contact sheets directly."

RAZORS EDGE HOUSEBAG (1997)
Jon Black at Vinyl: "This was the first housebag for the Metalheadz offshoot. I was supplied with a name and asked to submit a visual. The background image is of atoms colliding and splitting. I wanted to create something exact and technical to match the music of that period."

GOLDIE FEAT. KRS-ONE - DIGITAL (1997)
Jon Black & Sam Bennett at Vinyl: "This was a great photograph taken by Phil Knott. The concept was based around the construction of a b-boy. Goldie was always a hip hop fan, and by recording a track with KRS-One he was referencing his roots, which was why we used the map of the Atlantic and sound waves. We worked on several variations, with a mesh across his face but Goldie wanted direct lines."

VARIOUS - COLLECTORS TIN (1997)
Jon Black at Vinyl: "This was to be released as a collectors edition of 12"s with a drum & bass tune of one side and a downbeat track by the same artist on the flip. The tin was manufactured to hold the vinyl, but we had a real problem sourcing plastic sleeves to fit inside and eventually they were custom made by the printers. I designed the booklet using Phil Knott's photographs, and the idea of the very tight crops was to emphasise the focus was on the artists as individuals. The original tin was metal, but later they manufactured a white box version."

VARIOUS - PROTOTYPE YEARS (1997)
Jon Black at Vinyl: "The image used for this sleeve is an x-ray of a man's head. It's illegal for hospitals to give these out, so I had to donate some money to get my hands on the image. Grooverider then had some photos taken of himself, and I mapped them on top of each other. Grooverider had just signed to Sony, and this was a collection of old and brand new material. The idea was to look inside the Prototype label, which is why I chose to go with the lenticular CD case and x-ray theme. Sony originally wanted the skull to be wearing headphones and mixing with decks - I had to talk them out of that! The artist images inside were by Optical's brother, Fergus, who worked as The Plain Clothes Men design team."

PLATINUM BREAKZ (1996) /
PLATINUM BREAKZ 2 (1998) /
PLATINUM BREAKZ 3 (2001)
Sam Bennett: "I was working at Green Ink and Vinyl respectively when I did the first two sleeves. Goldie had commissioned a ring to be made, and the original 3D render became a basis for the PB2 sleeve. I worked on the third release independently at home. By this point, Goldie was really busy and less involved with the design. He gave me a brief that he wanted the head to look plastic and 3D. I used a 3D artist to try and get the right angle but ended up painting it in Photoshop."

PLATINUM BREAKS (JAPANESE VERSION)
Sam Bennett at Green Ink: "The idea for this? Explosions. At the time, it was pretty complicated to do because I was using early Photoshop."

TOTAL SCIENCE - SILENT REIGN (2000)
Jon Black: "Again, this was a sleeve done to a very tight deadline. I continued with a very technical and precise theme."

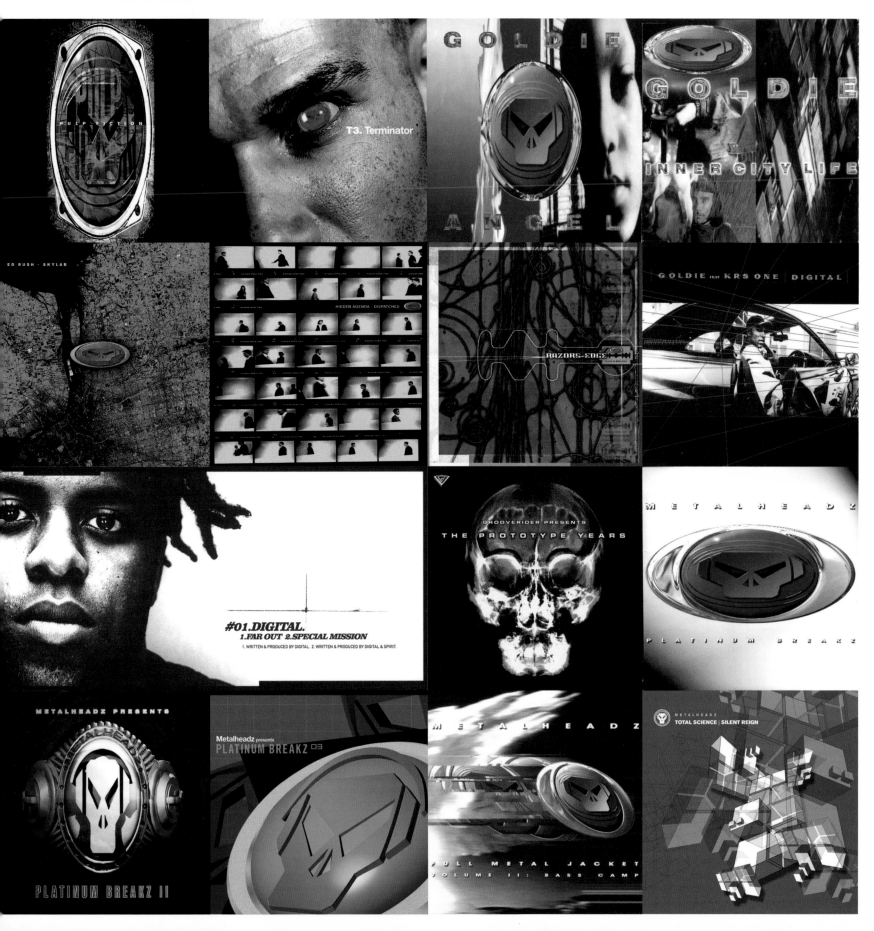

VALVE HOUSEBAG (1997)
Jon Black at Vinyl: *"The style for Valve was a lot more textured and analogue. I tried to give it a different look to most of the other sleeves I was doing."*

TEST HOUSEBAG (1998)
Jon Black at Vinyl: *"This sleeve for the experimental Valve offshoot is one of my personal favourites. The concept is based on crash test dummies, with numerous industrial warning symbols."*

CAPONE - HOMETOWN EP (2001)
Sam Bennett: *"This photo was taken driving down Brixton High Street. It was actually before Valve were running their nights at Mass."*

DILLINJA - CYBOTRON (2002)
Sam Bennett: *"Dillinja had helped Goldie produce 'Timeless' and on the back of that was signed to London Records/FFRR. The commission came through London, but I already knew Karl from the clubs. He lived down the road from me in a converted ice cream factory next door to Lemon D (they eventually sold their houses to build the Valve Soundsystem). Karl came round my house to work and was very involved in the whole process. He originally wanted the sleeve to look like Tron. London commissioned a photo-shoot in front of the Valve Soundsystem, and I made the images very raw and rough to play on the whole live aspect of their sound. This was one of the first albums I worked on with an artist image. That was a trend encouraged by the majors. I also designed logos for the Valve clothing line."*

DILLINJA - LIVE OR DIE (2002)
Sam Bennett: *"Again, I worked with the live element of Valve's music."*

DILLINJA - THIS IS A WARNING (2002)
Sam Bennett: *"The only brief I was given for this sleeve was to make it 'in your face'."*

LEMON D - GENERATION X (2003)
Sam Bennett: *"This tune sampled punk guitars, which is why I went for the neon pink and roughed up look. Lemon D did the original graff lettering. A lot of this was done manually then scanned into a computer. Lemon D is a sound bloke - we used to swap Dreamcast Mario Kart games."*

FRESH - DEAD MAN WALKING/FORMULA ONE (2003)
Sam Bennett: *"This was one of those urgent sleeves that had to be done in an afternoon! I was working on another project at the time and had a few visuals lying around. There was no time to listen to music - I was just supplied with the text."*

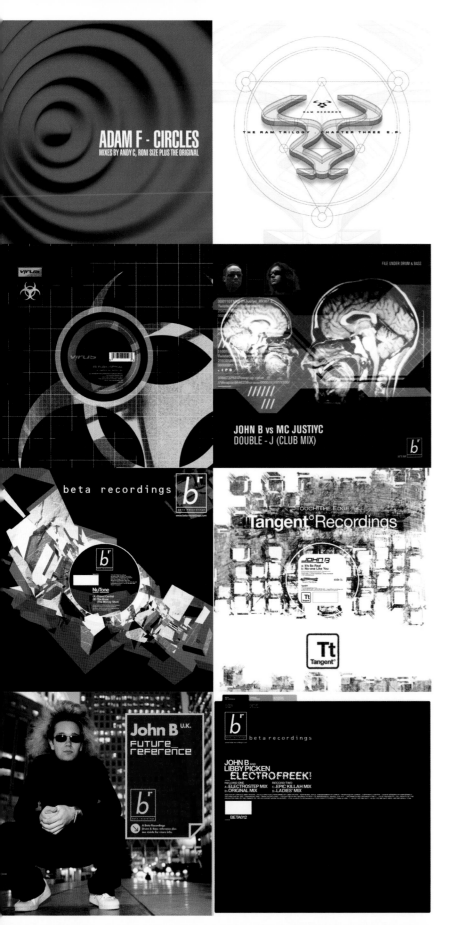

ADAM F - CIRCLES (1997)
Jon Black at Vinyl: *"I was supplied with the artwork for this sleeve, which was done in a 3D package. Adam F was a nice guy to work with and he liked to get involved with his artwork."*

RAM TRILOGY – CHAPTER THREE EP (1998)
Jon Black: *"I was supplied with the original Ram logo and given free range for this design. It was a three-part series - so I came up with something that could be adjusted for each release."*

VIRUS HOUSEBAG (1998)
Jon Black: *"The logo for this housebag was already designed. I just used a powerful industrial look."*

JOHN B VS MC JUSTIYC - DOUBLE J (1999)
Sam Bennett: *"At this point I'd left Vinyl and John B contacted me directly. This is a dark track, and I wanted something very technological. As it was a 'versus', I was thinking along the lines of a beat 'em up computer game. This version features statistics, but the original had just their heads. John B designed the Beta logo and chose all the photographs."*

BETA HOUSEBAG (2001)
Sam Bennett: *"This housebag was designed to reflect the dark, aggressive mood of the music. There was very little money involved, so I had only one colour to work with."*

TANGENT HOUSEBAG (2001)
Sam Bennett: *"This was John B's more experimental and jazzy offshoot. The music was more organic, so I wanted to design the sleeve along the lines of a painting."*

JOHN B - FUTURE REFERENCE (2001)
Sam Bennett: *"With this album, John B was keen to cultivate his image. He wanted something futuristic, so we chose to do the photo-shoot at Canary Wharf. Matt Crossick took the photographs over the course of a day - you can see the changing light in the album and EP images. Photographs of John B's kit fill the inlay - it was intended to show how he makes the tracks. I wanted the album to look like a drum & bass reference disk, by basing it on a series of files."*

JOHN B - ELEKTROFREEK / JOHN B - AMERICAN GIRLS (2002)
Sam Bennett: *"This was when John B started on his 80s throwback. He had photographs taken in his 80s gear, and I made the images look more punk and roughed up. I used a Mac Classic (once new technology, now considered retro) for the logo."*

RICH LOCK

Rich started his career designing t-shirts and album layouts at an alternative music distributor before setting up Devolution in 2006. He gained recognition working with a variety of drum & bass events and labels, before being asked to run the art department at Nu Urban Music in 2007. During his time working at Nu Urban, he worked with clients that included Ram, Good Looking, Full Cycle, Viper, Metalheadz and Playaz. Rich left in 2010 to establish himself as a freelance designer. Rich now works as creative director at the design agency co:lab and continues to work with music clients through Devolution Designs.

Contact: rich@devolutiondesigns.co.uk/ devolutiondesigns.co.uk

VARIOUS - RENEGADE HARDWARE XV

"This was one of the first designs I created for Renegade Hardware. I had been helping out with their overflow design work for a while and was allowed to design their XV album to mark their 15th anniversary. I ended up just keeping it simple. The H icon is one of the most recognisable logos in the scene and represents a rich musical legacy and a massively loyal following. I just wanted to take it and put my spin on it. I produced the logo treatment and then worked to create the various packaging designs based around it."

MIKAL - LIFTS ME UP

"I worked with Mikal a bit on his brand and artwork when he started, so it was great to be able to create the artwork for his first release on Metalheadz. The design idea was to create something based on the Metropolis movie artwork, art deco style. I was relying heavily on photography for the basis of the designs I did, so to create something completely graphic from scratch was a nice challenge."

ICICLE - PROBLEM

"This was a single taken from Icicle's Entropy album on Shogun Audio. They had a nice video shot already which they sent over. I took the essence of the video's aesthetic, creating a fragmented, distorted image of a policeman in riot gear. "

RIDO - TWISTED

"I wanted to avoid doing anything too photographic as sometimes it can end of looking a bit obvious. Instead, I took the iconic Headz logo and chopped it up, colouring each bit separately, giving the appearance that the logo had been twisted up, torn apart and broken up. This seemed to reflect the feel of the music nicely."

ARTIFICIAL INTELLIGENCE - FORGOTTEN TRUTHS EP

"I can't remember what the brief was for this release. I think it was pretty open from what I remember, so again it was really about my take on the music and title. I created something pretty abstract, incorporating themes that I felt resonated with the music. The title made me think of ancient religious cults, like the Mayans. I wanted this to be based loosely on that, like the religion had been rediscovered now. It needed to have an ethereal feel but have an underlying subtle, sinister edge to it."

MAZTEK - 3.0

"This is based on the idea of artificial intelligence and the next stage of evolution. Maztek's music is hard, relentless and very mechanical sounding, which reflects the theme perfectly. I created a design that took images of robotic elements and machinery, repeating, flipping and arranging them up to create a sort of futuristic, robotic tribal symbol."

NYMFO & BTK – DON'T STOP

"This sleeve resulted from experimenting with some chopped up images of fighter jet engines I'd found. At the time, I was doing a lot of work like this for Hardware and had a bit of a visual style going, for some reason, this one stands out. Again, it's really about just getting an interesting image that has the right feel to begin with, then using it to get a vibe going in the artwork."

DELTA HEAVY - SPACE TIME

"Think this was the first release I did for Ram Records. I remember slaving over this cover for quite a long time, combining photos with painted textures and processing them through various Photoshop filters and blends to create a wormhole image."

METHOD MAN - METH LAB

"I think I produced about 5 or 6 full artwork covers in the end with this being the chosen one. The theme is obvious, so it's not exactly the most creative cover conceptually, but as a big Wu Tang and Meth fan it was amazing to be asked to do it. I still have the other drafts, which I think might be a bit more interesting, but the Meth branding needed to be the main feature, so this is where we ended up."

ACTS OF MADMEN

"I've worked with Viper on and off for over ten years seeing them grow into one of the biggest labels in drum & bass. I created the original Acts of Mad Men artwork in 2009, and after designing the new Viper logo and website, I was asked to create the Acts of Madmen artwork. They originally wanted to create something with a political design like before, but with the way the world is at the moment, it was decided it wasn't a good idea! Instead, we ended up doing something that captured the live essence of Viper."

TRICKARTT

Ricky Trickartt's brother and friends were big drum & bass heads when they were teenagers, but it wasn't until he heard John B's Salsa that he found the fun in the music and began to love it. He talked John B into designing his album cover before he was even old enough to (legally) go out to the clubs. He dropped out of school as he was having so much fun designing record covers, and has been doing it ever since. He wouldn't recommend it.

Contact: ricky@trickartt.com / trickartt.com

LOGISTICS - NOW MORE THAN EVER (2006)

"This was one of my earliest album projects, and it set a good tone for how I work. Chris Goss, who was doing all the Hospital artwork before I worked with them, sent me a sketch for some typography from an old book. I turned this type into a physical matrix of LED lights I soldered together, which we then reflected in Logistics' sunglasses during the photoshoot. I found a webpage discussing the artwork after its release, full of people complaining that they could've done the same thing a lot faster in CGI, which taught me one of my mottos for design - you can't get more real than reality."

Q-PROJECT - CREDIT CRUNCH (2008)

"I LOVE getting good track titles to create artwork for. Q-Project would come up with great titles at the worst of times, and this was no exception. After seeing the recession being described in the news as the credit crunch for months and thinking how it sounded like the name of a bad cereal, the opportunity to realise that idea fell into my lap. Andrew Attah brought it all to life and staged a wavey breakfast scene to feature my packaging."

LOGISTICS - JUNGLE MUSIC / TOY TOWN (2009)

"This has become one of the defining covers of the Hospital catalogue, and it was a surprisingly tough sell at the time. Nobody really knew what they wanted the artwork for this to be, but I didn't want to make an ironic cover with hoodies and graffiti and stencil fonts out of fear of it being taken seriously. So I sidestepped the A-side and did the artwork to suit the B-side instead. Hospital has a history of toys and games in its artwork even before I started doing it, so I made this cover out of fridge magnets."

CAMO & KROOKED - EDGE OF MIND EP (2009)

"John B, aside from being an innovator himself, has a track record of picking up on artists early in their careers. I (humbly?) count myself among them, as he gave me my first job designing record covers! This was an early Camo & Krooked EP on John B's Beta label, where out of the fog of a load of differing ideas and opinions came this artwork, which somehow managed to please everybody."

PLAY:MUSIK HOUSEBAG V2 (2010)

"I was a faithful listener to Flight's 1Xtra radio show, which, in a roundabout way, landed me the job of doing the design for her label project. This is the second version of the housebag design, and it was such a nice opportunity to be able to have another go at a design after you've lived with the original for a few years. I managed to tighten everything up, and make it a little more play-ful too!"

UNQUOTE - REVERBERATION BOX (2011)

"When I'm asked what my favourite cover is, this one always jumps to mind. It fits the music to me so perfectly and was also designed entirely with practical effects too. It's all paper and wood and string and photocopies!"

EMPEROR & MEFJUS - HELLO WORLD (2014)

"I'm a long way from being an expert at computer programming, but I know enough to know that you start learning most languages with something called a 'hello world' script, and decided to make the artwork for this release like that too. Kasra, Emperor and Mefjus were kind enough to indulge me in a super-minimal cover, set only in programmer-favourite 9pt Monaco."

BINARY SERIES - CRITICAL MUSIC - (2014-?)

"While I get to indulge some of my sillier inclinations with some other labels, I get to exercise a bit of minimalism with Critical. When Kasra started a sub-label called Binary, I thought why not do the artwork in binary? Each Critical squircle denotes a 0 or 1, and eventually spells out the track information. I was happy when I found someone on the forums had figured it out and went to the effort of transcribing one of these covers to get the info on the next release - it justified the amount of time I spent setting each cover out the first place!"

HOSPITAL MIXTAPE - S.P.Y. (2016)

"I was given a bit of a head-scratcher of a brief by Hospital, who wanted to call their album a 'mixtape' but to somehow subvert the notion of cassettes. The packaging design for S.P.Y.'s recent 'Back To Basics' album was all about the production finishes and paper stocks, so I decided to use those same papers to make a 1:1 scale cassette tape for this album's artwork."

KRAKOTA - STRANGE SYSTEM (2016)

"A rare entirely-inside-the-computer design I'm happy with. I got to indulge my own fascinations with machines and cables, and mix in a few items from Krakota's own Instagram feed, into a design that made for a strange system itself."

BOP - NOT YOUR CUP OF TEA (2017)

"This cover ended up being a bit of a time-constrained compromise for Bop, which is a pity because I think the artwork smashes it. It's an entire galaxy in a teacup, but I think Bop found it to look more like something you *would* want to drink than the questionable substance he wanted."

ALEX EVESON

Originally hailing from Glastonbury and nurtured on a strict diet of mixtapes, raving in fields and doodling in school books, producer, DJ and visual artist, Alex Eveson (aka Eveson/Dead Man's Chest), has been making his journey throughout the deeper spectrums of drum & bass since the mid-2000s.

Cutting his design teeth at Renegade Recordings in 2003, Eveson went on to design sleeves for Exit, Metalheadz and Quarantine, whilst releasing music on the likes of Creative Source, Good Looking, 31 Records and V Records. After a brief hiatus in the French Alps, 2014 saw Eveson re-emerge as Dead Man's Chest; dropping a series of critically acclaimed EPs, singles and the Trilogy Mixtape on Ingredients Records before launching Western Lore, the current focus for his musical and visual creations.

Contact: www.westernlore.co.uk

INTRIGUE (2004-2005)

"I'd bailed out on a design degree the year previously and ended back in the attic at my mum's house in Glastonbury searching for freelance design work. Ben from The Insiders got in touch off the back of their Renegade Recordings 12" I'd recently put together, wanting flyer designs for their Bristol night, Intrigue. I had a completely open brief and as most d&b flyers at the time leaned toward a more atypical 'futuristic' aesthetic, I went in the other direction entirely. I scanned old nature books from the local library to create a more organic vibe that sat in line with the deeper sound the night was pushing. The flyers were a fantastic way to get my work around in those early days and got seen by a lot of industry heads that proved fruitful down the line."

L.I.S / CALIBRE - THE KEY / OVERATION (2006)

"I was living in Bristol, and the Intrigue flyers had attracted the attention of dBridge who'd also recently moved that way. He came to me with the idea for the first in a series of 'Aptitude' releases and, as per the definition of the word, wanted the artwork to reflect 'a natural ability' and gave me an entirely blank canvas to work with.

At the time, my style was heavily influenced by the classic art nouveau and modern street art movements, so I went to town creating something as visually arresting as possible. The 10" clear pearlescent vinyl came packaged with an A3 poster and the limited run of 1000 sold out in three days flat. However, a New Order - Blue Monday style accounting error at distro meant each record ended up costing the label money to release!"

STEVE SPACEK, DBRIDGE - BLACKPOCKET VOL.1 (2007)

"The only brief here from Steve Spacek was red, yellow and green to fit with his existing visual identity. After the sleeve for Exit Aptitude Vol.1, I felt it natural to continue with the figurative stencil style I was exploring. The B-side, Last Straw, was a silken smooth liquid anthem at the time, so I used plenty of textures and curves, bringing back the tones to more muted, earthy shades to reflect the warm organic nature of the music."

COMMIX - ELECTRIC / TALK TO FRANK (2007)

"This was my first sleeve for Metalheadz. I'd been designing flyers for their Herbal residency for a while and with Commix also being fans of the aforementioned Intrigue artwork, I was drafted in for the re-release of Talk To Frank. I remember being pretty stuck on this one for a while, holding Headz artwork in very high regard and wondering how I should come correct for such a prestigious label...

Inspiration struck in the form of my snapped snowboard leaning up against the wall (a Ride DH 2006 model) that I hadn't chucked out because I loved the graphics so much. I recreated the emblematic vibe of the design using the Headz logo as a centrepiece alongside various audiophile and street art elements."

GOLDIE & COMMIX / COMMIX - ENVIOUS / JUSTIFIED (2009)

"This sleeve is a nod to Banksy's stencil art that emerged throughout the streets of Bristol in the late 90s and was always a personal inspiration. I was into the idea of creating something spooky and shamanic but stripped back, much like the big track on this 12", Justified. The tune is littered with samples that sound like fighter pilot radio chatter, hence the helmet being the central focus of the design."

EVESON & REDEYES / EVESON - STATE OF MIND / HOTWAX (2009)

"I felt I'd gained enough experience working with design and releasing music to set up my own label where I could be a little more free in how I developed stylistically. Like many other teenagers at art college in the late 90s, I'd grown up being influenced by and messing around with graffiti and being a fervent d&b soldier. It was actually

GOLDIE & COMMIX

the pages of Knowledge Magazine and the doodles/illustrations of Mr Jago and Will Barras that first put me on to the modern street art movement.

I wanted to move away from the endless hours of vector tracing that I'd steered myself toward in my professional work and used Channel 82 as an opportunity to return to and explore that street art influence more directly. The image was created out of various sharpie drawings and spray-paint drips scanned from a sketchbook, then assembled and coloured in Photoshop."

EVESON - THE LAST SUMMER OF LOVE (2012)

"I was asked and honoured to write an album for V Records who were up for something a little more adventurous, exploring various styles and tempos throughout. I wanted to directly reference the 67 and 88/89 Summer Of Love counter-culture movements that inspired the theme of the LP. So the design is inspired by one of my favourite illustrators, Alphonse Mucha, whose work was drawn upon heavily for much of the psychedelic poster art of the era."

DEAD MAN'S CHEST - DREAMSCAPES EP (2014)

"After writing the album and finding myself unable to return to the more traditional sound and arrangements of my previous output, I went back to the French Alps, where years previously I'd established a long-standing DJ residency during snowboard seasons in Morzine. I was playing loads of house, techno and bass music and the weekly d&b night I was running had taken a turn towards retro jungle which all went into the pot and inspired a rebirth in sound as Dead Man's Chest.

I wanted this theme of rebirth to be reflected in the artwork as it represents both a personal journey and the nostalgic ethos of the music, based on hazy memories of mixtapes and raves and an aim to channel the ghost of hardcore junglism for the modern era. The skull, long being a periphery theme in my work, no doubt due to a life long fascination with pirates, now takes centre stage, something that's since become synonymous with the DMC alias."

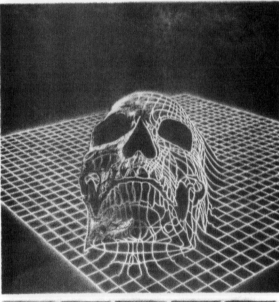

DEAD MAN'S CHEST EPS (2017-2018)

"In 2017, I launched Western Lore to further push the contemporary jungle sound and streamline my creative output. The label is heavily focussed toward the visual side of things and keeping traditional formats front and central, offering heavyweight vinyl in full art sleeves, limited edition prints, cassette tapes and other assorted collectables alongside releases.

The designs for the opening trio of EPs echo the early 90s references in the tracks, taking inspiration from and reworking classic rave flyers of the era. I created visual references in Photoshop which I then drew in pencil on A3 art paper, scanned, edited and printed on a Risograph printer, re-scanned and edited again, giving the final images the same ghostly, hazed out, textural aesthetic as the music."

SUPER SHARP SHOOTER

Words by: Dan Beale

DJ Hype amongst some interesting patterns and colours. His face is nice and clear, with an angled composition to create dynamism. You can see his hand movement is blurred as if he was scratching, which of course he was famed for.

ANYBODY WHO WAS IN THE SCENE DURING THE 90S WILL HAVE SEEN THE WORK OF TRISTAN O'NEILL, EVEN IF THEY DIDN'T KNOW IT. ALONGSIDE MIXMAG'S JONATHAN FLEMING HE WAS ONE OF, IF NOT THE MOST, PROLIFIC EVENT PHOTOGRAPHERS.
HIS WORK FEATURED IN ALL THE TOP RAVE PUBLICATIONS OF THE DAY AND HIS PHOTO ALSO GRACES THE COVER OF BRIAN BELLE-FORTUNE'S ALL CREWS BOOK. FLICKING BACK THROUGH COPIES OF DREAM AND ATMOSPHERE ALMOST EVERY OTHER PAGE SEEMS TO HAVE IMAGES CREDITED TO TRISTAN.
WE TRACKED HIM DOWN AND ASKED HIM TO SHARE HIS THOUGHTS ON HIS DAYS BEHIND THE LENS AND SOME OF HIS MOST TREASURED IMAGES WITH US. SOME OF YOU WILL RECOGNISE THEM AND FOR OTHERS, THIS WILL BE A HISTORY LESSON. EITHER WAY, ENJOY THESE FANTASTIC IMAGES WITH US.

How did you get into photography?

I've been taking pictures since I came to England when I was 13. I lived in Belgium before and only wish I'd had a camera then.

It seemed to be such a natural thing for me to take pictures. I enjoyed taking pictures of everything I did, including family and friends. I did a GCSE while I was at college at the age of 16 and that got me more into the technical side of photography.

I read every photography book in the library, which is where I would spend all my spare time, even missing classes to go there. As I learned what it meant for a picture to be good I realised that I had a natural talent. When I looked back at old pictures I'd taken, I could see that I had been doing all the things I'd been reading about.

Tell us a bit about how you got into the rave scene...

My friends and I used to listen to pirate radio in 1993 in the bedroom. We used to go to Blackmarket Records in Soho and used to pick up magazines. The one that stands out, which was free, was just a few black & white photocopied pages with no binding or pictures. It was really basic.

My friend Carlo said I should contact them and see if I could take pictures for them, so I did. I think the magazine was called Rave Scene. They invited me to Dalston to Club Labyrinth where they were doing a night. I went with Carlo and we stood outside for what seemed like ages in the December cold, having never been to a rave before and not knowing what to expect.

Anyway, we were finally greeted by the promoter of the night and the magazine. I took my first pictures there. We went to Bagleys for them a couple of weeks later to a bigger venue and took pictures there. I remember processing some in black & white at college.

After that, I had my eyes on Atmosphere magazine, which was much better. It was colour, had pictures and was about jungle, which we were interested

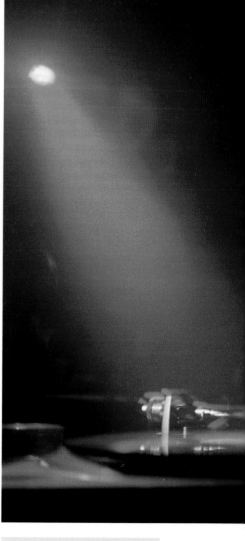

↑
Angelic picture of DJ Rap, the light from my flash on her face is soft and gentle, you can see her concentrating, and the red light shining down on her record balances out the shot well. Perfectly composed if I may say so myself!

←
This picture was taken at the Island in Ilford, probably at One Nation. I love the way the picture looks like it's a collage of different images. The front guy stands out and his two supporting mates behind make for a dynamic picture that takes your eye backwards and forwards from character to character. This shot was used as the cover of Brian Belle-Fortune's book about the history of jungle, All Crews.

Jack Frost, DJ Hype and Ellis D. The problem was I never used to know their names. I wasn't really interested in the DJs. I was only interested in photographing the crowd, non-stop. I had to ask my friends to remind me!

Which magazines did you work for, and which did you prefer and why?

I worked for every dance magazine that existed in the UK at that time, my favourites being Atmosphere and Dream Magazine. I loved Dream as they were local to me and practically the whole magazine was full of my pictures. I had a close relationship with them and enjoyed submitting my best images. Great days!

How did it work back then? This would have been the mid-90s when digital media was still in its infancy.

I only got a digital camera in 2006 and all my work was printed in magazines, not on the web.

How did you embrace the digital image revolution?

I was wary at first, thinking that the images wouldn't be as good with a digital camera. Then I went to Belgium to take some pictures in Antwerp and my friend had a digital camera. I tried it and that was it. I came home and bought one - boy was I excited!! I could see my pictures as I was taking them. I could take pictures 'til I dropped and that is what I did! I am a bit of an extremist in many ways - when I do something, I do it to the max! I've had loads of digital cameras and never had as many as I do now, I love them and love taking pictures of everything around me.

What did you look for in a good composition? Was it all pretty girls dancing in lazer beams, or was there a genuine artistic value to you work?

A picture has to be perfect, it has to be sharp, well-exposed, well lit and the subject matter has to be interesting. That might be a pretty girl, an interestingly dressed character, somebody well dressed, badly dressed, whatever catches my eye. I like abstract shots of interesting stuff. A good composition has to fill the frame, everything in the frame has to have a reason to be there and be well balanced and well proportioned. A picture needs everything to be right to be a top picture. I love to have foreground, background and middle ground in a shot, a horizontal shot of someone on the left, as if they were the main subject but then, in the middle, you have some people dancing to give depth to the picture and extra interest. In the background, you might have some amazing lights, or the DJ or a feature of the club for example.

So how did your work for All Crews come about?

I met Brian Belle-Fortune in Bagleys and we got talking about this book he wanted to publish. I met up with him and brought along a whole load of pictures, put them all on the floor and he chose the ones he wanted. We also did an exhibition after that.

As the 90s progressed, how did you and your style progress?

To be honest, when I first took pictures in clubs they were crap. The composition was fine, but the lighting wasn't great. Clubs are very difficult places to take pictures. To start with, you can't see a thing through your viewfinder. Then the smoke machine fogs up your shot if you don't know how to deal with it. Then you're trying to focus on a constantly moving subject that you can hardly see, not to mention the forever-changing exposures due to the lights, strobes and lazers.

When you have mastered all these things you can then take a picture and hope that it is a good one. You need to do everything you can to make it good. Probably my biggest discovery was using the flash remotely from the camera; in other words not stuck to the top of my camera where it usually was. That was just amazing. The pictures suddenly got a lot more interesting, like three-dimensional.

in. I must have spent about two months ringing the owner and asking to take pictures for him, but with no luck. Eventually, I thought 'OK, I'll go out myself and take some pictures and do a review and send it to him'.

I went out at 4am to Equinox in Leicester Square, which was hosting a night called Orange [legendary all-nighters run by London DJ and promoter Chris Paul AKA Isotonik]. I smuggled my camera in under my huge coat, but I hated writing so I asked Nicky Blackmarket if he would write the review for me. He was the busiest man, DJing at night and working in Blackmarket Records in the day, I can't believe he agreed to write it for me!

Anyway, I sent the review, Atmosphere published it and from then on I was out every weekend taking pictures and asking other people to write the reviews for me.

What styles were you into?

I was mainly into hardcore/jungle, then drum & bass - I loved the basslines! Any tune with a bassline is my tune! One of my nicknames is Tristan Bass. I liked Nicky Blackmarket, he always played a set that pleased everyone; he wasn't a show-off trying to play the latest tunes to impress the other DJs.

I also liked Andy C, Kenny Ken, DJ Trace on the radio, Slipmatt, Jumping

↑
And while I'm on the exhibition theme, here's another one called Lazer Raver. It was taken at Club U.N. in the mid-90s and was used in my exhibitions as well as on a poster I produced. It's a striking picture and makes me think of how much fun those people were having dancing on the podium and feeling on top of the world!

←
One of the highlights of taking pictures in raves was, of course, the many pretty ladies. If there was a pretty lady in the place, she ended up in my camera. Another picture taken at One Nation at the Island in Ilford. I like this picture because she's just dancing as if I wasn't there instead of posing. This main reason this picture is special to me because here I am almost 22 years later, living with her and four kids and happier than ever.

→ I love this picture because it's got so much going on in it. You have the background which shows the lighting rig, the lights coming off it, a person looks like the DJ, then the ravers bathed in the red, green lights and lazers all happily posing and, at the last minute, you just spot an eye poking through there from the horn-blower. I'm big on composition, it makes the picture if the balance is right. Just looking at it makes me smile and reminds me of how keen everyone was always to have their pictures taken. I used to be completely sober when I used to take pictures and I just fed off the crowd. It was an incredible natural high I'd get from them. When my film ran out, I would usually just put my camera away and go home, that was me done.

→ This is another exhibition picture and one of my favourites. I used to love naming all my exhibition pictures and this was simply called Sherbet World because of the mad colours as well as the obvious sherbet theme. This picture was taken at a club in Islington that has long gone and I forget the name of. So many clubs I took pictures in now don't exist; every club featured on this page doesn't exist anymore. I read a blog about that and I couldn't believe how many clubs have disappeared over the years and how many are always in constant threat of closure, Fabric being the most famous.

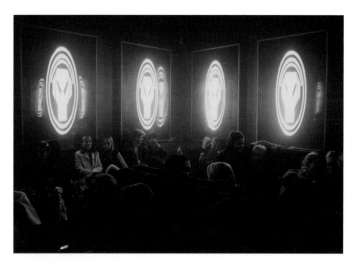

↑
This is Metalheadz when it was in the city at the Leisure Lounge I think. I love this one, the lighting is just nice, cosy and atmospheric. I like the people's heads popping up, everyone talking, chilling out.

What was the beginning of the end of your career as an event photographer?

Well, I was a dance photographer for 12 years in total but only a small portion of that was rave related, as I was also taking pictures for Muzik, Ministry, Seven, Mixmag and DJ, all of which mainly focused on house music. I pretty much went where they sent me. I didn't particularly like the music, but I got my buzz from seeing happy people and taking pictures, documenting the night if you like.

I guess most magazines I took pictures for went down in the end and I was left only with Mixmag and DJ. I wasn't too keen on Mixmag as I had to do short interviews with people and the brief was so precise. That left me taking pictures for DJ which I liked. When they went from bi-monthly to monthly I didn't get any more jobs from them. I never really pushed myself too much.

I haven't taken any pictures for any magazines for years now, but I would still do it if someone asked me. I am a photographer at heart and I treasure my memories. That will never stop. I hope to take more street life and other types of documentary shots again in the future, but with my full-time job and children, I was quite relieved to have the weekends to relax and spend time with them. I guess also digital photography changed things. Everyone takes pictures now and many with more enthusiasm to stay up late than me, so I guess that was also a part of it.

What are you doing now?

I make fitted furniture and run my own company doing that full time. Photography is now my hobby, but that it makes it more enjoyable as making money always takes some magic away as you have to do it, rather than want to do it. Don't get me wrong, I loved taking pictures in clubs and whenever you see me I always have a camera - any party I go to I'm taking pictures! I'll never lose that, I love it.

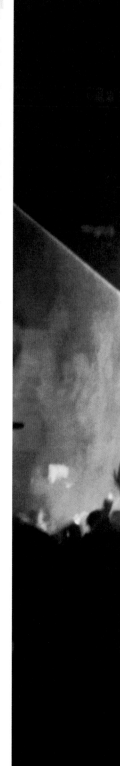

←
Stevie Hyper D! I love this shot. You have a mixture of the foreground with Stevie in his colourful shirt in action, there's lots of live-action here, with the crowd immediately behind him nice and sharp. Horns are being played, a couple of girls add a feminine touch and then it blurs into the background with colourful heads. That with the purple light shining on the crowd makes it all nicely balanced and composed. RIP Stevie Hyper D.

→
This is quite an early picture taken at Club U.N. in Tottenham in the days before digital. I would never know what I was going to discover when I developed the films as the lights changed so fast. All I could do was frame the picture as best as I could in the dark and hope for the best. Believe me, taking pictures in a club is a challenge because you have to be able to imagine the shot and frame it in practical darkness. This shot came out well; I love the different lights coming from different places creating a balanced shot. This was one of the pictures I used for many years when I used to do exhibitions.

SNAPSHOT

Words by: Colin Steven

Photography by: Cleveland Aaron / Courtney Hamilton / Naneen Rossi

JOIN US IN A TRIP DOWN MEMORY LANE THROUGH THE KNOWLEDGE MAGAZINE PHOTOGRAPHY ARCHIVE.

Photography has always been an important aspect of Knowledge. For the first few issues, we didn't have a photographer and relied on artists to supply us with photos. Let's just say some were better than others!

In 1996, my friend DJ Clarkee introduced me to Courtney Hamilton, who not only loved drum & bass but also was a photographer who worked for Dazed & Confused. Around that time, I would travel from Bristol to London every few weeks to do interviews and Courtney would join me and take pics. At that time, he was going out with another photographer called Naneen Rossi, and she ended up taking lots of great photos for us too. I have many happy memories of crashing on the sofa at Naneen's flat in Hackney while I was in London.

Using Courtney and Naneen's photos immediately made the magazine look much more professional, especially as Courtney also had access to the Dazed photo studio. Around the same time, Phil Rees from Azlan Design started designing the magazine, and the visual side of the magazine was totally transformed.

However, the photographer most associated with Knowledge is Cleveland Aaron, and it's a funny story of how we met. It was May 2000, and a PR company wanted to fly a photographer and me on a week-long all-expenses-paid to Las Vegas to interview DJ Rap who was playing at the Luxor hotel. Knowledge co-founder Rachel Patey who looked after advertising and marketing wasn't going to miss out on this trip, and so she became the Knowledge "photographer"!

Luckily, there were about four other magazines on the trip, and Cleveland was there working for M8 magazine. I remember telling Cleveland about our situation and asking if we could also use his pics. Of course, he didn't mind as he got paid twice! We became firm friends on that trip.

After that, he became our chief photographer. When we moved from Bristol to London in 2002, we made sure that Cleveland had a desk in our office with a photo studio downstairs. Cleveland had an incredible knack of putting people at ease, and the results were incredible as you can see over the next few pages.

Flight (2004)

Ed Rush (1998)

Jakes (1999)

Dr.S Gachet (1999)

Rebel MC (2005)

Grooverider (1998)

Swift (2005)

Jumpin Jack Frost (2005)

Kenny Ken (2001)

Doc Scott (2004)

London Elektricity (2005)

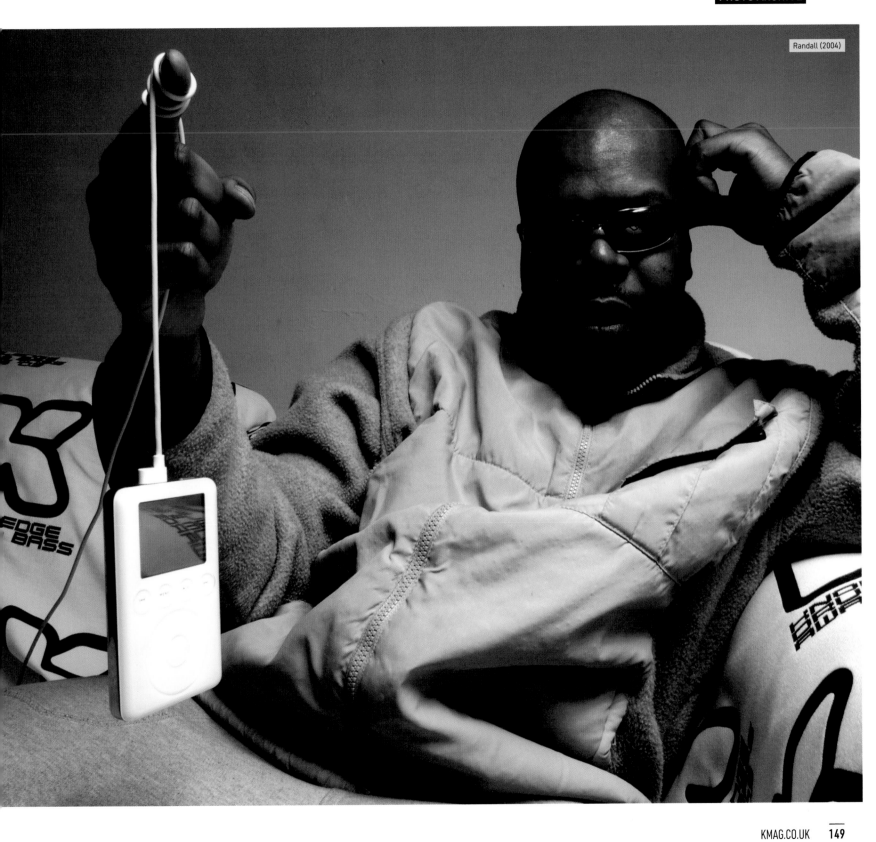

Randall (2004)

Bad Company (1999)

Substance & Decoder (2000)

Aphrodite & MickeyFinn (2005)

Wildchild (1998)

Storm & Bailey (2005)

LTJ Bukem (2004)

Peshay (1999)

Photek (2005)

Mistical (2006)

Dylan (1999)

Zinc (2004)

Matrix (1998)

Hype & Pascal (1999)

Chase & Status (2006)

Jenna G (2006)

MC Fats (2004)

High Contrast (2004)

DJ Ron (1999)

Break (2008)

Breakage (2006)